Broken Promises

Agrarian Reform and the Latin American Campesino

William C. Thiesenhusen

WESTVIEW PRESS

Boulder • San Francisco • Oxford

Dedicated to the memory of Bryant E. Kearl,
mentor extraordinaire

Copyright © 1995 by Westview Press, Inc.

Published in 1995 in the United States of America by Westview Press, Inc., 5500 Central Avenue, Boulder, Colorado 80301-2877, and in the United Kingdom by Westview Press, 12 Hid's Copse Road, Cumnor Hill, Oxford OX2 9JJ

A CIP catalog record for this book is available from the Library of Congress.
ISBN 0-8133-8458-3—ISBN 0-8133-2401-7 (pbk.)

Printed and bound in the United States of America

The paper used in this publication meets the requirements of the American National Standard for Permanence of Paper for Printed Library Materials Z39.48-1984.

10   9   8   7   6   5   4   3   2   1

Broken Promises

Contents

Tables

Preface

The purpose of this book is to introduce students and policymakers to the issues involved in granting access to agricultural land to the rural poor in Latin America. I summarize important aspects of rural poverty in the region and cite what scholars have written about agrarian reform in the recent past. The historical and social context is presented in subsequent case studies to aid readers in understanding some of the more significant agrarian reforms in Mexico, Bolivia, Guatemala, Chile, Nicaragua, and El Salvador. Peru and Cuba could not be included because recent, reliable field data on these countries are lacking.

I conclude that agrarian reforms in the region have not done very well in ameliorating rural poverty, improving equity, or creating employment largely because of the multiplicity of their expected accomplishments and because they are vulnerable as policy instruments. Although the agricultural sector was more "modernized" after the reforms, most of the change occurred in the nonreformed sector and benefited those who were not peasants (of course, the reforms in Nicaragua and El Salvador are too new to be able to apply this judgment). The region's agrarian reforms, many of them limited to begin with, included built-in features that were inequitable. Furthermore, most reforms were not supported with much credit or technology transfer to beneficiaries. In other instances, they were neutralized by macroeconomic policies that channeled expenditures away from farming in the reformed sector and/or drove down prices for goods produced there. And the context of economic populism surrounding some agrarian reform efforts caused help for the poor to dissipate in bursts of inflation, which had an especially devastating impact on nonbeneficiaries. In general, government took away by stealth what it had given with a flourish.

In most countries of Latin America, the prevailing patterns of land ownership and land use are still wasteful and hard to justify. Modernization of farming, now proceeding at a rapid pace, has not solved the problem of extensive land use coexisting with substantial agricultural underemployment. Land reforms of the past are unraveling with neoliberalism and free trade; land reforms of the future must cope with rural-urban and international migration, pressure from indigenous groups, and protection of the environment, all of which complicate their mission even further.

As if to underline the importance of issues discussed here, on the very day this manuscript was sent to the publisher, an uprising by ethnic Indians took place in Mexico's southern state of Chiapas. It reminds us that the problems that engendered agrarian reform movements—stark poverty, vast disparities in wealth, lack of productive jobs—have not been solved.

William C. Thiesenhusen

Acknowledgments

The author gratefully acknowledges those who read and made valuable comments on an earlier draft of this book, including Bryant E. Kearl, Peter P. Dorner, Jane A. Dennis, and Steven G. Smith.

The author also thanks the students in many classes who were a sounding board for ideas expressed here.

The College of Agricultural and Life Sciences of the University of Wisconsin-Madison, especially Jane B. Knowles, who helped arrange a sabbatical semester to do the bulk of the first draft; and the Land Tenure Center and its then-director, John W. Bruce, offered me time for revisions as well as encouragement.

The cover photograph was taken in Pichidegua, Chile, by Fritz Albert; I thank him for allowing me to use it.

Beverly Phillips and her Land Tenure Center library staff were, as usual, quick to help with bibliographic assistance. Marilyn Fruth picked up pieces from projects I dropped while working on this one. Without the patience of Jane Dennis, one of the few people in the world who can read my handwriting, the work would not have been possible.

W.C.T.

1

Introduction to Rural Poverty in Latin America

Like the homeless in U.S. cities, the rural landless in Latin America are people whom society chooses to ignore. Only peripheral vision catches them in the current debate on Latin America, focused as it is on postwar reconstruction in Central America, economic rejuvenation, the environment, drugs, free trade, privatization, and neoliberalism. Tragically, the chances today seem slim that the rural poor will be positively affected by public policy anytime soon. With slow recovery and declining foreign assistance at the beginning of the 1990s, the available means for public programs have diminished. The political will to ameliorate poverty is also weak. Meanwhile, rural poverty is particularly stubborn in Latin America, accounting for three-fifths of the so-called "hungry poor" of the region. Much of its intractability is due to the fact that it is spread over a large area among often unorganized *campesinos* (peasants). Those rural people who can mobilize the necessary skills, aptitude, talents, knowledge, and resources may see their incomes improve over the next decade. Lacking these—and the perspicacity to acquire them—the rural poor may do worse in the 1990s than they did in the 1980s unless policies change radically.

The problems of the poor have persisted for many decades. Impressive overall growth rates in Latin America from 1950 to 1970 had inadequate spillover effects on the alleviation of poverty. The Inter-American Development Bank (IDB) complained that

> The failure to achieve broader amelioration in the distribution of income and in the incidence of extreme poverty stemmed in part from the dimensions of the problem, but also from the strategy followed, which was to seek maximum growth, with the belief that more equitable distribution would follow automatically. The unprecedented financial and economic dislocations of the 1980s and the adjustment programs that were put in place in response to these problems exacerbated structural disequilibria and distributive inequities that had long existed within the regional economy (1990, p. 25).

1

In fact, the proportion of poor people did decline somewhat when economic growth in the region quickened during the 1960s and 1970s, but it increased when growth stagnated again in the 1980s (de Janvry and Sadoulet 1992). This trend was accompanied by "deepening dualism in the types of employment (precarious versus formal) and forms of economic activity (informal versus formal). The peasant and the urban informal sector have played an increasing role as a refuge for surplus population" (de Janvry and Sadoulet 1992, p. 4). Labor absorption in the commercial sector of agriculture dropped from an annual growth of 0.8 percent in 1950–1980 to 0.5 percent in 1980–1989; income inequality also grew during the 1980s (de Janvry and Sadoulet 1992, pp. 4–5).

According to the United Nations Development Programme, the number of persons in Latin America considered to be chronically poor (that is, earning less than the income needed to satisfy the essentials of consumption) rose from 128.8 million in 1986 to 143.4 million in 1990; the first figure constitutes 32 percent of the population and the latter 33 percent. Projections show that in 1995 this proportion should drop to 31 percent and in 2000 to 27 percent, where it was in 1980 (PRSP 1992, Cuadro 1, p. 381). The highest poverty levels—62 percent at the end of the 1980s—are found in rural areas (*LAC TECH Bulletin* 1994, p. 1); countries with the largest percentage of their population engaged in agriculture are most likely to have the highest proportions of poor people (Couriel 1984).

The incidence of rural poverty is vastly different from one country to another (Table 1.1), encompassing nearly 25 percent of the rural population in Uruguay and Argentina, 25 to 50 percent in Trinidad and Tobago, and over 75 percent in Haiti, Honduras, and Bolivia (IICA 1992, Table 1, p. 11; *LAC TECH Bulletin* 1994, p. 3), figures that seem to agree with those of de Janvry and Sadoulet, who concluded:

> The leading cause of rural poverty by far is the lack of access to sufficient land and low productivity of land use for the peasant population. Inequitable distribution of land resources is the norm in Latin America where a tiny minority of landlords hold a high percentage of the best land and the majority are crowded onto tiny holdings. There is evidence that large farms are coming to include even more acreage while smaller farms are subdividing. In Latin America there were somewhat more than 4 million subfamily farms in 1950 and about 8 million in 1980 (1989a, p. 1211).

Although the number of subfamily farms (units not large enough to provide year-round sustenance for a family) increased by 92 percent between 1950 and 1980, the average size of these holdings fell by 13 percent. They accounted for roughly half of the farms in the region but did not occupy more than 2 percent of the agricultural land area. Families living on these subfamily farms derived only about 40 percent of their income from their holdings; they worked for wages for most

TABLE 1.1   Population Below the Poverty Line, 1977–1991 (in percentages)

Country	Urban	Rural	Total
Ecuador	40	65	56
Paraguay	19	50	39
Dominican Republic	45	43	44
Costa Rica	25	22	23
Guatemala	66	74	71
Honduras	62	85	74
Panama	35	45	40
Nicaragua	N.I.	N.I.	50.3
El Salvador	N.I.	N.I.	60.3

N.I. = no information.
Sources: United Nations Development Programme, *Human Development Report, 1993*
(New York: Oxford University Press, 1993), pp. 170-71, Table 18; *LAC TECH Bulletin*,
no. 3 (March 1994), pp. 2–3.

of the rest of their earnings. Two-thirds of these farm households derived more
than half of their income from off-farm sources. At the other end of the
distribution scale, medium and large farms represented some 26 percent of total
farms and occupied more than 90 percent of the land (de Janvry and Sadoulet
1989b, p. 1398). Scholars often call this a bipolar agrarian structure (Johnston
1966; Johnston and Clarke 1982; Carter and Walker 1988). In the 1990s,
bipolarity remained in a moderately altered state and was essentially unbroken
by agrarian reforms, which affected only about 15 percent of the farmland and
22 percent of the potential beneficiaries (de Janvry and Sadoulet 1989b, p. 1398).

IS LAND REFORM STILL RELEVANT?

Agrarian reform has long been regarded as a powerful weapon against rural
poverty. Whereas affirmative action in industrial countries is a conscious,
government-sanctioned policy to redistribute opportunities more equitably,
agrarian reform in agricultural societies is a method to apportion land, a major
source of employment. Enough time has elapsed in some countries so that the
impact of these reforms may be tentatively evaluated. Even so, the 1990s are
a peculiar time to be discussing agrarian reform in Latin America. Distribution
policies are not very much in the public debate, as most countries are attempting
to accelerate their economic growth with variants of free-market and export-
promotion strategies after the disastrous 1980s—a decade in which debt and civil

war dominated events in the region. Furthermore, to the extent that increased commercialization of farms in Latin America loosened the peasants' ties to land, pressures for land reform were somewhat dampened. During the 1980s, with better markets and improved technology, capital—not land—became the most important factor of production.

Yet agrarian reform is a matter that tends to resurface, sometimes unexpectedly. Maldistribution of land was the fundamental cause of wars in Guatemala, El Salvador, and Nicaragua during the 1980s and 1990s; many resource problems still in those countries. Moreover, agrarian reforms that occurred in the past are now being reformed, reshaped, "individualized," and "privatized" in Mexico, Peru, Nicaragua, and Honduras. In Chile and Guatemala, where earlier reforms were reversed and beneficiaries repressed, there is renewed concern that *campesinos* are still not participating in the economies of those nations. In addition, the 1990s have brought new pressures to bear in the rural sector. Increasing numbers of landless or land-poor in agriculture, coupled with relatively high rates of population growth in some countries, are creating a torrent of migration to cities, frontiers, and other countries. As democratic institutions become more firmly entrenched in Latin America, deep rural poverty and extremely inegalitarian incomes and personal wealth become increasingly anomalous. The 500th anniversary of Spain's arrival in Latin America has brought new activism on the part of certain indigenous groups, who were largely excluded from earlier agrarian reforms and today are often discriminated against by dominant cultures. Moreover, land reform is at the forefront of discussions in newly independent states of the former Soviet Union, Eastern Europe, and Africa. Although no agrarian reforms are alike, Latin American counterparts provide comparisons from which to draw lessons; also, problems that reforms have had may have analogues in other policies meant to reduce rural poverty. Whatever the guise or origin of a resurgent concern about agrarian reform in Latin America, past shortcomings and accomplishments need to be analyzed.

LAND REFORM IN CURRENT EVENTS

The issue of the landless appears frequently in the media coverage of Latin America, especially in countries with insignificant agrarian reforms:

> Violence is reaching epidemic proportions in the Brazilian countryside as campesinos continue to invade land and landlords retaliate.... Land concentration continues to be the major issue. Just under 2 percent of farms occupy 54 percent of arable land 6,221 [and] 15 million campesinos work farms that have less than 10 hectares of land. As a result of the concentration of land in the hands of a few and inadequate agrarian laws, local campesinos resort to land invasions to obtain a parcel to farm.... In 1991 ... there were 383 land conflicts, landless campesinos received 253 death threats ... according to statistics from the Brazilian Council of

Bishops.... According to [a UN report] living conditions for those who benefitted from the government [land-reform] program are much better. For example, the average monthly income for these families is US$148, nearly four times the minimum wage, while 66 percent of other rural workers earn an average of $60 a month (Martins 1992).

The land-reform program in Brazil is tiny when measured by the enormous number of those who need land.

The agrarian-reform issue also complicates the peace process. The *New York Times* reported that "seven months into El Salvador's difficult peace, huge land claims by the former insurgents have become a major impediment to the demobilization of the nearly 8,000 Salvadoran guerrillas. Leaders of the former rebels say their people will give up their weapons only if several hundred thousand acres of land is legally turned over to them" (Christian 1992). Resolving the land issue is also central to the cessation of conflict in Nicaragua. The *Christian Science Monitor* reported in 1991 that the government of President Violeta Barrios de Chamorro was facing the challenge of unsnarling the tangled and politically explosive problem of property rights now that the civil war was officially over:

Chamorro has yet to resolve the basic question of who owns what in Nicaragua: Uncertainty over the matter has helped stall economic recovery....

The Chamorro government says it will not dispossess poor Nicaraguans, proposing instead to indemnify former owners in cases where the poor or peasant cooperatives occupy the properties. The government has also said it will not challenge those who benefited under agrarian reform. The administration has made it clear, however, that it wants to rectify abuses.

Such distinctions are lost on the Sandinistas, who view the initiative as an attempt to roll back the 1979 revolution....

Former landowners recently formed the National Association of the Confiscated. Association President Arjes Sequiera says local chapters of the group exist in almost every department in the country.

"The group is growing," says Mr. Sequiera. "I don't know how many members we've got, but it's in the thousands" (Hull 1991a).

The *Wall Street Journal* elaborated on the Sequiera story: "On the morning of November 23 last year, just outside the remote town of El Sauce, two men approached Arges [sic] Sequiera ... one of them shot Mr. Sequiera in the head six times. The Sequiera murder has become a symbol of the anguished political times Nicaragua is living through.... [T]he near-anarchy and conflicts about land ownership have stalled the country's economic recovery" (de Cordoba 1993). Land has also become a prime issue in the claims that indigenous peoples are making. James Brooks wrote from Quito:

To defuse tension over the 500th anniversary of Spain's arrival in the Americas, Ecuador's government is preparing a present for its Indian minority: stewardship over a swath of Amazon rain forest nearly the size of Connecticut. Land titles are the fruit of a two-week, 160 mile march that brought 2,500 Indians out of the tropical Amazon and into this chilly mountain capital.... Ecuador's move is part of a wider trend in the Amazon basin. In the last three years, the governments of Ecuador, Colombia and Venezuela have restricted most of their Amazon areas as national parks or as Indian reserves, as have Brazil and Bolivia (1992).

In Mexico, preparation for the North American Free Trade Agreement (NAFTA) opened the issue of reshaping the country's agrarian reform, which dates to 1917:

The problems of the current hand-to-mouth system of agriculture were very much on President Salinas' [Carlos Salinas de Gortari] mind when he formally submitted his constitutional reform package to the legislature last February 10. The changes —undoubtedly spurred on by [NAFTA] negotiations—which were approved on February 20 by an overwhelming 388 to 45 margin in the Chamber of Deputies, will allow *ejido* members to acquire ownership rights to their properties, opening the door to an increasingly capitalistic agricultural system....

Peasant groups are up in arms at Salinas' remedies, charging that he is the source of many of the problems he now eagerly seeks to rectify. They maintain that governmental neglect, and not the subdivision of lands, is the chief reason small-holders remain uncompetitive. Government expenditures on agricultural subsidies and technical assistance have been parsimonious at best, and only about 40 percent of Mexican farmers receive any credit at all. Overall, government allocations for rural development declined from 13.4 percent to 8.7 percent of the total budget between 1982 and 1988 (COHA 1992, p. 4).

DEFINITIONS AND THE DEBATE ON LAND REFORM

This book includes a rationale for agrarian reform in Latin America that incorporates environmental concerns, a discussion of basic issues involved in agrarian reform, some case studies of agrarian reform in the region, and a critique of these reforms.

Land tenure in this book refers to the legal, traditional, or customary ways of holding land and the behavioral characteristics stemming therefrom; it includes cash rental, sharecropping, usufructuary (use) rights, outright ownership (in fee simple), common property with open access, common property with restricted access, and so on. *Land reform* is any fundamental alteration of the existing tenure, usually understood to mean redistribution of tenure rights from one group (usually elite landowners) to others (usually peasants without land or with insecure access to it). Because land reforms are rarely all-encompassing, at least in Latin America, they tend to create a "reform sector" and a "nonreform sector." If the reform is ongoing, land moves from the nonreform to the reform sector. To a certain extent, capital formation decisions depend on whether this movement is occurring or is considered likely to occur. As reform proceeds, some owners in the nonreform sector hesitate to invest for fear of losing their venture capital; but if reform takes place as unused land is expropriated, some owners will press idle property into use in order to keep it. If owners in the nonreform sector perceive the reform as complete, they may invest in an "income maintenance" pattern—an all-out effort to intensify their operations—to bring returns back where they were before reform began by producing more on less land. Examination of agrarian reforms must not neglect the nonreform sector.

Bromley recognizes that four aspects of the human-land interface may be affected by land reform: "(a) who controls the land, (b) who may use the land, (c) who reaps the benefits of land use, and (d) who bears the costs of land use" (1984, p. 276). Similarly, land tenure is also sometimes analyzed via the "bundle of rights" concept. Differing tenures are distinguished by who owns what different sticks in the bundle. For example, even in outright fee-simple ownership proprietors do not always hold all the sticks. Local government may retain the right to tax; if the property is mortgaged, the bank holds some sticks; if there is borrowing for production purposes, the lending institution holds some rights when land is used as collateral; and so forth.

At the other extreme from individual ownership, Hardin (1968) maintains that property held in common provides no disincentive to overuse by the community, so when sticks in the bundle of rights are ill defined, the property is easily depleted; everyone exploits it and no one is concerned about such matters as sustainability and continued use. Ciriacy-Wantrup and Bishop (1975) counter Hardin by claiming that in discussing common property, he was really analyzing problems of "open access"—a situation that implies absence of property rights. They contend that communities that form the user group for a resource do indeed define the sticks in the bundle of rights by developing local rules governing its use. Bromley (1989) agrees that common property is often a functional and rule-governed institution and is as far from "open access" as private property. McGranahan (1991, p. 1285) shows the utility and adaptability of common property for such environmentally sustainable, subsistence uses as fuelwood foraging and implies common property may have other unrecognized and highly valuable functions for the rural poor. He asserts that too much power on the part of the central state may "destroy the ability of local communities to solve their own collective-action problems, the regulation of common property being one .... " He argues that private property may ultimately subvert the ability of the poor to solve their own problems locally as private (and state) property becomes ascendant and insists upon "the need for economic development strategies which do not undermine the subsistence strategies of the rural poor" (1991, p. 1285).

Worldwide, Latin America is a prime example of maldistribution of land resources, though countries in other parts of the world also have this problem.

Its agrarian structure is characterized by the extreme concentration of landholdings (*latifundios* which increasingly are large commercial holdings) in the hands of a few alongside holdings (*minifundios*) too small to maintain the families living on them. Eleven of the sixteen countries with the most land concentration listed in Table 1.2 are in Latin America. In the region, large numbers of people who work in agriculture have only usufructuary rights to land or no rights at all. Resident farm laborers are called by a variety of terms. In some countries they are called *colonos,*; in others *inquilinos* (Chile), *peones acasillados* (Mexico), and *huasipungueros* (Ecuador). Landless, migratory, seasonal workers are referred to as *afuerinos*, *golondrinas*, and the like. Sharecroppers, cash renters, and squatters are among the others with markedly restricted access to land.

The *latifundio-minifundio* or, increasingly, "commercial farm-microfarm" land-tenure structure is as common in Latin America as the family farm is in most parts of the United States. It is also in evolution. Resident farmworkers have all but disappeared as an employee group as large farms become more mechanized and commercialized; these farms depend more and more upon seasonal wage workers. Modernized farms are overwhelmingly oriented to the market. Compared to just a decade ago, they are using more farm implements and more land-saving and purchased inputs (like fertilizers and pesticides) and are also participating in more international sales in the increasingly interdependent global economy. But because of the historically backward nature of Latin American agriculture, its potential is a long way from being realized.

In articulating demands for more land, *campesinos* have often focused on the fact that many sizable estates have cleared large parcels of agriculturally suitable land yet fail to farm them. In Brazil, some 33 million hectares may fall into this category (see Table 1.3). (Clearly *some* of this land should be used only for swidden agriculture.) Other land, though not idle, is used in ways that do not realize its sustainable potential. For example, one-third of the farmland in Brazil is unimproved pasture. Meanwhile, many *campesinos* who have been forced off the good farmland they formerly worked now cultivate steep slopes and other lands that are marginal for farming and often divided up into tiny farms that destroy ground cover and forests and promote soil runoff.

Landowners usually exhibit enormous solidarity in their efforts to circumvent or repel reform, arguing the sanctity of private property and the safeguarding of their investments on the land. As a rule, Latin American landowner organizations are much stronger than those of the *campesino*. In Brazil, for example, where 2 percent of all farm operators hold over half of the farmland, landowner organizations created in the mid-1980s joined forces under the umbrella of the União Democrática Rural (UDR), a political party that has played an important part in blocking agrarian reform since its inception. Today, the UDR is playing a key role in the central-west, southeastern, and southern regions of the country (Martins 1992).

TABLE 1.2 Inequality in the Distribution of Landholdings in Selected Countries

Country	Year	Gini Coefficient*
Very high inequality (Gini above 0.75)		
Paraguay	1981	0.94
Brazil	1980	0.86
Panama	1981	0.84
Uruguay	1980	0.84
Saudi Arabia	1983	0.83
Madagascar	1984	0.80
Kenya	1981	0.77
High inequality (0.51 to 0.75)		
Colombia	1984	0.70
Dominican Republic	1981	0.70
Ecuador	1987	0.69
Grenada	1981	0.69
Chile	1987	0.64
Honduras	1981	0.64
Yemen	1982	0.64
Sri Lanka	1982	0.62
Peru	1984	0.61
Nepal	1982	0.60
Uganda	1984	0.59
Turkey	1980	0.58
Jordan	1983	0.57
Pakistan	1980	0.54
Philippines	1981	0.53
Medium inequality (0.40 to 0.50)		
Bahrain	1980	0.50
Bangladesh	1980	0.50
Morocco	1982	0.47
Togo	1983	0.45
Ghana	1984	0.44
Low inequality (below 0.40)		
Malawi	1981	0.36
Mauritania	1981	0.36
Egypt	1984	0.35
Niger	1981	0.32
Korea, Republic of	1980	0.30

* The Gini coefficient is a measure of inequality in distribution. It ranges from zero to 1: the closer the value to 1, the greater the inequality.

Source: United Nations Development Programme, *Human Development Report 1993* (New York: Oxford University Press, 1993), Table 2.2, p. 29.

TABLE 1.3   Fallow and Unused Agricultural Land, Brazil, 1970 and 1980

Farm Size (in hectares)	Fallow and Unused Land in 1970 (ha)	% of Total Ag. Land	% of Total Fallow and Unused Land	Fallow and Unused Land in 1980 (ha)	% of Total Ag. Land	% of Total Fallow and Unused Land
Under 1	4,895	2.1	*	4,625	1.6	*
1–10	788,539	9.0	2.4	593,804	6.8	1.8
10–50	5,624,318	15.6	16.8	4,594,370	12.2	13.7
50–200	7,189,530	13.4	21.5	6,778,832	10.9	20.3
200–2,000	11,871,069	11.0	35.5	11,114,144	8.6	33.2
2,000–10,000	4,594,040	9.0	13.7	5,372,879	8.0	16.1
10,000 and over	3,338,070	9.2	10.0	4,965,601	8.3	14.9
Nation	33,410,460	11.4	100.0	33,434,255	8.5	100.0

* Less than 1%.
Source: W.C. Thiesenhusen and J. Melmed-Sanjak, "Brazil's Agrarian Structure: Changes from 1970 through 1980," *World Development* 18 (1990): 399, Table 4. Reprinted with kind permission from Elsevier Science Ltd., The Boulevard, Langford Lane, Kidlington OX5 1GB, U.K.

ARGUMENTS FOR AND AGAINST LAND REFORM

Land reform is sometimes deemed necessary when agriculture is doing poorly and food prices for city consumers rise. When industrialists must raise wages so workers can afford higher-priced food they jeopardize profits for reinvestment. Suggested remedies for this situation fall into two categories. When the first set of policymakers see a great deal of acreage within large farms that is underutilized and yet capable of being farmed to meet food needs, they urge that it be redistributed to smaller holders in an agrarian reform. Their argument is supported by strong evidence of an inverse relationship between production per unit of land and farm size; as farms get larger, production per hectare falls (Arulpragasam 1966; Dorner and Kanel 1971; Berry and Cline 1979; Parthasarathy 1979; Herring 1983; Cornia 1985; Thiesenhusen and Melmed 1990). One reason for higher production per land unit on small farms is that smallholders utilize a higher proportion of their farmland (leaving a smaller portion idle) than large farmers (even though large farmers often obtain higher yields per hectare planted). Net income per land unit is also greater on small farms because unpaid family labor is used whereas labor is hired on large farms. The "inverse relationship" argument is also often extended to show that small farms provide more employment per hectare (for owners, family workers, or hired laborers) than large holdings.

A second set of analysts claim that when farming is slow to respond to heightened demand for food, something is wrong with price structure and macroeconomic policy. They fear that agrarian reform might place land in the hands of an uneducated peasantry, a group unused to making management decisions (Schultz 1964; Bray 1961; Schuh and Branadão 1985).

Production of a marketable surplus of food often drops after agrarian reform, but, if postreform policies are favorable to the sector, it soon rebounds. Falling production is a particular concern when the method for organizing production after reform results in a significant departure from the prereform situation (for example, when haciendas are divided into family farms). In fact, other reasons may be responsible for the drop in marketable production. Sometimes consumption was severely depressed under the former ownership regime, and because of the freedom that agrarian reform affords, beneficiaries consume more at the expense of marketed production. Furthermore, there is little empirical support for the contention that *campesinos* do not make good managers. Through generations of observing farm administrators and doing the work themselves, most peasant farmers make excellent managers. Even in some rather drastic reforms, production has been maintained regardless of a radical change in ownership rights, operatorship, and production structure (Brown 1989). When land reform means a small and, for the peasant, more secure change in land tenure (such as a small renter being transformed into a small owner on the same land as in Taiwan and South Korea), production usually increases immediately (Dorner and Thiesenhusen 1990). In the short run, at least, this generalization seems to hold even when Latin American estates are transformed into production cooperatives, as in Chile and El Salvador.

Maintenance or improvement of production during and after agrarian reform usually requires a mix of policy alternatives. Once *campesinos* are settled on the land, proper price incentives, credit, and technical assistance are of prime importance. Over time, increased production has been found to be possible on both large farms and smallholdings in a variety of Latin American land-tenure types. As modern commercial farming techniques come to the region, production defects of large farms tend to lessen, though the idle land and social problems tend to persist in some countries.

More often, grassroots demands for land reform come not from a concern for problems of production shortfalls but because equity is at issue; under the existing system, the majority of *campesinos* don't share in the benefits of economic growth. Thus the problem for public policymakers is how to give *campesinos* additional resources and income while overall production is maintained or increased.

In Latin America, pressures for land reform also are frequently a recognition that the rural poor suffer because they are denied basic human rights:

> In some sense the poor in Latin America are the objects of racial discrimination as blatant as that in South Africa.... Inadequate incomes, illiteracy, landlessness or near landlessness, and dark skin are closely correlated in all the countries of

the area. In general, the closer the relationship to European stock, the more apt a population cohort is to have a high income level, land, and education; the closer the relationship to indigenous or African stock, the more apt the group is to lack land, to have a low income level and little schooling, and to suffer discrimination in the workplace, in the schools, and at sites where public services are dispensed (Thiesenhusen 1990, p. 26).

Although the distribution of land is the most contentious part of *agrarian* reform, the concept is broader than merely *land* reform (even though in Spanish and Portuguese there is only one term for the process, *reforma agraria*). Agrarian reform includes both redistributing land and assisting new landowners by assuring them inputs and markets, extending credit, and imparting certain technology that will help them to become agricultural producers.

Indeed, a land-tenure system can be likened to a prism through which government policy must pass on its way to delivering a product or service to the recipient farmer. In traditional Latin American land-tenure systems, government policy is so refracted that most benefits go to an elite group—the larger and more capitalized landowners. Credit, extension help, market openings, less expensive inputs, irrigation water, and agricultural research are facilitated to dominant elites as major resource holders. Agrarian reform changes the shape of the prism so that the rays fall on a wider group of farm people, including at least some of the poor.

The prism does not broaden its focus easily. As Kanel (1971) shows, third world land-tenure systems often reflect the social structure and hence must not—in fact, cannot—be changed capriciously. Therefore, one cannot think of land tenure in terms of technical inputs such as seed and fertilizer. Although one can change the levels of technical inputs fairly easily, it is much more difficult to alter an established land-tenure system that replicates social structure. But as farms commercialize, land tenure is stripped of some of its social imperatives.

Until recently the environmental aspects of land reform were neglected. This was an error, for if agricultural land were pressed into cultivation for its "highest and best use," the large amounts of unused arable land in Latin America would be farmed while land in ecological peril might be conserved. It was not until the UN Conference on Environment and Development in June 1992 that ecological destruction and poverty were internationally recognized to be parts of the same problem, especially in rural areas.

The link between rural poverty and environment was clearly articulated as early as 1987, however. The World Commission on Environment and Development notes, "Those who are poor and hungry will often destroy their immediate environment in order to survive: they will cut down forests; their livestock will overgraze grasslands; they will overuse marginal lands; and in growing numbers they will crowd into cities" (Brundtland Commission 1987, p. 28). If people are poor, they tend not to plant trees and give little attention to maintenance of nearby forestland. Instead, small-plot farmers will exploit forests by pruning, often indiscriminately, for firewood. They frequently destroy trees to establish cropland. They may also allow animals to graze low branches, weakening the trees. Short-term income—how to feed the family today—is a major goal for these peasants and little heed is given to the longer term.

If these farmers had a slightly larger landholding, they might be encouraged to remain on it year-round; as it is, small farmers and family members often seek wage work elsewhere, especially during harvest and planting seasons. A full-time, on-farm labor force that also has security of tenure often busies itself with long-term projects, some of which might be important to conserving forests.

Furthermore, if landless *campesinos* were granted farmland in an agrarian reform, or could buy land in a market transaction, they would not be as apt to move to the fragile frontier, clear land, and farm it. This puts a priority on reforming those farms with fallow and unused agricultural land. Land reform could also be used to resettle peasants who presently work highly erodible hillsides and land in other precarious locations, thus making small-farm agriculture more sustainable. In contrast, most current land reforms contain auxiliary colonization provisions, meant to take the pressure off privately owned property and which grant parcels of public land in ecologically fragile areas. This practice, except in relation to indigenous peoples (who live there already), is usually environmentally dangerous and should be halted (Thiesenhusen 1991; Dorner and Thiesenhusen 1992).

STRATEGIES OF DEVELOPMENT

In the 1980s, the debate surrounding rural development and land reform in Latin America disappeared into discussions of how earlier government debts, accumulated in the surge and decline of import-substituting industrialization (ISI), could be repaid. This industrial development strategy—manufacturing at home what used to be imported behind high tariff walls—had slowed and foundered as domestic markets filled and high-cost products proved uncompetitive internationally. Meanwhile, the import content of local manufactures grew, as did the commensurate debt from credits used to pay foreign trade bills.

The debt was compounded by the worldwide recession of mid-1982, and Mexico led other Latin American countries in announcing its inability to pay its loans. To recuperate, policies emphasizing export diversification and economic liberalization followed; the idea was that increased competition could reduce manufacturing costs if economic activity were moved to the private sector, state intervention minimized, and trade barriers lowered. Attrition would be the fate of those enterprises that could or would not adjust.

Accordingly, government expenditures (for example, on schools, health facilities, and infrastructure) were pared to the bone and local currencies were devalued to more or less equal level with the dollar. In the process, inflation would be controlled, exports increased, and imports curtailed. This tough neoliberal medicine was frequently imposed by the International Monetary Fund (IMF) as a condition to additional loans, but sometimes countries enacted these rules on their own. As a by-product, most governments cut expenditures for agrarian reform (which involves considerable up-front funding) and accompanying subsidies for farm credit and inputs to *campesinos*. Moreover, since agrarian reform represented too much out-of-favor government intervention, Latin American political leaders proclaimed faith in the land market as a mechanism to place property in the hands of the *campesinos* (largely in vain, it turns out).

As the 1980s wore on, the "free-market" model, with privatization as its keystone, received added impetus in Latin America thanks to new governments in Eastern Europe and the newly independent states of the former Soviet Union, which began unraveling years of government intervention in the name of neoliberalism and the free market.

It is worth remembering that the now-discredited development strategy of ISI in Latin America was initially a reaction to overreliance on an undiversified export sector that moved primary products from enclaves in the region to industrial countries for purposes of economic development. ISI stemmed from the dual notion that the monoproduct export economies of the region were prone to cyclical price variations and that terms of trade were systematically turned against the less developed nations as a group (the periphery) and toward the developed countries (the center); some felt this was an inexorable trend. (In fact, the terms of trade are also cyclical, as later economic analysis showed.) ISI led to rapid growth in Latin America in the 1960s and 1970s, though it was more robust in some countries than in others. When domestic markets were filled with high-cost merchandise, the strategy faltered and stagnation ensued. Dynamism in growth was not really possible without market expansion.

The recent history of Central America (and much of South America) may be read as an effort to expand markets: Each republic is severely limited by a small population so that firms always confront high long-run average operating costs and are unable to reap economies of size. The market is further constricted when an extremely inegalitarian income distribution limits meaningful participation in the money economy to a small fraction of the population. Efforts to enlarge the market could have led to a push for more equality of income distribution, which would, in turn, have led to more simple consumer goods being manufactured economically in the domestic market. But this would have meant programs aimed at redistributing resources, raising effective demand (agrarian reform), and increasing public savings (progressive taxation), actions anathema to the elite. Export promotion thus came to be the successor as well as the predecessor development strategy to ISI in Central America. Creating free trade represents the favored future way of market enlargement.

Today the high tariff walls and other barriers that protected ISI production in the 1960s and 1970s are regarded as anachronisms, and the promotion of traditional and nontraditional exports is now the most common rural development strategy. The worry concerning this approach is that peasants may be bypassed, untouched by income benefits, unless they are explicitly included by public policy. Although free markets may be a necessary condition for growth—and without growth, problems of poverty will never be solved—when unaided, the same inequitable markets distribute small amounts of newly generated income to society's poorest rural citizens.

The 1990s continue to be characterized by the "liberalization" and "structural adjustment" efforts of most Latin American countries. Revitalization of growth requires new foreign investment together with a reactivated private sector. The notion is that the export sector will be the workhorse of growth, the assumption being that development of the domestic economy will trail close behind.

The *Economist* captured the spirit of neoliberal policy outcomes in an enthusiastic editorial entitled "Latin America Cheer Up": "While the world's eyes were turned towards Eastern Europe and the former Soviet Union, an equally bold revolution has spread through Latin America. From the Rio Grande to Tierra del Fuego, governments have started unwinding their old interventionist, protectionist policies. If—still a big if—the reforms are carried through, they offer Latin America its best hope yet of sustained prosperity" (1992, p. 11). *Economist* editors believed that real progress was beginning to be made: "The fruits of this hard struggle are beginning to be seen. Latin America's real GDP rose by 3 % in 1991. Private capital is flowing in from abroad—more than $40 billion of it in 1991, three times the sum in 1990—to seek out the opportunities reform has opened up. At least half of the money belongs ... to Latin Americans, from the $200 billion or so they have salted away against home-grown hyperinflation" (1992, p. 11). In 1992, "[d]espite sluggish economic conditions worldwide, regional GDP rose for the second consecutive year by approximately three percent" (IDB 1993, p. 1).

AGRO-EXPORTS

ISI never was a self-sufficient development strategy; it was always supplemented by exportation in Latin America. In small countries, like those of Central America, ISI did not make much headway because markets were too small and common-market efforts were too weak. Agro-exporting was the predominant model and seems to have proceeded in an anti-*campesino* manner in at least two ways: it allocated state resources away from peasants and displaced peasants from land they formerly farmed. Sanderson's (1986) work on agribusiness in Mexico may be used to illustrate the former and Williams's (1986) work on agro-exports in Central America the latter.

Sanderson (1986) decries the advantages the state gave to agribusiness at the beginning of the Miguel de la Madrid presidency in Mexico. He also documented that discrimination against *campesinos* (many of them land-reform beneficiaries), who grow the lion's share of the country's staples, has been an enduring feature of contemporary agricultural development policy: "If the agricultural leadership of the Mexican state is to manage a real food security program ... it must challenge those leading elements of agricultural internationalization which have led to ... the dependence of Mexico's peasantry on a propitious future niche in agricultural capitalism.... [T]he 'commanding heights' of the agricultural economy cannot continue to be the exclusive domain of the agribusiness giants" (Sanderson 1986, p. 281). Sanderson noted that "[o]ften this [policy emphasis] has meant that *campesinos* have gone without credit ... or improved seed" (1986, p. 281). Sanderson (1986, p. 281) believes that the Mexican state should revise the policy of allotting scarce resources to the production of luxury agricultural exports (he uses the example of white asparagus) by large growers and using the foreign exchange thus earned to import staples. He feels the government should assist traditional peasant producers to obtain the necessary inputs to be productive.

Williams (1986) writes that displacement of peasants from land they traditionally farmed characterizes the various Central American export booms. In the 1950s and 1960s, for example, cotton replaced corn on some of the richest land on the isthmus. As Williams remarked, "The switch would not have mattered much if the persons who ended up raising cotton were the ones who used to raise corn" (1986, p. 55). As it happened, the introduction of cotton along the Pacific strip of Central America represented the eviction of small-scale corn-growing peasants in favor of plantation-type cotton farmers.

In times past, large landowners often gave out plots of land in usufruct to *colonos* in order to guarantee a needed labor supply. This done, landlords knew that laborers would be available to care for their livestock. Other plots in the littoral strip were ejidal (town property), and peasants may have obtained access to them through the municipal government. In some cases *campesinos* squatted on government and even remote private land; a few had title to a *minifundio* of their own.

This settlement pattern changed when cotton became profitable during the Korean War in the early to mid-1950s. The price of land rose in response to increased demand for cotton on the world market, and estate owners engaged in wholesale usurpation of peasant farms in order to take advantage of the economies of scale in cotton production. Ejidal lands were snapped up quickly by plantations and titled to estate holders as soon as peasants could be evicted. Although the labor displacement pattern may have been somewhat different in detail from country to country, a process of the same nature took place throughout the flatland cotton belt in Honduras, Nicaragua, El Salvador, and Guatemala. Roads were cut through the rich farmland and *campesinos* were notified that they would have to pay rent in cash before planting (instead of in-kind with the harvest, which was the traditional arrangement). Since *campesinos* had no up-front cash, many left. And the state, anxious as it was to assist the landowning elite in taking advantage of the newest boom and to earn export revenues, called on local public authorities to evict recalcitrant peasants. During the first decade or so after the advent of cotton, some peasants were allowed to remain on their usufruct plots if, in return, they plowed the landlord's fields, cleared forests, cut roads, and dug drainage ditches. But when tractors and mechanized planters became available in the 1960s, landowners almost completely replaced year-round workers with seasonal hires for harvest months only and folded the remaining peasant land into the plantation. In the 1960s, "workers were expelled from the estates in droves" (Williams 1986, p. 59). In 1965, a minimum-wage law was extended to resident workers in El Salvador, leading to another wave of expulsions. In Guatemala, a similar law extending social security was the final excuse for *colono* eviction (Williams 1986, p. 59). Meanwhile, "the people evicted by cotton began to swell the rocky riverbeds, the edges of mangrove swamps, and other areas unsuitable for mechanized agriculture.... Shantytowns of the landless sprang up along the national road rights-of-way near the cotton farms, and slums formed around the villages, towns, and cities of the Pacific coastal plain.... Wherever the cotton revolution could not go, the common man sought refuge" (Williams 1986, pp. 59 and 73).

Today's export strategy includes traditional products but also encourages nontraditional exports—for example, fresh fruit and copper in Chile, broccoli, snow peas, and coffee in Guatemala, and fresh flowers, bananas, and coffee in Costa Rica. Visionaries believe that as individual economies become more attuned to the world market and more integrated, a free-trade area stretching from the Yukon to Tierra del Fuego will be forged. The United States and Canada, which had several years before established free trade between themselves, found another partner in Mexico; NAFTA began to operate in January 1994. A free-trade area encompassing the rest of Latin American would, it was hoped, eventually challenge the European Economic Community and the Pacific basin. Perhaps the most powerful contemporary factor fueling change in Latin American agriculture is its increasing integration into the worldwide economy.

POVERTY AND THE FREER MARKET

The danger of espousing a free-market ideology is that some hard-fought twentieth-century lessons of contemporary developed countries may be forgotten in the process. For example, most believe that governments have an obligation to function as a kind of mutual insurance society, providing nonparticipants in growth with some protection in the face of inevitable disasters. The free market, they feel, should not be presented as a "total ideology"—a system where any outcome is presented as an unalloyed societal benefit, when in fact it is incapable, without government assistance, of focusing on such reforms as poverty alleviation. The state, therefore, must not abrogate its legitimate functions in the face of an increasingly unfettered market (for the true measure of a society, it is sometimes noted, may be taken by how it treats the young, the ill, the aged, and the forgotten).

John Kenneth Galbraith (1990) writes that governments must also, even in the world of the free market, function effectively in the areas of education, health, infrastructure, agricultural research, market regulation, and the like. Regarding privatization and laissez faire, he warned that it is not true that "out of unemployment and hunger will come a new and revitalized work ethic" (Galbraith 1990, p. 51). Even in an economy that is "privatizing" and in other ways making a transition to freer markets, there is a place for social expenditures on such matters as poverty alleviation. Galbraith concluded, "In a very real sense ... our task is ... to seek and find the system that combines the best in market motivation and socially motivated action" (1990, p. 51).

There were stern reminders in the early 1990s against a free-market philosophy that was "too pure." In Venezuela, a coup—the product of those disenchanted with dropping wages and souring benefits to workers—almost toppled the country's president early in 1992 and again later that year. Drug exports and a Maoist insurgency caused Peru's president to dissolve parliament and remind the world that structural adjustment was not the only factor moving events in Latin America. Critical in all of this was the issue of poverty, both urban and rural, sometimes exacerbated by neoliberalism and the cuts in public programs enacted to bring about renewed growth. Although some rural poverty is sharpened by neoliberal policies (and some is even created by them), it is partly a carryover from previous ISI policies, reflecting an urban-biased development strategy that routinely turned the internal terms of trade against farming to favor city-based economic activity. Much poverty in Latin America is simply chronic, continuing as obdurately under export promotion and neoliberalism as before under ISI. De Janvry and Sadoulet claimed: "Even before the crisis of the 1980s, rural poverty evidently had long-run structural determinants that made its eradication resilient to economic growth" (1989a, p. 1209). Despite its zealous enthusiasm for the free market, the *Economist* concluded,

> The reforms of the early 1990s have made the rich better off, but they have as yet done little for those at the bottom of the pile. In Latin America the gap between rich and poor is wider than almost anywhere else in the world, and complicated by racial differences. In Brazil the richest (and palest) 20% of households have incomes 33 times as high as those of the poorest 20%. Across such a divide it takes an awful lot of growth to make the poor feel happier. Venezuela's economy grew by 9% last year, but most people remember it as a year when wages lagged behind prices.

Here is Latin America's toughest challenge.... [T]hat choice is ... between reform for the few and reform for the many. The political picture is mixed, but the economic need is clear: growth must be sought, and it must help the poorest too (1992, pp. 11-12).

Whereas it is all but impossible to treat problems of poverty in the absence of brisk economic growth, it is not inevitable that growth brings poverty alleviation. The World Bank (1990, pp. 46–55), in its analysis of a dozen or so countries in which data have been relatively good over a fairly long contemporary period, argues that changes in the incomes of the poor can be explained by decomposing them into that part attributable to overall economic growth and that part ascribed to differences in the inequality of income distribution.

Although poverty persisted in Latin America during the 1960s and 1970s, a few advances were recorded. There were substantial improvements in health and education: infant mortality abated; life expectancy lengthened; and rates of illiteracy fell, in some countries significantly. Whatever the evidence to the contrary in the 1980s, a frontal attack on poverty in Latin America was often shunned as unnecessary concern with a transitory phenomenon that would disappear if economies grew again. Therefore, governmental welfare budgets dwindled during the 1980s (expenditures for health declined by 5 percent in Costa Rica, 15 percent in Chile, 10 percent in Brazil, 22 percent in Venezuela, and 30 percent in Uruguay), so past progress was in jeopardy: public services were allowed to deteriorate; education got worse nearly everywhere; and health, water, resources, and the environment were allowed to decay, bringing demands for tax reforms as soon as the region could be pronounced "in recovery."

Problems of malnutrition, lack of education, low life expectancy, illness, and substandard housing were more severe in rural than urban areas. The World Bank (1990), for example, showed that even before the Salvadoran conflict began in earnest, the infant mortality rate was 81 per 1,000 live births in the countryside in 1980, and 48 per 1,000 in the cities. The incidence of malnutrition was 5 times higher in Peru's sierra than in Lima. The bank concluded:

Many of the poor are located in regions where arable land is scarce, agricultural productivity is low, and drought, floods, and environmental degradation are common.... [T]he worst poverty occurs predominantly in arid zones or in steep hill-slope areas that are ecologically vulnerable. Such areas are often isolated in every sense. Opportunities for nonfarm employment are few, and the demand for labor tends to be highly seasonal. Others among the poor live in regions that have a more promising endowment of natural resources but lack access to social services (education and health) and infrastructure (irrigation, information and technical assistance, transport and market centers) (World Bank 1990, p. 30).

Much regional poverty is due to too few jobs. Despite the steady economic growth and the high rate of urban labor absorption from 1950 to 1980, the overall level of underemployment in Latin America remained almost constant. Because of labor-saving technology and labor union activity, Latin America, like most of the world, is experiencing a phenomenon that the United Nations Development Programme (UNDP 1993, pp. 36-37) euphemistically calls "jobless growth," in which gross domestic product (GDP) grows at a faster rate than employment.

Agricultural modernization made labor redundant in the countryside by two major mechanisms. On the one hand, it forced traditional agriculture onto inferior land, where peasants were obliged either to work part-time for wages to support their families or abandon their plots completely and move to the city. On the other hand, it failed to absorb the labor force that resulted from the surge of population growth in the 1960s and 1970s. Employment in commercial agriculture increased by only 16 percent between 1960 and 1980 while numbers in the peasant sector increased by 41 percent and rural-urban migration increased by 65 percent. Between 1950 and 1980, employment in the modern sector of farming grew hardly at all, with an annual cumulative rate of 0.5 percent (Couriel 1984). Couriel stated:

> [T]he peasant sectors ... have not benefitted as they should from land distribution, water supply, access roads, financial and technical assistance, price ratios, or wage levels when they undertake occasional labor.... Even in countries in which extensive agrarian reforms were implemented, such as Peru and Chile, large sectors received no benefit from the measures of the state. In Peru the agrarian reform of 1969 failed to reach 75% of the agricultural population, which did not enjoy the advantages of land reform.... In Chile close to 80% of the agricultural labour force had no share in the redistribution of land (1984, p. 50).

Despite a relatively dynamic performance between 1960 and 1980, when the agricultural product in the region rose at a cumulative rate of 3.4 percent per year while nonagricultural product grew by 6 percent annually, the rural underemployment problem remained obdurate; in 1980, 65 percent of the Latin American rural population was underemployed (Couriel 1984).

Meanwhile, in the 1980s, *campesinos* came to depend in increasing measure on securing seasonal wage work either to serve as an exclusive source of income or to supplement production revenue from a cultivated plot. Although agricultural wages in Latin America registered gains between 1965 and 1980, they fell sharply in the 1980s. In a sample of thirteen countries, wages grew by 2.5 percent per year from 1965 to 1980 and fell by 6 percent annually from 1980 to 1984 (de Janvry and Sadoulet 1989a, p. 1212, and Table 10, p. 1214).

The factors that alleviated rural poverty from the 1960s to the 1990s lay largely outside of agriculture in the urban sectors of the economy to which peasants migrated. Several labor-market developments in rural areas stimulated increased poverty by fostering underemployment and outright joblessness. Temporary wage work, for example, increasingly displaced permanent on-farm employment so that the resident farmworkers were for the most part removed and replaced by wage laborers, who did not have to be paid year-round. At the same time, in some countries (Chile, for example) a pool of ready workers lived in rural towns—and sometimes even in cities (the *bóias frias* of Brazil)—ready to be mobilized for seasonal farm work.

With cruel irony, as these factors accentuated off-farm migration, the amount of urban work available was abating because of the exhaustion of ISI, resulting in a rapid growth of the city "informal" sector, that is, economic activity dominated by petty commerce or uncontrolled and unregulated services, a sort of black market in labor.

As soon as the first Latin American country defaulted on its external debts in 1982, it became clear that such action would exact a particularly heavy price from the poor. Later, organizations and professionals began to argue for "adjustment with a human face," which the United Nations Children's Fund (UNICEF) said should include: (1) the goal of protecting the poor and vulnerable as a basic objective of economic adjustment alongside the longer-term goal of human-focused sustainable development; (2) adjustment programs that are recast to incorporate specific measures for investing in the poor, including credit for small-scale agriculture and traders and support for enterprises that women carry out; (3) monitoring of human indicators as well as economic variables—nutrition as well as inflation, food intake as well as balance of payments, and so on (UNICEF 1990, p. 10).

National income figures during the 1980s dropped significantly throughout Latin America due to recession, lack of external demand for traditional commodities, debt, and structural adjustment. Of twenty-two countries in Latin America, only Chile, Paraguay, Barbados, Colombia, and Jamaica registered positive economic growth for the decade. In the 1980s—often called the lost decade of debt—some argued that the rural poor with some land (*minifundistas*) were less impacted by the debt crisis than the urban poor, because agriculture was doing relatively better than city-based economic activities; agriculture was, in fact, the most dynamic actor in a dismal overall economic performance. As income dropped during the decade at the rate of about 1 percent a year, value added in agriculture grew slightly. As a result, urban poverty grew faster than rural poverty during the 1980s (IICA 1992, p. 32).

But the effects of favorable domestic terms of trade for the farm sector were sometimes nullified by falling international prices for traditional exports. Some economic weakness was also instigated by imports of highly subsidized European and U.S. farm commodities that were substituted for domestic products. Falling government expenditures on health and education damaged the quality of the rural work force. Also, rising commodity prices were sometimes obliterated by rising production costs. As the financial market was liberalized and interest rates rose from subsidized levels, production credit came to be more severely rationed to small farmers.

Nonetheless, some of the urban bias characteristic of ISI disappeared in the 1980s as export promotion—often of farm products—merged as a prominent development strategy. Small farmers were helped if they grew staples, for which there was little competition from abroad, and whenever their potential margins were not captured by intermediaries.

Furthermore, prices for nontraditional exports (temperate climate fruits, flowers, shrimp in lagoons, chicken, and vegetables), the growing of which was highly promoted in the 1980s, remained generally favorable. The rural poor benefited to the extent that small-scale farmers could enter these markets. Although small scale may offer some economies since it tends to involve crops that need to be meticulously tended and carefully watched (for signs of disease, insect damage, and the like), in general, engaging in production of export nontraditionals was a big step for peasant farmers, made more difficult by the technology costs and quality controls demanded and the terms of credit offered by international purchasers. In Chile, peasant farmers found they could not afford the investment in orchards—and the wait for trees to bear fruit—together with the riskiness of production. These would-be producers were afraid that the market would close to them even if they did master the technology and meet the capital requirements. In contrast, there was evidence in Costa Rica and Guatemala that some small farmers did benefit from growing nontraditional vegetables for the U.S. winter market. Here contract farming was established; the *campesinos* were loaned capital and technology packages and were assured of a market for their products. The problem with this arrangement is the great temptation of the contracting companies to bilk the *campesino* growers, who are often unfamiliar with real input costs and product prices (Carter et al. 1993).

Meanwhile, capitalized farmers and agribusinesses were always searching for more land to put into high-profit, export-crop production and were eager to purchase the property of failed smaller farmers. The Latin American agricultural organization known as IICA documented this problem:

There is some indirect evidence of land reconcentration. There is, for example, the growing tendency for those who work in agriculture to work for wages. These jobs are generated by the expansion of export agriculture and the intensive use of technology and capital in nontraditional exports. Also there is the fall in grain production in Central America that has been traditionally associated with small producers; as *campesinos* lost their farm plots, this land came to be used for more profitable crops. There is also evidence that some crops that require large farms (like citrus in Brazil and bananas in Central America) are being planted on properties recently acquired from small and medium agriculturists. The movement toward neoliberalism probably obliges the less efficient slowly to leave the market. This means that smaller producers who have little aid will not be able to survive the new model. Also liberalization of the land market will probably accelerate the process of reversing past land reforms (1992, pp. 38–39, translation by the author).

Whereas free markets and privatization might well have been the best ways to get economies moving in the 1990s, "trickle-down" has not alleviated the problems of the poor and will not in the future. An attack on rural poverty will have to be an explicit policy goal in Latin America if the poor are to escape the continued burdens of the agricultural version of a Dickensian existence.

POVERTY ALLEVIATION

There are four major ways in which the condition of the rural poor in Latin America might be improved, and specific poorest-group targeting (to those in arid zones, to landless, to women, for example) is possible in all cases: (1) increasing the productivity of those with some land by channeling more inputs, credit, technology, and techniques to them and by raising their skill (education) and health levels; (2) offering rural poverty groups more employment opportunities, whether farm, nonfarm, agro-industrial, urban, or international; (3) subsidizing the poor through food rations, food stamps, and the like; (4) giving the peasants more land resources through land resettlement, agrarian reform, land market activity, or a mixture of the three. Realistically, of course, a combination of these methods is used in most real-world situations (for example, integrated rural development was a prominent regional agricultural development strategy in the late 1970s).

Schuh and Branadão (1991) concentrate on the first method, increasing output from agriculture. They feel that if prices and macroeconomic policy were calibrated correctly, unhindered by subsidies and according to the free market, proper technology would be used, agriculture would grow, and income and employment would increase the peasants' share of income. They write that the history of agriculture over the last three decades or so in Latin America is a chronicle of lost expectations. There was inadequate local investment in research (biological technology is very location-specific), which would have translated into abundant production and lower food prices to domestic consumers. They imply that had agricultural productivity risen, something free-market prices would have brought about, industry could have become more internationally competitive. They also believe that farming in the region suffered for lack of investment in education and decry the fact that foreign-aid agencies are turning away from Latin America and the agricultural sector.

Schuh and Branadão (1991) believe that because food prices were artificially depressed, the sector expelled capital and labor too rapidly. In the course of ISI, exchange rates were overvalued, which was tantamount to placing a tax on agricultural exports (it was sometimes also an explicit policy choice meant to keep food at home) and a subsidy on imports. The low food-price problem was accentuated by Western European and U.S. food subsidies meant to protect their own farmers. The authors show that through much of the period, Latin American countries imported foodstuffs and that these products out-competed domestically grown food, thus imperiling local farmers. They further argue that better technology and improved farmer education would have brought about a cheaper food supply, thus improving income distribution (assuming constant income) since a larger relative portion of the incomes of the poor is spent on food when compared to the rich.

Schuh and Branadão continued: "Agriculture [in Latin America] has suffered serious neglect and outright discrimination during most of the period since the end of World War II.... Thus agriculture has not been a dynamic force for economic development. By the same token, it has not been the constraint to development that it is often alleged to be" (1991, p. 177). On the latter point, they state that, during the 1960s and 1970s, food production grew at roughly the rate of population (the major growth period was in the first fifteen years; the rate fell markedly during the latter part of the 1970s), calories consumed were somewhat higher at the end of the period than at its beginning, and diets were becoming more healthful as the decades progressed. Unfortunately, as international trade in agricultural products boomed in the 1970s, Latin America did not participate as actively as it might have because of its protectionist policies. In regard to the 1980s, Schuh and Branadão concluded that "agriculture neither contributed to the solution of the debt problem as it might have, nor did it provide the impetus for general economic development that it could have" (1991, p. 180). The rate of growth of the sector declined a full percentage point in the 1980–1988 period from what it was in the 1965–1980 time span. (But given the dismal performance of the other sectors of the economy in the 1980s, this rate was almost stellar.)

The second solution focuses on increasing all-around employment as a primary goal. Adelman saw danger in promoting this goal through off-farm employment in manufacturing and believed that this type of job creation early in development would sharpen inequities: "Great Britain, Belgium, France, Switzerland, Germany, Denmark, Sweden, Norway and the U.S. all experienced declines in the shares of income accruing to the poor and increases in absolute and relative poverty during the early phases of their industrial revolutions" (1989, p. 2). She notes that those periods of maldistribution were long-lasting—from two to six or seven decades—but estimates that they might be confined to one generation in the contemporary third world. Yet industry and agriculture are quite different in this respect. Adelman (1989) argues that since agricultural development uses precisely those factors that the farm sector has in abundance—unskilled labor—job creation should focus on farming. For example, "planting of HYV [high-yielding varieties] on irrigated land can produce an increase in the demand for labor by a factor of 7.5" (Adelman 1989, p. 5).

Contemporarily, urban employment in the informal sector, where barriers to entry are low, is a common and less expensive alternative to industrial work. Marginal or petty business activities are employing more and more people—

including many recent migrants from agriculture—and are allowing the battered Latin American economies the extra time they need to attract more foreign investment, modernize industry, and find new sources of development. The informal economy flourished significantly during the recent recessionary years. Employment in the informal sector rose from 20 percent of all jobs at the end of the 1970s to about 35 percent today. The sector represents up to 40 percent of urban employment in many Latin American countries (Nash 1992). The *Christian Science Monitor* (Gannon 1988) described the informal market phenomenon: "Fruit sellers stake out curbspace with blankets, patchwork shoe repairmen set up sewing machines at street corners, and black-market buses, which account for 90 percent of Lima's transit system, carry the urban poor to and from their black-market real estate—shantytowns built on invaded land." Bolivia exemplifies the importance of the informal sector; its unemployment rate of 7 percent would have been 35 percent if such a sector did not exist. De Soto (1987) estimates that the informal economy accounts for more than half of Peru's production. In Argentina and Colombia, the figure is at least one-third and rising.

De Soto (1987) shows the formal-sector inhibitions that Peru places on the establishment of a small business and land purchase. It required 289 days and the equivalent of $1,231 in lost wages to register a small business in Lima; in the United States, a comparable procedure took just 3½ hours. To buy a piece of private property would take 7 years and countless papers generated at a variety of ministries, de Soto estimates. Because the informal sector operates without "rules," many of which are useless, bureaucratic steps, it is the most flexible part of Peru's economy, de Soto (1987) believes. There is by no means universal acceptance of his contention that the informal sector can and should be controlled—and somehow harnessed for the good of society as a whole. De Soto is criticized as neglecting the reality of the matter: Since the informal sector is very large and unwieldy, made up of thousands of minuscule transactions, there are few levers that those in power can use to force it to serve a more focused "social good."

For example, critics debate the desirability of encouraging an informal sector that gives little attention to worker health and safety standards. Enterprises in the informal sector have low operating costs so they compete easily with legitimate businesses. Indeed, the underground economy may thrive because it can drive regulated firms out of the market, inter alia, robbing the government of tax revenues. The paradox is that if society attempts some sway over the informal sector, it may augment poverty and social discontent by abolishing needed jobs.

The third method of poverty alleviation is direct subsidy of the poor. A number of policies have been attempted: food stamps, input subsidies, price controls, and income transfers. In general, these policies in Latin America have been associated with "economic populism" and inflation, to be discussed later. They are criticized for being too expensive for fragile, poor economies.

This book focuses mainly on the fourth method: broadening access to the factors needed for agricultural production as a way to improve the condition of the rural poor in Latin America. This approach, commonly called agrarian reform, is seldom effective unless combinations of strategies are used, and the difficulties and strengths of a land-reform approach must be recognized and taken into account.

Those who write favorably about agrarian reform tend to cite the contributions that *campesino* agriculture makes. Emiliano Ortega (1982, 1985) concludes that it is not correct to assume that the contribution of crops that peasant agriculture produces *on land it owns or controls* is insignificant given the small amount of resources available to it. Classifying about one-fifth of the farmland in the region as "peasant agriculture," Ortega (1982) shows that in 1972, 30 percent of marketed agricultural products in the region were grown on small farms. He also shows that as income rises after reforms, more crop marketing occurs (Ortega 1982). Some basic crops are more apt than others to be produced by the peasant sector. In Mexico, for example, 70 percent of all corn, two-thirds of all beans, and one-third of the wheat crop are produced by the peasant sector. In some countries peasant contributions to exports also have been large; in Costa Rica, for example, nearly 30 percent of agricultural exports is attributable to the peasant sector; in Honduras, the figure is 25 percent (Ortega 1982, esp. pp. 82-94; Ortega 1985; see also López Cordovez 1982). In Brazil, 80 percent of peasant sector production is marketed (Thiesenhusen and Melmed-Sanjak 1990, Table 8, p. 402).

Furthermore, increasing incomes for benefited farmers would change the composition of demand and give new dynamism to industrialization. As low-income farmers increase their earnings, they enlarge the market economy for simple consumer goods—often the starting place for establishing a viable manufacturing sector. Also, agrarian-reform beneficiaries would begin to demand farm inputs like fertilizer that could increase per-acre yields. With linkages forged between the new agrarian-reform sector and manufacturing, economic growth should ensue (Dorner 1992, pp. 18-19).

Others have argued the case for agrarian reforms in Latin America on the basis of the region's excess capacity. It has land that is suited for agriculture but is unutilized or underutilized, land that could be used for production and job creation. Lacking access to that land, *campesinos* are moving to cities, which are overcrowded and increasingly ungovernable, or they are migrating across international borders. Thus it makes perfect sense to utilize unused rural land to solve pressing social problems.

As Prosterman et al. noted:

Land reform can generate increased overall economic activity, including the creation of nonagricultural jobs. As a broad base of agricultural families benefiting from land reform receive higher incomes, they enter the marketplace for a range of locally produced goods and services, from improved housing to schoolbooks, from bicycles to sewing machines. Development theory has rediscovered agriculture, recognizing that a dynamic agriculture has significant forward and backward linkages to broader societal development (1990, p. 312).

The ways in which the Latin American countries have approached land reform are quite different, ranging from the revolutionary situations of Mexico, Bolivia, Nicaragua, and Guatemala to the legislated reforms of Chile and the quasi-military, authoritarian reforms of El Salvador.

The rationale behind the reforms presented as case studies, beginning in Chapter 2, is often as different as the manner in which they evolved, though there are surely some commonalities. Although Guatemala's and Chile's reforms were stopped dead in their tracks and largely reversed, in Guatemala the semifeudal agrarian structure continues in many parts of the country today, and in Chile's Central Valley a highly modernized agriculture oriented to world markets is one legacy of the reform period. Mexico's agrarian reform continued into the 1990s along a slow, evolutionary path. Bolivia's reform sector was especially neglected since it occurred in the mid-1950s whereas today El Salvador's and Nicaragua's are caught up in the peace-and-privatization process.

The reforms of Mexico, Bolivia, Guatemala, Chile, Nicaragua, and El Salvador are given detailed treatment here. In very important ways land reform is a manifestation of the historic and social background of the country in which it takes place. In each case, attention is given to historic background, description of the reform, economic contributions of reform including its effects on *campesino* beneficiaries, and current problems. Chapter 8 draws together reform lessons.

The rationale behind agrarian reforms in Latin America has been made in the literature on the basis of their being able to utilize fallow land, stabilize the peasantry, alleviate poverty, assist the country in making the transition to capitalism, add to production, augment employment, add to effective demand, improve equity in the economy, and save the environment. What is the record?

2

Early Revolutionary Reforms: Mexico

Mexico's agrarian reform was used by most Latin American countries as a template for parts of their own programs. Unfortunately, the Mexican land reform did not give *campesinos* the equality and social justice that some advocates had promised. Although Mexico's land reform paved the way for present-day economic growth and the appearance of a vibrant middle class, farm workers, small-farm operators, and indigenous cultivators still live in dismal poverty relative to the opulence of the upper classes. In late 1991, speaking to a country fast emerging from its debt crisis via free markets and trade, President Carlos Salinas de Gortari announced his goal of amending the Mexican Constitution of 1917 to end over seventy years of agrarian reforms. A news magazine displayed its story on the event under the headline, "The unfinished revolution: Economic reform in Mexico has yet to reach the grassroots." It continued:

> The market-oriented economic miracle wrought by President Carlos Salinas de Gortari has yet to trickle down to the countryside, where the vast majority of Mexico's poor live. Half of Mexico's 81 million people still live in poverty, and pulling them into the emerging market economy is the key to sustaining both Mexico's growth and Salinas's success.... In an attempt to attract investment to the countryside, a constitutional ban on the sale of [land in agrarian-reform communities] has been dropped to encourage creation of larger, more-efficient agricultural units. Salinas is thus dismantling a pillar of stability that ended Mexico's long and bloody revolution (Robinson and Dabrowski 1992).

In the mid-1990s, agriculture in Mexico is at a turning point. According to Cornelius (1992, p. 6), fewer than half of Mexico's *ejidos* (agrarian-reform settlements) employ any kind of modern technology; 58 percent, in fact, still keep oxen for plowing. Although sparse rainfall characterizes much of the country, only 17 percent of *ejido* land is irrigated. Of the 50 percent of Mexicans who live below the poverty line, 70 percent reside in rural areas. Per capita incomes of the agriculturally employed average one-third of the national mean. Most of the 10 million whom the Mexican government deems "critically nutritionally deficient" live in rural areas.

THE *PORFIRIATO*

During the latter part of the nineteenth century and the first decade of the twentieth, Mexico had surged ahead of most countries of Latin America in terms of economic growth yet remained the prototype of an underdeveloped country. The country was characterized by technological dualism, domination of leading sectors by foreign interests, a small middle class, and quasi-feudal agriculture with a large, backward, poverty-stricken rural sector (Singer 1969, p. 15). During the long dictatorship of Porfirio Díaz, which ended with the outbreak of revolution in 1910, the state supported the privileged few while preventing the vast majority from realizing improvements in their welfare. On the other hand, the government of Díaz (the *porfiriato*, as it was known) encouraged development in mining, transportation, commerce, and banking as well as in textile manufacture. Although most Mexicans missed out on this activity, the economic infrastructure that Díaz helped to create—though some of it was destroyed in the revolution—provided an important backdrop to Mexico's achievements after the war (Singer 1969, p. 16).

Nevertheless, upon Díaz's exit, the agricultural sector was a shambles, characterized by lack of direction and stagnating production. Fewer than 11,000 *hacendados* controlled 57 percent of the national territory; 834 of these landowners held 1.3 million square kilometers (one of them being a landholding as large as Costa Rica). Meanwhile, some 15 million peasants were landless. Much common village land[1]—a buffer for *campesinos*—had disappeared in the years after 1857. Beginning in that year, the *Ley Lerdo* (liberal reform legislation) caused much land to be individually titled and appropriated from peasants, often by nearby landlords (Singer 1969, p. 49).

Capitalism did not work equitably in this setting; economic growth accentuated income disparities. In general, landowners were more interested in avoiding risk than in entrepreneurial activity and often rented their properties to other cultivators who were even less innovative. Singer claimed: "The system ... left in its wake an illiterate, poorly productive work force, constantly in debt to the plantation, with no capital to speak of, and with no motive or opportunity to experiment" (1969, p. 50). After 1890, Mexico began to import staples. While money wages remained stable between 1810 and 1910, prices for foodstuffs rose almost 300 percent.

Peasants labored on landlords' property on set terms; they had little incentive to work efficiently. Singer described the life of the hacienda-dwelling *campesino*, the *peón*: "He was paid in corn, pulque, the right to live rent-free on property and petty cash.... He was perpetually in debt. The debt could be his or his father's, or it might even be older. His labor was unfree.... His working hours were from dawn to dusk. He could be flogged for requesting an auditing of his account at the store, failing to meet quotas, and not kissing the master's hand" (1969, p. 50).

THE HACIENDA

The Mexican hacienda, which evolved from the even more extensive operations called *estancias*, is usually dated from the depression at the end of the sixteenth century, when, instead of producing for the market, the farmers turned inward and grew crops and livestock for estate residents. Concurrently, the ownership structure of farming areas was evolving from usufructuary to private rights. The Spanish crown began to distribute *mercedes*, or land grants awarded to notables, in a process known as *composición*. Previously it had made supposedly temporary grants of jurisdictions (*encomiendas* and *repartimientos*) to individuals; these included both villages and the *peones*. Accordingly, grantees could levy taxes and demand labor of the villagers living within their *encomiendas* or *repartimientos*. In areas of more dependable rainfall, the haciendas that developed were smaller; in the desert north, very large estates were the rule. *Hacendados* soon began to take up residence in towns, spending time on their estates only during planting and harvesting. Sometimes their absence left a breach that was filled by an enduring type of local boss known as the *cacique*. (The Salinas reforms in 1992 were made primarily to increase agricultural production but also to rid the countryside of *caciques*.) Initially the haciendas that evolved were controlled by merchants, the church and clergy, royal officials, winners of major battles, and mine owners.

Historian Frank Tannenbaum set the hacienda in context: "The hacienda is not just an agricultural property owned by an individual. The hacienda is a society under private auspices. It is an entire social system and it governs the life of those attached to it from the cradle to the grave" (1962, p. 80).

Until the revolution, a typical hacienda in Mexico may have incorporated as many as 200 peasant families scattered in five to ten groups residing within its borders. The landlord furnished the land and contributed the working capital; the *peón acasillado* (peasant resident on the hacienda) provided the labor and delivered a predefined share of the harvested crop to the owner. In addition, the *peón* or his wife may have supplied maid service to the landlord for a specified number of days each month. The husband and older male children, in addition to sharecropping land with the owner, worked on the demesne of the proprietor, the part of the farm reserved for the master's own crops, orchards, and livestock. Usually the *peón* and his family labored six days in the landlord's fields and one day on the plot allowed for individual cultivation. The wife and daughters often performed household tasks for the landowner on a rotation basis. If the *peón* needed something from the company store (*tienda del raya*), he bought it with the few chits he earned by working on the demesne. Also, landlords paid their laborers' taxes, arranged for families' clothing, and supplied medical attention when ill. They also paid the parish priest to give mass in the church within the hacienda boundaries.

These goods and services often resulted in continuing debt, which the *peón* was endlessly paying off. The relationship was one of paternalism. Landlords "protected" the *peón* and his family from the exigencies of the market—indeed, from having to cope with the world outside the hacienda gates. Frequently the landlord became the *compadre* of the *peón*'s children for the Roman Catholic baptism, giving rise not only to coparental relationships with the children but also to a set of fictive kinship duties, obligations, and privileges with the parents. In return, the *patrón* demanded allegiance and labor. The paternalistic hacienda exchange relationship was asymmetric: *campesinos* gave more up more in dignity and labor than they received in benefits.

Given the weakness of state power in Mexico, the end of the seventeenth century and beginning of the eighteenth saw the zenith of the Mexican hacienda. Although it was still a viable institution at the time of the revolution, the state had reclaimed some of its powers (such as judicial functions), which the *hacendado* frequently had asserted in the absence of local courts. Tannenbaum, noting that people on haciendas were born there, observed: "They cannot leave because they may be in debt, or because there is no place to go. This is home and every other place is foreign. Here too their fathers and grandfathers were born and are buried. If the place changes hands, they change with it" (1962, p. 82). He added, "The hacienda is, however, not merely an economic enterprise. It is also a social, political, and cultural institution" (Tannenbaum 1962, p. 85). Indeed, work roles on the hacienda defined a class structure, one in which those who worked at manual tasks on land that belonged to others were always lowest in status.

THE REVOLUTION

The Mexican Revolution was far from a simple battle over land. Mainly it was a middle- and upper-class revolt against the thirty-year *porfiriato*. Obtaining land for *campesinos* and relieving rural poverty was merely a subplot in a complex drama begun in northern Mexico by a group of landowners and intellectuals who wished to establish a liberal democracy that provided for universal suffrage and no presidential reelection. Led initially by Francisco Madero, a politically progressive landowner, the revolutionaries were "a heterogeneous conglomeration of sectors of a number of different social classes, each with its own grievances against the Díaz regime and its own set of demands to press" (Hellman 1983, p. 4). The group was prepared to take up arms because its own economic and political advancement had been thwarted by the Díaz dictatorship. Furthermore, the loose coalition was angry that Díaz had allowed foreign capital to control the country's infrastructure and dominate its growth industries. But when it came to specifics, Hellman stated that the revolutionary goals were as varied as the groups around Madero:

The middle- and upper-class liberals were calling for political reforms to broaden the base of political participation, for anticlerical legislation to curb the power of the Catholic Church, and for nationalistic legislation to impose state control over foreign investment and ownership. They were concerned with putting an end to some of the glaring abuses of the Díaz regime: forced military conscription, suppression of the press, the total neglect of public education, and the maintenance of order through the use of ... a militia of mercenary soldiers (1983, p. 5).

Meanwhile, appeals to a mass base that called for social justice and "land or liberty" perplexed and even frightened the middle- and upper-class leaders of the revolution. Those who farmed had demands that varied according to their relation to the land. For example, agricultural laborers who worked for wages on commercial estates carried petitions that resembled those of urban workers in industry: better pay, shorter hours, more benefits. *Peones* and sharecroppers wanted their own land (Hellman 1983, p. 6). Those who had their land sequestered by the "liberal reforms" wanted justice—the return of their property.

The revolutionary message found special resonance in the state of Morelos, where "[o]f the hundred pueblos ... there was probably not one that was not involved in a freshly embittered legal dispute with a neighboring hacienda" (Womack 1967, p. 61). The cry for land thus came to be a critical demand of the southern front of the revolution. Here the revolutionaries had a more focused, coherent, and radical ideology than elsewhere in the country. "[T]he movement was shaped by the charismatic qualities of its undisputed leader, Emiliano Zapata, whose name came to represent all that the southern peasants, or *zapatistas*, were fighting for" (Hellman 1983, p. 7). Zapata and his guerrilla troops fought from the mountains and the forests, never attracting much nonpeasant support except for a group of radical intellectuals who helped him draft the documents that called for a breakup of the *latifundios* and a restoration of village lands to their rightful owners. Through it all, Zapata never broadened his appeal. Whether this was by choice—because it would dilute his call for land—or by fate—because his appeal was always doomed to be local and even parochial—is unknown, and fuels scholarly argument to this day.

Another revolutionary leader, Venustiano Carranza, also a landowner of substance and a conservative who first fought alongside Madero, despised radicals like Zapata for demanding social change. Even Francisco (Pancho) Villa, whose origins were as humble as those of Zapata, did not join ideologically with Zapata until relatively late in the conflict, preferring instead to found schools among the poor to overcome social injustice. As Hellman explained, "even at the height of his military strength, Villa never attempted to seize landholdings and distribute them to the landless in a systematic fashion as Zapata had done in the south.... [N]either Villa nor the generals who fought under him were much interested in establishing the legal bases or the mechanisms for a full scale land reform program" (1983, p. 11).

When Madero became president of Mexico, he was strongly opposed by U.S. President William Howard Taft, who worried that the revolutionary government would not continue to grant special concessions to U.S. capital. But after Madero was killed and counterrevolutionaries took over the Mexican government, Woodrow Wilson was U.S. president; he would not recognize the new government, deeming it a throwback to the *porfiriato*. American policy toward Mexico soon emphasized arms sales to favored revolutionaries and shows of force. The counterrevolutionaries were able to govern only eighteen months, from February 1913 to July 1914 (the short-lived U.S. invasion of Veracruz took place in April 1914), after which Carranza emerged as leader of the revolutionary armies.

THE WAR ENDS: GAINS AND LOSSES

Started in October 1910, the war finally ended with the proclamation of the constitution in February 1917. The Mexican economy lay in ruins. Basic infrastructure had been destroyed in the conflict, and public utilities needed major reconstruction. Mining was in severe decline, and corn production had dropped to dangerously low levels. Few cattle remained, having been either consumed by the combatants or driven across the U.S. border in exchange for arms. With such severe dislocations in agriculture, food prices soared, prompting food riots in the cities. Although peasant-guerrillas and soldiers had died in large numbers, survivors found themselves no better off than before the revolution. Gains "made by the peasant armies ... were undermined or neutralized by the manipulations of politicians like Carranza, who represented the aspirations of land owners, industrialists, and a highly mobile middle class" (Hellman 1983, p. 15). Indeed, there had been no time during the conflict for peasants and workers to consolidate their gains; in 1920, Zapata was assassinated and after that many *villistas* and even some *zapatista* officers picked over the spoils of war to enrich themselves.

But for the *campesinos* there had been an important glimmer of hope—in September 1914, when Zapata renounced Carranza because of the latter's lack of interest in land reform. Villa had met secretly with Zapata and the two agreed that Carranza was not to be considered a trustworthy revolutionary leader. Afterward Carranza called a meeting with the *villistas* to discuss his plan for governing Mexico. Against Carranza's wishes, *villistas* brought *zapatistas* to the discussion and they presented a draft land reform, the *Plan de Ayala*, which they felt should be a plank in Carranza's platform. Meanwhile, Zapata had already begun instituting land reform informally and extralegally in Morelos.

Carranza thought that he could easily dismiss the results of the tripartite meeting, particularly the agrarian reforms set forth by the *zapatistas*. But the *zapatista/villista* forces staged such an enormous display of force in Mexico City that Carranza's troops were obliged to move to Veracruz. Back to the sea, Carranza issued a decree—often considered the beginning of official recognition of agrarian reform in Mexico—on 6 January 1915, which restated the *Plan de Ayala*. Paradoxically, Carranza had undercut *zapatista* demands yet became the first Mexican president to proclaim the country's land reform.

Increasingly desperate, Carranza secured Alvaro Obregón to dismantle the solidarity organized labor had displayed with forces under Zapata and Villa. For rather small concessions, some members of organized labor joined with Carranza, but most still favored unity with Zapata and Villa. When Carranza held another meeting in Querétero to draft a new constitution, he felt that he had finally bested the *villistas* and *zapatistas*. But by this time a group of those who had fought with Carranza—and even General Obregón himself—regarded themselves as *agraristas*, determined to see the basic principles of the *Plan de Ayala* incorporated into the constitution. In the end, they succeeded (Hellman 1983, pp. 17–28).

Alvaro Obregón became president in 1921 after the death of Carranza, and his term is known for expanding the system of mass education. He also cleared up some of the Mexico-U.S. diplomatic debris left over from the revolution. President Plutarco Elías Calles (1924–1928, plus the series of puppets he installed from 1929 to 1934) established some weak benefits for and stronger controls of the labor movement. He is known primarily for giving shape to the institutional structure of the country's political system and the party now called the Partido Revolucionario Institucional (PRI) (Hellman 1983, pp. 29–33). Calles also determined to enforce constitutional restraints on the Catholic Church, and his anticlericalists were soon countered by conservative *cristeros*, giving rise to a brief religious war between Right and Left in parts of central and western Mexico (Cline 1963, pp. 32–33). This movement slowed any progress toward agrarian and other liberal reforms, for the *cristeros* were adamantly anti-*agraristas*. Even though his policies became ever-more conservative, Calles distributed some 3 million hectares of land in a nascent program of land reform. Nonetheless, after eight months in Europe witnessing the production problems that small farmers faced in France, Calles returned to call the Mexican agrarian reform a failure (Craig 1983, p. 58).

In general, the northern dynasty—Carranza, Obregón, and Calles—"were or had become large landowners ... and they were supported by large landowners from all parts of the republic. It was in their personal interest to leave large landholdings intact. And these men ruled Mexico until 1934" (Hellman 1983, p. 27). Landowners fought *agraristas* through a terrorist organization called the White Guards, specializing in assassination. Another barrier to agrarian reform was foreign ownership of land. At the outbreak of the revolution, 40 percent of the land was owned by U.S. citizens. By 1923, 20 percent of the land still belonged to foreigners, with Americans owning the greatest part.[2]

The Mexican Revolution "still stands as the bloodiest conflict ever witnessed in the Western Hemisphere. Of the 14.5 million Mexicans when the struggle broke out in October 1910, one millon and a half lost their lives. By 1920, 8000 villages had completely disappeared as a result of the conflagration" (Hellman

1983, p. 3). Although peasants were only one small group fighting the corruption and selfishness of those in power, the revolution eventually forced post-*porfiriato* Mexico to come to terms with its land problem.

THE MEXICAN LAND REFORM

Farm production, especially in central parts of the country, remained low until Lázaro Cárdenas took power (1934–1940). Rural unrest resulted in premature urbanization (people moved to towns and cities before there were jobs to absorb them), deterioration of physical assets (including irrigation works, granaries, and the like), and low levels of savings and investment, all of which slowed postrevolutionary recovery. In a sense Calles was compelled to arrange for a more liberal successor for the new party was deeply divided between liberal and conservative factions. But when Cárdenas assumed power in Mexico, policies changed more sharply than ever thought possible. Calles reacted with such disapproval that Cárdenas eventually had him removed from the country. The more Calles attempted to control Cárdenas, the more Cárdenas exerted his fierce independence.

Still, what Cárdenas wanted was reform, not new revolution, and land reform was an important part of his program. On the agrarian question, "Cárdenas stood firmly by the principle that the land belongs to those who work it. In the Constitution of 1917, he found the concrete mechanism through which agrarian justice could be achieved. Cárdenas clearly meant to throw the full power of his office behind a dramatic, large-scale land distribution" (Hellman 1983, p. 35). If peasants, speaking through rural union movements, could articulate their need for land, Cárdenas was determined that they should have it. "[H]e was not setting out to destroy the bourgeoisie. He was, rather, attempting to shake up a social, political, and economic structure that had grown rigid since the revolution.... Cárdenas's vision of Mexican development was a capitalist one" (Hellman 1983, pp. 37–38).

Cárdenas had run on a platform of "cooperative socialism" (but it more aptly could have been called "capitalist reformism"), endorsing collective agricultural communities or *ejidos* as an antidote to the tiny farms that Calles had railed against after his European sojourn (Craig 1983, p. 112). Cárdenas also institutionalized the role of workers, giving them visible, often vocal functions that they had never had in the Calles party organization. Also, Cárdenas "extended education to the remotest parts of the country, and, in many other ways, rekindled the sparks of hope of 'los de abajo'—the underdogs.... As a climax, Cárdenas at a stroke expropriated the foreign petroleum holdings, long a symbol to Mexicans of exploitation" (Cline 1963, p. 33).

Cárdenas's program of agrarian reform was not a top-down effort. The Great Depression had sent home from the United States many rural workers who had been accused of taking jobs that U.S. citizens should have. When these former peasants returned to Mexico, they were not ready to accept life once again as *peones* on haciendas or even as sharecroppers or seasonal laborers, so they helped change the rural society around them. These returnees spearheaded the *campesino* organization that was crucial to the land reform (Craig 1983, pp. 91–94).

Thus land reform was implemented where the rural population concentrations were located—in the central and the southern parts of the country, which had the highest *campesino* population density and where the mystique of the revolution's *zapatista* Southern Front was strongest. There were fewer and larger *ejidos* in the north, where irrigated commercial agriculture was favored.[3]

In a backlash to Cárdenas during World War II, landlords threatened to withdraw support from the war effort if not placated by a cessation of agrarian reform. In fact, the landlords' self-serving cry fit into the general economic plans of the governments that followed Cárdenas. These administrations saw greater development potential in an economic strategy that favored manufacturing over farming and building infrastructure and promoting commercial agriculture instead of fostering rural reforms.

Closely associated with the immediate post-Cárdenas period was an ambitious plan to expand rural infrastructure, especially roads and irrigation works. Reynolds felt this expenditure "did more than anything else to bring about rapid growth of crop production after 1940.... [Indeed,] the years 1935 to 1955 saw the government involved in a major transfer of resources from urban to rural activities" (1970, p. 155). But resources did not follow the agrarian-reform beneficiaries. Reynolds (1970, p. 158) generalized that "those regions with the highest concentration of *ejidos* (the Center and the Gulf) received a disproportion-ately small share of public investment in irrigation" in the decades after 1940. Investment in roads during the 1940s and 1950s similarly favored the north and north-Pacific. These areas also accounted for two-thirds of private investment in agriculture from 1940 to 1960, with benefits largely accruing to commercial growers. Meanwhile, the *ejidatario* or landless laborer, the *minifundista*, and the *comunero* remained immune from these developments.

Under Article 27 of the Constitution of 1917, the agrarian reform in Mexico establishes that all natural resources belong to the state, which can assign them as private and social property; land in *ejidos* and Indian communities cannot be sold or transferred and corporations cannot own land (Vargas 1992, p. 5).[4] Land-reform communities were created in three ways: by *restitución*, by *dotación*, and by *amplificación*. The first method restored property to groups of *campesinos* whose land had been taken by others (it was recognized that especially during the *porfiriato* some landlords had moved their fences to take holdings from villagers),[5] but the petitioning peasant communities were expected to prove that they had once owned the area in question. Although the original reformers thought that *restitución* would be the most important way of allotting land to *campesinos*, many of the early records were destroyed in the revolution and some ownership documents had never been issued in the first place.

The principal *ejido*-granting mechanism, the one responsible for some 80 percent of the Mexican land reform, was *dotación*, an outright award of land to an indigenous community. Communities of no fewer than twenty *campesinos* could petition for hacienda land located within a 7-kilometer radius of their village, provided the land claimed was owned privately by an individual. *Campesino* communities could request that the government expropriate parts of any holding over the legal limit of 100 hectares of irrigated land to yield a total of 20 rain-fed hectares (or 10 irrigated hectares) for every family in a claiming community.[6]

In cases where more public land became available or if more affectable private land were found in the 7-kilometer radius, land could be added to either *dotación* or *restitución* ejidal grants in a process known as *amplificación*.

If no claimable land existed, communities could be granted land in a *centro de población*, often on the forested frontier, at the discretion of the government. If no land was available either within the 7-kilometer area or as a *centro*, *campesinos* were placed on a waiting list. With rapid population growth in the rural areas of Mexico, the waiting list quickly grew; in fact, once enrolled, the peasant had slim chance of ever obtaining land. Petitions for land first went to the state government, giving political units (and *caciques*) inordinate powers of patronage, for they made the initial decisions concerning exactly which landlords would be expropriated and which *campesinos* would benefit.

Agrarian law introduced many ambiguities regarding hectares permitted for holding as it sought to preserve economies of size for farms growing agricultural export crops and for other commercial endeavors. Legislation permitted the issuance of *certificados de inafectabilidad* (exemption certificates) to larger holdings for crops such as cotton and for cattle ranching. In cotton, properties of 150 hectares of irrigated land or its equivalent in rain-fed land were allowed. In livestock, the ceiling was "the land area needed to support 500 head of cattle," but owners were in peril of losing their land if they intensified their operations by improving pasture or growing grain instead of grass.[7]

After the government processed an expropriation claim on the part of the peasant community and land was finally granted (a long and tedious process), the *ejido* was expected to elect a governing council and individuals were to begin farming. If there was not enough land to provide each beneficiary family with a minimum of 20 hectares of rain-fed land (and there seldom was), *campesino* recipients divided the available land according to rules they established. The problem with this informal procedure was that an official parcel title (*título parcelario*) could not be awarded. The result was that nearly 90 percent of *ejidatarios* never got property titles (though official *ejido* membership was duly recorded).

Although land distribution brought a certain amount of insecurity to the landlord class and *campesinos* tended to grow subsistence crops (corn and beans, especially), Reynolds claimed:

> These costs must be set against the eventual benefits of agrarian reform in terms of more equitable distribution of the returns from the land to the peasant; a higher ... rate of return for his labor and hence more labor-intensive cultivation of peasant holdings, increased output per hectare in all regions, greater stability of rural incomes, wider participation of the rural population in national politics, identification of the peasantry with the goals of the federal government, and freedom of the government to engage in large-scale investments in commercial agriculture once it had attacked the problem of rural land hunger (1970, p. 140).

Eventually land reform brought both economic security and political stability, traits historically related in the minds of those who supported small-scale agriculture (Huntington 1968). Such an ambience was required to create the security of expectations needed to improve the prospects of investment and to stimulate development. In the end, however, the proliferation of smallholdings together with a reduction in the size of haciendas (in the nonreformed sector) confirmed the bimodal structure of agriculture in Mexico on a different scale.

Landlords could retain a preferred part of the farm, invariably containing the bulk of the infrastructure and the best soil. The hacienda remnant was called a *rancho* or a *pequeña propiedad agrícola* (small agricultural property), though it may not have been "small" by most definitions. Aside from the *ejidos* and *pequeñas propiedades agrícolas*, indigenous reservations (*comunidades indígenas*) were also a component of Mexico's land-tenure panorama. The *comunidades* persisted in more remote places, where their isolation enabled them to remain aloof from central government policies. Sharecroppers and many other combination-tenure categories filled out the complex scene of land tenure relations that came to make up contemporary Mexico.

Ejidos were designed to be usufructuary property, and *ejidatarios* could not mortgage, rent, or sell the land (though in practice, and without the blessings of law, they did lease and alienate).[8] If any ejidal plot were not farmed for two consecutive years, it was subject to forfeiture to the *ejido* government and could be repartitioned among members.

In fact, it proved impossible for the government to prevent subdivision of *ejido* parcels upon inheritance. John Heath (1990, p. 4) notes that the Mexican land reform failed to halt the spread of *minifundia*: on holdings up to 5 hectares, the average farm was 2.4 hectares in the *ejido* sector and 1.7 hectares in the private sector. By 1981, there was no significant difference between the *ejido* and the private small farm in crop mix, proportion of cropland left in fallow, and number of cattle per hectare. At the same time, there was proportionally somewhat more land in production on *ejidos* than on small private farms (Heath 1990) (see Table 2.1).

TABLE 2.1   Land Use by Tenure Category, Mexico, 1991

	Ejido*		Private	
	000 ha	*(%)*	*000 ha*	*(%)*
All farms				
Total	15,235	(100.0)	73,862	(100.0)
In production†	12,975	(85.2)	54,200	(73.4)
Cultivated	8,279	(54.3)	8,753	(11.8)
Fallow	1,733	(11.3)	1,675	(2.2)
Natural pasture	2,154	(14.1)	27,427	(37.1)
Forest	2,588	(16.9)	26,426	(35.7)
Other	481	(3.1)	9,599	(12.9)
Irrigated	1,878	(12.3)	9,133	(12.3)
Head of cattle (000)	7,613		14,067	
Farms up to 5 ha				
Total	2,952	(100.0)	982	(100.0)
In production†	2,778	(94.1)	919	(93.6)
Cultivated	2,294	(77.7)	699	(71.1)
Fallow	259	(8.7)	69	(7.0)
Natural pasture	189	(6.4)	93	(9.4)
Forest	172	(5.8)	80	(8.1)
Other	38	(1.3)	41	(4.1)
Irrigated	464	(15.7)	104	(10.5)
Head of cattle	2,387		855	

* *Ejido* refers to the aggregate of individual parcels; it does not include collective *ejidos* or the communally worked area of parceled *ejidos*; according to Agrarian Reform Ministry statistics, there were 101.3 million hectares in the land-reform sector in 1982 (INEGI 1986). "Cultivated" includes planted pasture; "other" refers to land that is not being farmed and/or is inappropriate for agriculture.

† Refers to land that was being used in April-September 1981 for crop, livestock, or forest activities.

Source: John Richard Heath, "Evaluating the Impact of Mexico's Land Reform and Agricultural Productivity," *World Development* 20 (1992): 704. Reprinted with kind permission from Elsevier Science Ltd., The Boulevard, Langford Lane, Kidlington OX5 1GB, U.K.

Today, about half the farmland in Mexico is occupied by 23,000 *ejidos*. Most are "parceled *ejidos*," that is, they are divided into individual family-farmed plots, often with some land, usually forest or pasture, held in common (Heath 1992, p. 695). Some 3.1 million peasant families are *ejidatarios*. There are a few collective *ejidos* (perhaps 3 percent of the total) located in areas where there seem to be economies of size in farming, especially in the Laguna region of north-central Mexico.

While Lázaro Cárdenas conceived of *campesinos'* farming collectively, the ensuing PRI government insisted on policies that fostered individual farming within the *ejido*. Although the original idea was to grant loans to the *ejido* as a unit for individual members of the collective to share, in time credit came to be allocated to subgroupings of the most creditworthy *campesinos*. The initial practice of giving special assistance in farming techniques to collective units of farmers was also changed in favor of offering aid to the most able *ejidatarios*. The unity of the *ejido* organization was accordingly weakened through the factionalism and class consciousness that resulted.[9] Furthermore, since the most skilled *ejidatarios* tended to find individual farming—where they were not held back by laggards—more remunerative, those who withdrew into family operations were no doubt the same talented individuals most needed to keep the group farm functional.

Today's small farms (private and *ejido*)—that is, those under 5 hectares—still grow more than their proportionate share of corn and beans, the country's staples, whereas larger private farms tend to cultivate higher-value crops and exportables. Although Mexico pegged its prices for corn and beans at about double the world market price during the 1980s, it imported a good supply of both staples. Throughout the decade structural adjustment policies called on productive sectors to reduce imports and government subsidies while increasing exports; agriculture in general and the *ejido* sector in particular were seen at the time as not doing their share to reinvigorate the flagging economy.

The poor performance of farming today stands in stark contrast to the period during and after the golden age of Cárdenas reforms, from 1934 to 1965, when Mexican agricultural production increased by 325 percent, better than any other Latin American country in the same span. After the mid-1960s, farm production slowed, increasing only 1.2 percent a year from 1965 to 1970. Performance in the 1970s and 1980s was erratic; by the 1980s, in fact, farm-sector production growth had been negative for five years out of ten.

Although *ejidos* contain, on average, poorer soil than private farms, they consistently have a higher proportion of cultivated land. In addition, *ejidos* obtained higher output per purchased input during the 1950–1970 period when compared to private farms over 5 hectares, even though private farmers within the small-farm category got more credit than parcelized *ejidatarios* since they were able to use their land titles as collateral (the distinction is less clear for farms under 5 hectares).

The 1970s were characterized by substantial government investment (made feasible by favorable petroleum prices) aimed at reinvigorating peasant agriculture via large-scale development projects and a variety of incentive and subsidy programs. The result of this intervention (which, of course, came to an end with the austerity of the 1980s) was a more compliant peasantry and a better PRI orchestration of *ejidatarios* at the grassroots level. These initiatives were accompanied and followed by policies that emphasized commercial agriculture and production in the nonreform sector: increased farm exports and more domestic agribusiness particularly (Barkin and Suárez 1982; Sanderson 1986).

Measuring performance of the small-farm sector becomes more difficult in the post-1970 period because of fewer available case studies and gross inaccuracies in the 1981 agricultural census. Within this limitation, Heath (1992) determines that parcelized *ejidos* were just as productive as private farms of the same size after 1970. As in the 1950–1970 period, the private sector, dominated by larger farms, had a smaller proportion of area cultivated—12 percent of total land compared to 54 percent in the *ejido* sector (see Table 2.1). Heath (1992) concludes that farm size is more important to factor productivity than whether the farming unit is an *ejido* or a private enterprise. This evidence led him to predict, "the economic return to privatizing of the *ejido* is likely to be small" (Heath 1992, p. 706).

Since *ejidatarios* usually have no document to prove individual land ownership, they cannot borrow from commercial sector banks. Their options are therefore limited to middlemen, friends and relatives, and the undercapitalized Banrural (formerly called the Banco Nacional de Crédito Ejidal). Access to credit in the late 1960s and the 1970s was especially important because it determined which farmers could use the emerging green revolution technology. Loans from the Mexican government tended to focus on large, irrigated, private farms and not on *ejidos* (Heath 1992, pp. 700–702). Only about 40 percent of *ejidatarios* received government credit after allocations for rural development fell from 13.4 percent to 8.7 percent of the state budget between 1982 and 1988 (COHA 1992, p. 4). There was a decline of 20 percent of production credit to *ejidatarios* between 1980/1982 and 1986/1988 and medium- and long-term credit declined even more sharply (Heath 1992, p. 706).

Three-fourths of Banrural's borrowers are *ejidatarios*. In cases of default, the major sanction is to refuse further loans to the *ejido* group, a blanket punishment that falls on innocent *ejidatarios* and dilutes incentives for the solvent to repay. Sometimes Banrural, which has a chronic problem with late credit delivery, causes the default. The bank is also apt to spread its limited credit widely, an action that opens the institution to charges of giving more attention to political influence than to economic impact. When there is rural unrest, for instance, the government has been known to increase the flow of subsidized *ejido* credit from Banrural (or to give more attention to small-scale irrigation works or increase marketing subsidies). Indeed, credit to *ejidos* doubled in the first half of the 1970s when peasant protests were numerous (Heath 1992, p. 703).

This lack of institutional credit has caused the reappearance of *latifundios*, or *neolatifundismo*, a process that matches *campesinos* who have land but no credit with entrepreneurs who have capital but not enough land. *Neolatifundismo* occurs when capital-strong *ejidatarios* add other *ejido* plots through purchase or rental, reducing former colleagues to *peones*. It also happens when *pequeñas propiedades agrícolas* reconstitute their farms by buying out nearby *ejidatarios*, who may be so credit-starved and desperate that they will exchange their land for guaranteed employment as hired laborers. In other instances, well-to-do farmers rent as many *ejido* plots in an area as they can and work the land with tractors and implements. Also, foreign firms have recently begun operating on Mexican *ejidos*.

Until the reforms of Carlos Salinas de Gortari in November 1991, successive PRI governments paid lip service to the revolution and its land reform and continued to distribute land to *campesinos*. During the two presidencies that spanned the 1960s, for example, some 33 million hectares were apportioned. At first glance this compares favorably to the 18 million hectares given out by Cárdenas, but over 90 percent of the land allocated in the later years was not usable for cropping and probably represented a threat to fragile natural resources at a time when environmental matters were not high on the country's agenda. Hellman described this process:

> Each new administration continued to repeat the rhetoric of the past, asserting the government's commitment to land reform as a "major goal" of the Mexican Revolution. At the same time, each of these administrations pursued specific policies which, logically enough, reflected the interests of the dominant bourgeoisie. Taken as a whole, these policies undercut peasant gains of the past, and slowed the process of land reform until the trend culminated in the 1980s ... with a virtual abandonment of the *agrarista* commitment (1983, pp. 92–93).

Even when Salinas was about to proclaim an end to agrarian reform, he did not slight its role in Mexican history, claiming that changes were now necessary "[n]ot because agrarian reform failed, but because of the social, demographic, and economic dynamic the reform contributed" (Salinas de Gortari 1991, p. 28). Although land distribution provided a cloak of national symbolism and was often referred to in reverential tones, as a practical measure it prevented peasant unrest and, from time to time, provided an excuse for repression in the countryside. Without an agrarian reform, peasant pressure would surely have instigated the destabilization of more than one modern-day Mexican government and caused the unraveling of its economic development aspirations.

To summarize, the major strengths of the Mexican agrarian reform are:
- It served as an incentive for those who held *pequeñas propiedades agrícolas* to intensify and commercialize their farms so they could maintain their incomes while cultivating fewer hectares;
- it held some people to the land who otherwise might have been unemployed in the cities;

- it provided supporters for successive PRI governments and deterred rural unrest while the remainder of the economy could develop; and
- it allowed its beneficiaries to become the major producers of staples in the country.

On the other hand:

- Some marginal lands containing natural resources that should have been conserved, restored, or preserved were put at the disposal of farming;
- slow government title provision and late and inadequate input, credit, and technical assistance delivery left the sector with many disillusioned beneficiaries and short of its economic production potential;
- some landlords were untouched by land reform because of political connections or subterfuge, giving an undercurrent of unfairness to the process;
- land delivery was used as a form of patronage, often functioning to keep peasants politically repressed and "in their place" [one opposition party member claimed, "The *ejidos* replaced one *cacique* with PRI *caciques*" (Asman 1991)]; and
- many peasants did not benefit from the agrarian reforms (those belonging to Indian *comunidades*, for example, and the many landless peasants on the waiting list).

INCOME DISTRIBUTION

Between the revolution and 1934, very little asset redistribution took place and only 6 percent of the area ultimately to be affected by land reform was allocated. During the Cárdenas presidency (1934–1940) income distribution in Mexico became more egalitarian as land reform progressed. After that period the trend was toward increased inequality, however. Cole and Sanders (1970) calculate that salary and wage shares of national income, usually more equally distributed than profits, exceeded profit shares in 1940 (29.1 and 28.6 percent, respectively), but decreased to 23.8 percent as profits rose to 41.4 percent by 1950.[10]

Table 2.2 shows the increasing inequality in size distribution of income between 1950 and 1975 and the return of somewhat more equity in the 1980s. (For purposes of comparison, most figures for size distribution of income in Brazil and the United States are also given.)

Even though farm-level prices were favorable when compared to industrial prices (that is, internal terms of trade turned against manufacturing) during the 1940s, increased inequality accompanied economic discrimination against the peasant class after Cárdenas's presidency. Reynolds (1970, pp. 107–115) calculates that the internal terms of trade between the urban and the rural sectors shifted in the 1950s away from rural and toward urban areas to support import-substituting industrialization; productivity changes reinforced the switch.

TABLE 2.2 Distribution of Family Income After Taxes (in percentages)

Economic Level	Mexico						Brazil			U.S.
	1950	*1958*	*1963*	*1968*	*1969*	*1975*	*1977*	*1984*	*1989*	*1985*
Lowest 20%	6.1	5.0	4.2	(3.7)	4.0	(4.1)	2.9	4.1	2.1	4.7
30% below median	13.0	11.7	11.5	(10.7)	11.0	(10.1)	} 39.4*	40.0*	30.6*	53.4*
30% above median	21.1	20.4	21.7	(22.5)	21.0	(19.4)				
Top 20%	59.8	62.9	62.6	(63.1)	64.0	(66.4)	57.7	55.9	67.5	41.9
Gini index	.50	.53	.55	(.56)	.58	(.58)				

* Includes 30% below median and 30% above median. In Mexico, Brazil, and U.S., disaggregated data not available.

Sources: For Mexico, William C. Thiesenhusen, "The Illusory Goal of Equity in Latin American Agrarian Reform," in *International Dimensions of Land Reform*, ed. John D. Montgomery (Boulder, Colo.: Westview Press, 1984), p. 46; for Brazil and United States, World Bank, *World Development Report, 1993* (Oxford: Published for World Bank by Oxford University Press, 1993), Table 30, p. 297.

In postrevolutionary Mexico, economic growth did not raise the real incomes of the lower classes as much as it did those of the middle and upper classes. Hellman showed that in the forty years after 1940, the income of upper-class and upper-middle-class Mexicans grew steadily in both relative and absolute terms: "While workers' wages have declined ... [t]he government has placed almost no limits on profits.... Indeed in 1958 the incomes of the richest 5 percent of all Mexicans were 22 times those of the poorest 10 percent; by 1980, the gap had more than doubled and the rich enjoyed incomes 50 times greater than those of the poorest sector of the population" (1983, p. 61). Earlier Reynolds had observed, "Subsistence agriculture is widespread in Mexico, and real per capita output for these poorest families has not risen significantly for the past fifty years" (1970, p. 88).

One usually associates the Mexican Revolution with more cataclysmic and radical change in social relations than actually took place. Even literature reflects the gradual alteration of the country's social fabric. In *The Death of Artemio Cruz*, Carlos Fuentes examines the life of a landlord and lays bare the contemporary social structure of Mexico. By the book's conclusion we have learned that Don Artemio was a revolutionary in his day, but in contemporary times offers only the rhetoric of revolution while thwarting its purpose with every action. New tyrants replaced old ones to repress the beneficiaries of land reform and the landless. Through Artemio, Fuentes muses: "Unfortunate land ... where each generation must destroy its masters and replace them with new masters equally ambitious and rapacious. The old man thought of himself as the final product of a peculiarly indigenous culture: that of illustrious despots; as a kind of father, at times hard, in the end a good provider, and always the custodian of a tradition of good taste, gentility, and culture" (1964, p. 45).

REFORMS OF THE REFORM

Reforms were demanded before the ink was dry on Article 27, but serious efforts to change the legal basis of agrarian reform were slow in coming. Amendments in 1971 to agrarian-reform legislation permitted rental of ejidal property under certain ambiguous circumstances. In 1981, a law of agricultural development (*Ley de Fomento Agropecuario*) facilitated joint ventures between *ejidos* and outside parties. Reversing postrevolutionary proscriptions on international investment in the *ejido* sector, President Carlos Salinas de Gortari came to encourage *ejidos* that lacked funds for capital formation to team up with foreign agribusinesses (Golden 1991). Although only 110 such partnerships were in operation as of January 1992 (Cornelius 1992, p. 4), numbers may increase as private-sector confidence grows in response to new policies. An example is the arrangement in San José Vaquerías (in Nuevo León) where Mexican cookiemaker Empresas Gamesa (now owned by Pepsico) gives *ejidatarios* credit, equipment, management advice, and know-how in exchange for land and labor to grow wheat; *ejido* members, in turn, get half of the profits from the grain (Angel Garza 1991, pp. 14–15; Solis 1991a).[11]

In November 1991, during his traditional State of the Union message, President Gortari announced that, preparatory to signing NAFTA and in the name of privatization, significant changes would be made to Article 27 of the Mexican Constitution and the country's large body of agrarian law and enabling legislation. He noted that emphasis in agrarian matters should be shifted from distribution of farmlands to increasing agricultural productivity: "In the past, land distribution was a path of justice. Today it is unproductive and impoverishing" (Salinas de Gortari 1991; see also Golden 1992). In January 1992, amendments to Article 27 passed in the Mexican Congress.

Cornelius summarized the key provisions of new agrarian legislation:

1. The government's constitutional obligation to distribute land has ended.
2. Private landowners are now able to make capital investments on their land without fearing expropriation.
3. Land rights disputes between *ejidatarios* and between *ejidos* and private proprietors are to be settled by local, presidentially appointed, agrarian tribunals.
4. *Ejidatarios* are able to sell, rent, sharecrop, or mortgage their land parcels as collateral for loans, though land sales to outsiders must be approved by two-thirds of the *ejido*'s general assembly.

5. *Ejidatarios* are no longer required to work their land personally in order to retain it.
6. The government will continue to enforce farm maximums to avoid excessive concentration of landholdings: individual farmers are limited to 100 hectares of irrigated land; no single *ejidatario* can purchase more than 5 percent of the land in an *ejido*; and corporate farms are limited to 2,500 hectares of irrigated land.
7. *Ejidatarios* who opt not to sell may enter into joint ventures with outsiders or can organize themselves into an association of producers to reap economies of scale (1992, p. 75).

These land-reform modifications altered macroeconomic policy and, together with freer trade, are meant to address lack of competitiveness stemming from low productivity and high production costs in farming. Costs of producing chickens, for example, are 27 percent higher in Mexico than in the United States (due mainly to the price of imported feed), and Mexican bean farmers harvest only one-third of the U.S. output per acre. There is also a large technology gap between the two countries. Mexico uses two tractors per every 100 farmers whereas in the United States there are 1.5 tractors to every farmworker on average. Mexico's farm-equipment imports will decrease in cost as NAFTA eliminates tariffs and the need for import permits.

Cuauhtémoc Cárdenas (and Lázaro's son), opposition candidate in the last two Mexican presidential elections, expressed alarm at *ejido* privatization, worrying that haciendas would be reconstituted as a product of transnational corporations and calling the amendment "a betrayal of the fundamental principles of the revolution."[12] He predicted: "This measure is going to be the source of agrarian social explosions for years to come" (Ross 1991, p. 1). The Chiapas rebellion that began 1 January 1994 makes his statement seem prescient.

Anticipating Salinas's reforms, Grindle (1988) argued that in the absence of a dynamic industrial sector, privatization of agrarian-reform farms would add markedly to the unemployment and underemployment problems that plague Mexico. She observed, "Mexico's major cities are already stretched far beyond their capacities in human terms" (Grindle 1988, p. 155). She believed that temporary migration is an underanalyzed but important feature of Mexico's contemporary rural landscape:

[T]he *ejido* structure is important in keeping the households rooted in rural areas. *Ejidatarios* are frequently involved in temporary labor migration, but they structure their migration around the need to maintain access to the *ejido* plot and to insure they are able to leave it to their heirs.... Moreover, the greatest number of labor migrants come from landless households; in the event that *ejido* land is made more subject to market forces, land concentration and consequent landlessness is a likely result. Thus altering the structure of the *ejido* could easily increase the incidence of labor migration, and there is little evidence that such a change would create the kind of economic opportunities that would provide more local options to those who engage in temporary labor migration (Grindle 1988, p. 60).

Intertwined with privatization is the matter of the price of corn, a crop that most *ejidatarios* grow. Not only are price subsidies presently awarded to Mexican corn farmers, but grain imports are strictly licensed. The United States wants the liberalization of corn prices and free cereal importation. If this happens, *ejidatario* incomes will fall and another wave of exits from the *ejido* sector will undoubtedly follow. However, if enterprise diversification in Mexico results, it will allow at least some farms to hire more workers. If foreign capital creates job growth in the manufacturing and services sectors, the agricultural unemployment effects of privatization and falling corn prices will be mitigated. (Mexico will continue to grow corn for human consumption regardless since U.S. varieties make satisfactory animal feed but poor tortillas.) One study estimates that some 850,000 farm families will leave agriculture as a result of falling corn prices. Of them, 60,000 will probably head for the United States every year over the next decade (Solis 1991b).

Scott (1992a) forecasts that Mexico's economy would have to grow about 7 percent per year to absorb *campesinos* into domestic jobs. [Mexico's average annual growth rate from 1980 to 1991 was 1.2 percent (World Bank 1993, p. 241); the country's 1990 growth rate was 4.4 percent, its estimated 1991 growth rate 3.6 percent (IDB 1992, p. 133).] As a stopgap, the Mexican government underwrites a multibillion-dollar public works and antipoverty program. Still, Mexican agriculture is in trouble, the *Wall Street Journal* reported: "Mexico is facing its worst agricultural crisis in 50 years. A sluggish domestic economy, reduced subsidies and foreign competition are bearing down hard on the Mexican farmer. Banks are seizing property from farmers delinquent on loans, many of which are at high interest rates.... But today's farming failures only propel more illegal immigration to the U.S." (Solis 1993).

Cornelius (1992) cautions against exaggerating the landlessness created by current agrarian reform, however. He argues that fewer laborers will be rendered jobless by privatization because of four significant obstacles to the transfer of *ejido* land to outsiders. First, legal property boundaries for individual plots are demarcated in only about 2,000 to 3,000 *ejidos* in Mexico, which serves as an impediment to selling plots. Second, much *ejido* property is of poor quality and so there are likely to be few buyers. Third, selling and moving are not especially attractive options for most *ejidatarios*, who have few alternatives to farming. Fourth, firms with capital would rather lease than buy land, preferring instead to invest in food-processing and distribution facilities.

Cornelius (1992, pp. 4–6) recounts that the new legislation represents a compromise between policymakers who recognize the necessity of substantial *ejido* reform and those who would abolish *ejidos* outright. One faction, he notes, sought to reshape the basic goal of the *ejido* from a means of social control and pernicious paternalism to a vehicle for grassroots participation (also see Otero 1989).

In contrast, technocrats within Mexico believe that unadulterated private property and a complete phaseout of commodity subsidies is necessary for the increased competition that NAFTA will induce. Luis Téllez argues that NAFTA requires Mexico to "have institutions that are compatible with free markets" (quoted in Cornelius 1992, p. 5) and that the *ejido* is not such an institution. Both schools of thought concur that the new legislation will bring clandestine rental contracts and quasi-sales into the open.

How the new agrarian legislation will be administered is still unclear. Also, some of its implications are ill-defined. The effects of the new constitutional provisions on natural resources are an example: At least 16.5 million hectares of forestland (of Mexico's total of 37 million hectares) are on *ejidos* and *comunidades*, some of which were set up under *centro de población* provisions of the agrarian laws (Vargas 1992). Whether *ejidatarios* will be able to divide up their heretofore common forest and sell it, or at least arrange with a transnational who might wish to clear-cut, is a matter for current speculation—and probably future legislation.

Mexico's agrarian prospects are at a turning point. Institutions and laws that have governed the peasantry for seventy years are very much in flux. The producers of its staples and preservers of many of its other natural resources are facing a new and uncharted future.

3

Early Revolutionary Reforms: Bolivia

Although Bolivia is known as a mining country, most of its citizens depend on agriculture. Today, children of many *campesinos* who benefited under the Bolivian agrarian reform in the 1950s probably live wherever their parents got land, usually a small farm now subdivided among heirs. This new generation does not have to contend with the abuse, service obligations, and high rents that typified their parents' existence until they received land. But reform beneficiaries got little else but land; they received few productive inputs, insufficient credit, and not enough technical assistance to launch productive, independent careers in farming. Nor is Bolivia much better at feeding itself as a nation because of reforms, which froze *campesinos* into a permanent relation with land in the mountainous highlands while the government used the resources at its disposal to develop commercial agriculture in the tropical lowlands. High inflation at the time of reform, together with subsequent policies favoring cheap food imports instead of basic domestic production, affected *campesinos* negatively. As a result of the agrarian reform, Bolivian beneficiaries often retreated into subsistence, living marginally better than before.

The emphasis of Spanish colonial rule in Bolivia, or Upper Peru as it was originally called, was on exploitation of rich mineral deposits through forced Indian labor and even slavery, together with the exploitation of peasant agriculture (Klein 1982, p. 17). The highlands and surrounding valleys of Bolivia became labor pools and food-supply centers for the mines. Silver mining in Bolivia was so important that by the middle of the seventeenth century the Bolivian desert town of Potosí was one of the most densely populated urban areas in the Western Hemisphere. But silver production declined, and European diseases began to decimate the native population. To ensure a labor supply, the colonial government began to implement *mita*, or forced labor, to compensate for declining numbers of indigenous workers. The first silver veins were rich but were soon exhausted, and further mining required deeper shafts and new exploration; both were expensive and required more labor than the original finds. However, workers were not available, and as a result mining did not revive until the eighteenth century and then only with government subsidization, which was not sustainable. The beginning of the nineteenth century saw another precipitous decline in silver exports.

BACKGROUND TO THE REFORM

Bolivia was importing food by the end of the colonial period. Mineral resources, moreover, were not valuable enough to offset the high transportation costs involved. Facing few alternatives, the Bolivian government demanded head taxes and placed a levy on consumption by the native population, which then constituted two-thirds of the country's inhabitants. This highly regressive tax system made up the largest share of the government's revenues until the latter part of the nineteenth century. Meanwhile, other nations in the vicinity were depending on export and import taxes for government revenue and enjoying a thriving international commerce. Of the new, independent republics in Latin America, Bolivia was one of the most backward. In the 1820s and 1830s, Andrés de Santa Cruz reorganized Bolivia and Peru into a confederation, which Chile subsequently destroyed. Bolivia turned inward, losing the desire and ability for international expansion. Although the country wanted to secure its Pacific and Amazon boundaries, sparse population made that impossible. In the Chile-Bolivia War in 1838–1839 and in the War of the Pacific in 1879, Chile expanded its claims against Bolivia; in the latter war, Bolivia lost both the Atacama nitrate fields and its route to the sea.

Although a controversial notion, Klein (1982, p. 18) believed that the loss of the Pacific coast for Bolivia was a "blessing in disguise"; it enabled the country to rid itself of the regime of *caudillos* that had plagued successive governments between the confederation and the War of the Pacific. The war also fostered the development of a key group of mining entrepreneurs who captured political control of the country. In 1880, the country began a period of stability and governance by civilians; correspondingly, the upper class divided itself politically into Conservative and Liberal factions. As in most other Latin American countries, there were few ideological differences between them; both, of course, favored economic growth. Personalities were the real distinction, but Liberals clearly favored disestablishment of the Roman Catholic Church. From 1880 to 1899, the Conservatives ruled; their governments promoted increased mining activities, for which they built a rail network to Antofagasta and Arica. With the revival of mining, city populations grew, resulting in increased demand for food. Meanwhile, as roads and railways penetrated the frontier, new land was opening for agriculture; as the end of the nineteenth century approached growing numbers of *latifundios* were cut out of the frontier. At the same time, settlers were establishing farms by grabbing land belonging to Indian communities. In

1846, over 63 percent of the indigenous population lived in freeholding communities; by 1900, only 27 percent did.

In 1900, the mestizo or *cholo* class represented over one-quarter of the national population and filled in the middle reaches of the otherwise bipolar Bolivian society. When the Liberals took over the government in 1899, they found a nation where *cholos* were shielding the enormous gap in wealth between Europeans and Indians (a gap that was expanding as a result of international commerce in metals and an increasingly viable agriculture). The Conservatives had lost power because of their tenacious adherence to the declining silver-mining sector and their location in Sucre-Chuquisaca. The Liberals, on the other hand, found their strength in La Paz, which had become a much larger and more cosmopolitan city. At this point, tin mining on the altiplano foretold Bolivia's future; by 1900, tin made up over half of Bolivia's exports. Whereas silver mining was controlled by members of Bolivia's old elite, tin mining had more international cachet at the time and rested in the hands of a small cadre of Bolivian entrepreneurs, who introduced modern, technologically oriented methods. The Liberal leaders of the twentieth century were not tin titans in the way that Conservative presidents of the nineteenth century had been silver czars. Rather, Liberals governed by pressure-group politics by way of the *rosca*, a cadre of the oligarchy who combined with their lawyers and other supporters.

An early task of the twentieth century was securing Bolivia's borders, which the government did poorly. In 1899, Brazilian settlers forced the secession of the province of Acre, which was annexed by the Brazilian government in 1903. In 1904, the Pacific littoral was officially sold to Chile. With the payment, the Liberals continued to build railroads; by 1920, the major urban centers of Bolivia were connected with rail lines. Tracks had also laid from La Paz to Tarija and the Argentine border. The stability and success of the Liberal party, which also concentrated on school and city construction, led to its overwhelming dominance over the Conservatives. It was not until 1914 that the country's two-party system was reborn.

Klein (1982, p. 20) characterizes the period from 1880 to 1932 as a time marked by see-sawing power in ten- and twenty-year intervals in an environment of stability and economic growth interrupted by a limited number of bloodless, civilian coups d'état that led to minor repression. The disputes occurred between *cholos* and whites, with Indians receiving neither voice in government nor arms. There were several revolts, but the Indians fought with primitive tools as the whites and *cholos* battled with modern weapons. As the national economy changed, the white consensus gradually crumbled, which allowed a somewhat greater role for the Aymara- and Quechua-speaking peasant populations. Although tin enjoyed great success until the late 1920s, when depression in industrial countries led to a breakdown of the market, the tin companies consolidated into three large firms. In addition to falling prices on the world market, the ore became less rich in tin as time wore on and capital investment plummeted.

By the time of the agrarian reform in the 1950s, 70 percent of the Bolivian population lived in the high mountain valleys and the altiplano; prior to the 1952 revolution, agriculture existed to serve the mines and took place mainly on haciendas. As in the case of prerevolutionary Mexico, land was concentrated in the hands of a few: 92 percent of the farmland in the country was owned by 6 percent of the landowners, whereas 80 percent of the smallest units had access to only 1 percent of the land (Burke 1971, p. 302). Workers were given a small house and a plot of land on the hacienda for growing their family's crops, but they were, in exchange, expected to labor in the landlord's fields for a specified number of days. In some cases the *campesinos* may have worked for five or six days a week during the growing season and every day during the harvest. This labor-for-land arrangement was called the *colonato* system; the peasant was known as a *colono* or *arrendero* and his borrowed plot an *arriendo*. As in Mexico, other goods and tasks were expected of the peasant family; often domestic service was required in the landlord's house on the hacienda, with men acting as busboys and women serving as maids. This kind of service was known as *pongueaje*. Sometimes livestock and crops were turned over to the landlord in lieu of money and labor. Instead of working on the *hacendado*'s fields, each *campesino* may have been given a sack of seeds to plant wherever no one else was farming. This was known as the *yanapacú* system and was used by haciendas where land was not a limiting factor. Or the peasant may have had to look after a hacienda animal that needed fattening, replacing it if it died. If the landlord did not reserve land for himself to be farmed by the peasants, who would deliver crops or animals in exchange, he needed no *colono* labor and tended to impose a tax, called a *catastro*, on the *campesinos* for their privilege of living on the hacienda. Sometimes *cacha*—the transporting of agricultural products to the *hacendado*'s store (*aljería*) in town—was required, as was *muqueo*, the making of *chicha* (beer) for the landlord. The *colonos* were sold with the land in the rather rare instances when haciendas changed hands. They were frequently kept in debt peonage by the *hacendado*, who tended to monopolize the few articles of consumption goods—kerosene, salt, and matches—that the workers needed to buy.

Wages did not constitute significant income for most *colonos* before the revolution. In most parts of the country, only the upper echelon of hacienda administrators received a salary. However, on some haciendas *campesinos* did receive small cash payments to cover their expenses while transporting the estate's products to market. When haciendas took on temporary help during harvest time, there was a tendency to pay workers in-kind.

The Chaco War, which broke out in 1932 between Bolivia and Paraguay, presented a major challenge to the hacienda system. It proved costly for Bolivia; 65,000 nationals died and the country ceded more of its national territory. The war was a bitter blow, since Bolivia had entered it with better materiel than Paraguay and supposedly a superior army. It also offered the first opportunity for indigenous and *cholo* troops to have broad contact with others like themselves (the hacienda system deliberately kept peasants from different farms apart, thus discouraging both cooperation and organization) and with foreign challengers.

Although calamitous in terms of lost lives and property, the war turned out to be a modernizing experience for Bolivians. Nothing was quite the same in this isolated, landlocked country after hostilities ended in 1935. José Romero Loza wrote:

> The disaster of the Chaco struck to the depths of the Bolivian spirit. It was like raising a curtain which revealed the entire intimate moral and material misery of an inconsistent society. The public conscience awoke, wishing to smash the elements of the social and political tragedy in which the country was enmeshed.... All the social sectors, the political parties, the press, the universities, etc., began to think in a profoundly nationalistic way.... Great change appeared that would integrate the society (1974, p. 223).

The fact that Bolivia lay defeated made common people critical of the weakness and vulnerability of their own rural social system. In the midst of the war and depression, the international price of tin had dropped precipitously, affecting the entire economy. Laid-off miners attempted to find work in the countryside, intermingling with peasants who had just shared life experiences with both miners and young officers during the Chaco War. After the hostility, former soldiers and miners joined in common cause with peasants, demanding a basic change in society.

The war was also an eye-opening experience for the elite young officers, who had always backed the traditional party system. Soon a number of small, radical parties and left-wing splinter groups emerged to sap strength from conventional politics. The regimes that followed were unlike the conservative-minded military governments that had dominated the country's political life in the former century. From 1936 to 1939, government was led by the "Chaco generation"—young officers who, with their socialist ideas, were frightening to the traditional elites, though they usually were offspring of that same establishment. These more egalitarian administrations made a conscious effort to incorporate sectors of society heretofore excluded. In addition to spawning political parties, the Chaco generation military governments enacted a labor code, wrote a constitution that proclaimed land ownership as dependent on landowners' carrying out their social responsibilities, and proposed modest welfare measures. Also, some U.S. oil holdings were nationalized.

Indeed, the end of the Chaco War in 1935 began a twenty-year period during which the 1952 revolution germinated and developed. After the war, the middle class, factory workers, miners, young officers, and the rural poor came to be genuine power contenders and, according to Lagos, "issues that had never been previously addressed came to the fore. These involved the land question, the

Indian problem, the organization of labor and the fact that the most important source of foreign exchange was in the hands of the so-called Tin Barons" (1988, p. 69).

The first acts of *campesino* rebellion occurred in 1936 in Ucureña, near Cochabamba: a group of *campesinos* founded a school on the Hacienda Cliza, owned by the Santa Clara monastery. Parts of this *latifundio* were rented to a private landlord who exploited his *colonos* in an especially abusive manner. *Campesinos* rebelled against the *hacendado*, founding a union. Some speculate that this unaccustomed action was possible because the peasants did not have the personal allegiance to the renter that they might have felt to a longtime *patrón*. Another factor was that the monastery had sold plots to a few *campesinos* (peasants in Bolivia who had been able to claim a plot of land before the war were known as *piqueros*). When the *piqueros* returned from the war with Paraguay, they discovered that their plots had been reabsorbed into the hacienda. The union petitioned to rent their own usurped properties. Leasing functioned reasonably well for a few years, but neighboring landlords were increasingly threatened by the growing *campesino* independence it represented and by ever-more vocal union activity, the leadership of which was provided by José Rojas (Bolivia's Zapata), assisted by a schoolteacher (a landlord's son) and a group of middle-class students from Cochabamba. In 1939, landlords prevailed upon the monastery and, with government help, bought for themselves the land that the *campesinos* had rented, burned the peasants' homes, and drove them away, an act that merely stiffened the rural unionization movement. In 1940, the schoolteacher assisted some 200 *campesinos* in their purchase of small farming plots, helped channel complaints about the landlord to proper authorities, and fostered increased unionization of the countryside by founding more schools. Meanwhile, some young officers, disillusioned by the Chaco War, together with liberal intellectuals, out-of-work tin miners, labor leaders, and other members of the Marxist Leftist Revolutionary party (Partido de la Izquierda Revolucionario, PIR) formed a rather uneasy coalition and founded the Nationalist Revolutionary movement (Movimiento Nacional Revolucionario, MNR), led by Víctor Paz Estenssoro.

The national political scene veered right, however, and in 1939, senior officers took power, inviting back the traditional political parties. Between 1939 and the outbreak of the revolution in 1952, the old guard attempted to defuse the political forces that had been aroused by the Chaco War, and many socio-politico-economic gains were erased in waves of repression. Still, by the early 1940s, tin miners were organized into powerful unions and participated in violent, disruptive strikes. With this example, peasant unions began organizing in the Cochabamba Valley, demanding their own land and sponsoring land invasions. Some of these activities were supported by increasingly radical groups and individuals within the white and *cholo* populations.

In 1943, an army disagreement brought Gualberto Villarroel to the presidency, with the MNR serving as his civilian ally. The MNR succeeded in organizing the first national federation of mine workers, but Villarroel's pro-Axis stance alienated the PIR and the traditional parties, which, with U.S. backing, formed a strong antifascist alliance. Villarroel took Paz into the government, and Paz presented a moderate proposal for land reform. Although the proposal was shouted down, the publicity surrounding this act gave peasants moral support. With government concurrence, the first Indian Congress was held in 1945, attracting delegates from all the provinces. Anxious to appear moderate to the wider Bolivian public, which feared *campesino* rebellion, the delegation declined to call for agrarian reform, instead requesting more educational facilities in the countryside and the abolition of the most onerous forms of servitude. The government responded with Decree 319, which declared *pongueaje* illegal and reduced the number of days per week that a *colono* was obliged to work for the hacienda (see Antezana and Romero 1973, pp. 119–217). The effects of this legislation are unknown, for enforcement methods were lacking. At the very least, however, the government had deprived some anachronistic practices of their former legitimacy. More strikes followed and fear of a widespread indigenous revolt spread to the middle class. The Villarroel government was overthrown in 1946 and the president was assassinated as jacquerie mounted. The antifascist alliance that followed Villarroel enabled the PIR, together with traditional parties, to rule for six years, but the government became steadily weaker as the period drew to a close, the oligarchic parties insisting that the working classes be neutralized and that middle-class radicalism be eliminated.

Various intellectuals wrote of the necessity of agrarian reform in Bolivia in the early 1940s, but, at the same time, the Society of Bolivian Landowners (Sociedad Rural Boliviana, SRB) pressed its demand that government protect private property, a call echoed by most of the press. In response, peasants no longer asked for reform of the *colonato* system; by the late 1940s and early 1950s, they wanted its complete abolition. There were sit-down strikes (*huelgas de brazos caidos*) and land invasions through which peasants aimed to make their point; *campesino* petitions increased as their unions became more cohesive. Despite the frequency with which the army was called in, order was not often reestablished during this prerevolutionary period. Of all Latin American countries marked with a hacienda system, Bolivia's rural social situation was considered by historians of the era to be the most regressive. As Zondag noted, "With the landlord having virtual control over life and death in his area and the Indians living in abject misery, the system was repulsive to anybody interested in even a modicum of social justice" (1982, p. 30). Romero Loza stated the case simply: "The roots of the problem in the countryside lay in the system of land tenure, in servile work forms, in the incredible backwardness of technology, and in the unequal distribution of income..." (1974, pp. 280–281).

Thus MNR, without its fascist elements and after the absorption of the Trotskyite Revolutionary Workers party (Partido Obrero Revolucionario, POR), assumed preeminent power among the nontraditional parties. As such, MNR led the middle and working classes in a program of social reform and became the leading opponent of the country's elites. On 9 April 1952, having seized the armories of La Paz, insurgents distributed weapons to the civilian populace. The Bolivian army lay defeated after several days of fighting; the miners and civilians had won. Víctor Paz Estenssoro took over the presidency.

It appears that inflation, which grew rapidly beginning in 1950 and remained high until about 1957, may have contributed to the revolutionary spark. As Wilkie observes:

> Inflation, of course, could not automatically cause a full-scale social upheaval, for many countries in Latin America lived with inflation as a fact of life without revolution during the same years. Given the dramatic rates of change in the price index, however, the conservative governments, which sided with the "tin oligarchy" without seeking to alleviate economic causes of social stress in Bolivian society, inevitably lost support among the middle sectors, government bureaucrats, and workers who made up the bulk of the economically active sector of the country's population.... [T]he revolution of 1952 ... [came] as a result of a sudden deterioration of the social and economic situation after a prolonged period of improvement (1969, pp. 3–4).

Although *colonos*, sharecroppers, *piqueros*, and village Indians did not participate in the revolution, they reorganized their unions and took over the vanguard of the peasant movement, especially in the altiplano and upper valley area. Following the example of Ucureña, and often promoted by MNR, unions became primary supporters of the revolution. Major union leadership positions came to be held by *piqueros* and sharecroppers and *colonos* were in charge of organizing agrarian reform on haciendas. Under union leadership, it was not unusual for acts of violence to be perpetrated against non-MNR *hacendados*. At this time some landowners left their properties, never to return; others went into hiding until the discord passed.

OUTLINE OF THE AGRARIAN REFORM

During the period of repression from 1946 to 1952, many peasant leagues were forced underground or disbanded, but after the short revolution, *campesino* unions and their provincial and departmental federations reappeared; within a year or two, most haciendas in Bolivia became organized by efforts spreading outward from La Paz and Cochabamba. To cope with this resurgence of rural organization, President Paz created the Ministry of Campesino Affairs (Ministerio de Asuntos Campesinos, MAC) as one of his first acts. Although there was a strong tendency of local unions to be independent and autonomous, Paz recognized that they were excellent vehicles for promulgating MNR's political message. The challenge for the party was to co-opt the union movement. In this spirit, the new government eliminated the literacy requirement for voting, increasing the national electorate from 200,000 to 1 million.

Even so, local police units continued to harass individual *campesinos* who engaged in union activity. The Bolivian right, led by the Bolivian Socialist party (Falange Socialista Boliviana, FSB) and the SRB, plotted the overthrow of the new government. Meanwhile, *campesinos* were arming themselves through the purchase of weapons confiscated from the army, and miners and laborers joined them in forming a loosely structured militia, which aimed to protect the interests of the working class (Dorsey 1975).

From 1952 to 1956, the basic revolutionary institutions were put in place, including land reform (Zondag 1982). In the immediate postrevolutionary period, destroying the feudal system and its abuses and restructuring the society was to have been the major thrust of public policy. In fact, nationalizing the tin mines, dealing with a raging inflation, and simply surviving were full-time tasks for the MNR government. Agrarian reform, therefore, was pushed into the background by more pressing concerns; the founding of MAC, however, signaled peasants that they had the power to play a key role in the new government. Even so, the short revolution had not completely broken the potency of the elite, and, had the *campesinos* taken a conciliatory stance, Paz might have bypassed agrarian reform entirely.

Instead, working through unions, *campesinos* forced landlords to confront land reform by means of renewed land invasions, strikes, and armed acts of violence—especially in the northern altiplano, the upper Cochabamba Valley, and the *yungas*. Paz soon realized the strength of the peasant union movement and its potential for disrupting his new administration. Accordingly, in March 1953, he appointed a commission to draft an agrarian-reform law. The commission was chaired by Hernán Siles Zuazo, who was to succeed as president in 1956. The FSB and the SRB argued that *campesinos* lacked sufficient education to run their own farms and that agricultural production would fall as a result of an agrarian reform. A stronger current of political thought in the country believed that some type of agrarian reform was inevitable, though all parties had their own idea of what would be most beneficial. The ordinance that emerged, signed into law by President Paz symbolically in Ucureña on 2 August 1953, provided for dismantling the *latifundio* and the *colonato* system and parceling land among its current users—a land-to-the-tiller program—while recognizing the sanctity of private property in the nonreform, commercial sector of agriculture.[1]

Unfortunately, even a crisis of this magnitude did not impel raising taxes on the rich to pay for social programs. Instead, it implied more reliance on Bolivia's recently nationalized tin sector and on U.S. aid, the World Bank, and the Export-Import Bank (Wilkie 1969, Table 9, p. 29).

To cope with the lack of government resources, the MNR government decided that the country's *campesino* problem had been solved with land redistribution (Cariaga 1982). Indeed, Cariaga (1982, p. 151) calculates that even though the agricultural sector produced 50 percent more of GDP than mining from 1967 to 1973 and employed two-thirds of the country's labor force, it received only 6–8 percent of total public expenditures, an amount hardly befitting its strategic importance. Since redistribution had left beneficiaries with land but not the inputs, credit, and technical assistance they needed for successful conversion into productive farmers, peasants who received parcels had a disappointingly small impact on Bolivian economic growth.

The Agrarian Reform Law (Decree Law No. 3464) provided that those who tilled the hacienda land prior to reform would be new owners, thus legitimizing the land invasions that had occurred just before and after the revolution. The maximum amount of land that could be transferred to beneficiaries varied by geographic zone, ranging from 0.5 hectare in the rich and crowded Cochabamba Valley to 2,000 hectares in the sparsely settled eastern lowlands (where the government wished to encourage farming so the area would not be claimed by a neighboring country in yet another encroachment).[2] The abolished "latifundio" was distinguished in the law from the legal "agricultural enterprise" by the latter's substantial capital investment and its use of modern technology and salaried (not *colono*) labor. Since these differentiating conditions were vague, land reform was far from universally fair in its application. If the hacienda in question happened to belong to a member of MNR, that person may have been afforded the luxury of the government's classifying it as an agricultural enterprise (see Lagos 1988, p. 84).

According to the Agrarian Reform Law's preamble, areas subject to expropriation were those "which inefficient landlords hold in excess, or from which they enjoy absolute rents not earned by their own personal labor in the field" (D. Heath 1990, pp. 4–5). Landlords were expected to forfeit that portion of their land on which *campesinos* were raising subsistence crops. Exacting which landlords could be labeled inefficient was as legally ambiguous as it was economically questionable, though old-style, feudally organized haciendas clearly qualified. The specified measures of efficiency included rather gross and imprecise indicators: amount of capital investment, number of paid workers, and use of modern technology. Land actually planted to crops by the owner's family was exempt from expropriation (D. Heath 1990, p. 5).

The Bolivian reform was designed not only to rid the country of *latifundios*, unpaid labor, and the accompanying feudal accouterments, but also to diversify agriculture, expand the export economy into the *Oriente*, and provide cheap food for urban areas. These latter goals were left to be achieved on nonreformed land.

Under the terms of the Agrarian Reform Law, five forms of land tenure were legal in Bolivia:

1. smallholdings: plots large enough to meet the food needs of the owner-operator family;
2. medium-sized holdings: farms larger than the former, capable of producing for the market and worked with the aid of wage workers;
3. commercial farm enterprises: large-scale farms worked with wage-earning employees, using modern technology and equipment, and requiring substantial capital investment;
4. community holdings: legally recognized Indian-community land worked for communal benefit; and
5. cooperative property: land worked jointly by individual farmers.

Because all of these descriptions were vague, there were boundless opportunities for arbitrariness in the law's administration.

As one might suspect, in the altiplano and the high temperate valleys, where *campesinos* revolted against owners who extracted exorbitant rents in labor and produce, coverage was much more complete than in the *Oriente*, a vast and underpopulated expanse that was hardly touched by redistribution. (Estates were immense in the eastern part of the country, and *campesinos* could often squat for years unnoticed by landlords.) Indeed, in contrast to the altiplano, some of the relatively few landowners in the *Oriente* needed to attract labor, so they presented *campesinos* with inviting promises, not onerous servitude. In the *Oriente*, landlords could not abuse workers with impunity, lest the property be left without a labor force. Thus, the prerevolutionary relationship between the land, the owner, and the tenant was quite different in this region than in the highlands. There was little rebellion here, so the land reform of the 1950s was largely irrelevant—except that landowners, fearful of the law, became more diligent in not allowing *campesinos* to cultivate remote plots for personal use. Moreover, *Oriente* estate holders tended to welcome *campesino* farming of unclaimed land because they could then tap this labor reserve (D. Heath 1990).

Legal specifications included maximum acreages allowed for landlord retention, designated in the law by region (Santa Cruz, 50 hectares; altiplano near Lake Titicaca, 10 hectares; and so forth). Yet the citing of geographic zones merely exaggerated the law's ambiguity (D. Heath 1990), since the delineation of their boundaries was not widely accepted (a local topographer was given the task of assigning a farm to a particular region). Moreover, the list of zones differed in each of the law's three articles (D. Heath, pp. 5–6), and no cadasters existed to show official farm sizes.

Expropriation did not take place at a single point in time in order to build up a land bank of reserves that could be distributed to needy *campesinos*. Rather, as in the Mexican reform, the mechanics of the process were set in place only when organized groups of *campesinos* requested particular properties. Since usually illiterate *campesinos* were not by themselves in a position to mount very focused and articulate demands, MNR routinely organized petitioning *campesinos* to secure the land and helped to partition it into individual family units. In this manner MNR got the patronage it sought, and peasants joined unions for the obvious material benefit of doing so.

Since agrarian judges and members of the National Council on Agrarian Reform (Consejo Nacional de Reform Agraria [CNRA], the highest court of appeal in land cases) were appointed, it was through them that MNR-member landlords were protected from expropriation. Conversely, many non-MNR landlords—even those who by any standard seemed "efficient"—were expropriated. Whether the land-reform program was a "revolutionary" matter or just the best means to garner wide political support for the MNR and its fledgling government is still being argued.

In order to retain land once it was allocated, *campesinos* were required by law to work the fields (new owners had to forfeit the properties if they did not begin farming within two years). Drafters of the law had assured that even this provision was ambiguous, however; they indicated no precise beginning for the two-year period. Did it start with the judge's award of land to the new beneficiary, with the allocation of provisional title, or with the date of granting final title (D. Heath 1990)? This point was all but moot, though, since most beneficiaries did work their land—they had no other means to support their families. The legal proviso that beneficiaries pay for the land was ignored; landlords were not indemnified, either.[3]

As with most agrarian-reform legislation, the Bolivian law included special measures to preclude the reemergence of inequitable distribution of land. The law prohibited the renting of beneficiary property; furthermore, the holding could not be subdivided, sharecropped, or mortgaged (World Bank 1992a, p. 17). Nonetheless, land distributed in the reform could be resold.

Although the first land titles were distributed to *campesinos* less than a year after the Agrarian Reform Law was signed, by late 1972 titles had reached only 30 percent of beneficiaries (and few have been added since). The easiest cases took from three to four years to advance from request to title; disputed cases took six or seven years, with many taking upward of a decade (Dorsey 1975, p. 35). Lagos (1988, p. 85) documents the tedious mechanics of granting agrarian-reform land in the community of Tiraque, outlining a process typical of other places in the altiplano and the high valleys. First, a claim was filed with the National Agrarian Reform Service (Servicio Nacional de Reforma Agraria, SNRA) by the leader of the peasant union. Field-level details on the physical attributes of the property were then obtained by a topographer, and relevant information was gathered on the *colono*'s labor relations with the landlord. A technical report, submitted to the agrarian judge who was to hear the case, was prepared by the *sindicato* in behalf of the *colono*; the landlords, if they wished, could formulate a rejoinder to the *colono*'s case. After the judge's verdict, the case was reviewed by CNRA, which might either uphold or reverse the judgment;

the president of the country, finally, was required to sign each document. Thome (1970, pp. 34–40) found twenty-nine steps in a contested case between the *campesino*'s initial request for a title and receipt of the final certificate. (Mobile brigades, which functioned for a time in the late 1960s and early 1970s, speeded up the process somewhat, but funding for these units ran out.) In Tiraque, CNRA reviewed sixty-four cases involving mainly medium-sized and large haciendas (Lagos 1988). Twenty-seven of these properties were ultimately classified as *latifundios*, on which only 21 percent of the land was cultivated by the holder. Accordingly, the remainder of these estates was available for distribution among the *campesinos*.

At the time of the revolution, some Indians lived on haciendas and received land whereas others, who resided in traditional *comunidades*, did not obtain property. Before the reform many *hacendados* had encroached on Indian-community lands, but at the time of reform whatever *campesino* was currently farming the property got it; no effort was made to grant land to its rightful owner if that person turned out to be another peasant. Also, some Indian families farmed plots in both the altiplano and the lowlands to spread risk (if one crop failed, the other might not). Legally they could receive but one fragment and were prohibited from obtaining titles to parcels in other geographic areas.

REFORM RESULTS

The agrarian reform in Bolivia ultimately granted land to about 256,000 families or 1 million peasants (Simmons 1974; World Bank 1992a, p. 17). One benefit of the reform was economic stimulation of local markets that either were reinvigorated or sprang up near beneficiary communities. The mining-agricultural town of Sorata near Lake Titicaca is an example. Middlemen and merchants stepped into the breach left by the landlords, and peasants entered into a vigorous consumer market for radios, bicycles, tin roofs, medicines, and store-bought clothes (McEwen 1974; for general discussion, see Clark 1968).

Dwight Heath (1970) emphasizes more continuity than change, however, concluding that, although the agrarian reform brought economic progress, social relations were less affected than may have been originally estimated. The agricultural union movement increasingly took on the patron-client role formerly played by landlords. Some *campesinos* who rose to *sindicato* leadership assumed the landlord's position of domination—sometimes exhibiting more guile than the former *hacendados*. Nonetheless, in the absence of viable local governments, the *sindicatos* often organized *campesinos* to build schools and other public works. More recently Heath (1990) documents reform reversal, citing as an example a citrus grower near La Paz who rents back land from his former *colonos*, now beneficiaries of agrarian reform, to maintain himself as a wealthy autocrat. Whether *neolatifundismo* is widespread in Bolivia is a matter for speculation.

In the upper valleys and the altiplano, landlords who were disenfranchised by the reform began to work full-time in urban occupations, which some held before the agrarian reform. Middle-level landowners who had their properties expropriated often went into smaller businesses in local towns or in the country-side; some became active in buying, assembling, transporting, or simply dealing in crops grown on their former holdings. They frequently found themselves able to control "their" former peasants by monopsonistic market power.

The effects of reform on agricultural production has been a hotly debated issue in Bolivia. Although official statistics show less marketed farm output after the reform, Clark (1968) contends that peasants were merely consuming more of what they produced. Whitaker and Wennergren (1982), in contrast, maintain that it took until 1961 for Bolivia to regain 1952 levels of agricultural production. Others respond that production shortfalls resulted from some land not being worked immediately after the reform, because former *colonos*, not believing their good fortune, thought that the landlords would inevitably return. In discussing this issue, a U.S. Department of Agriculture publication reported a more conventional view: "Due to the scarcity of land in heavily populated areas, many land grants were so small as to permit only subsistence farming. As a conse-quence, in place of production increases, output decreased sharply following enactment of the law. In recent years, however, production of some crops has turned upward, mainly as a result of the opening of new areas of production in the lowlands" (Lynch and Ferree 1961, p. 5).

Whitaker and Wennergren (1982) point out that production from Bolivia's agriculture expanded somewhat during the 1960s and 1970s when compared to the immediate postrevolutionary years but that overall farm performance remained poor. Demand for agricultural products increased by about 4.3 percent but output of food crops grew at about half that rate. The prices of staples were maintained at artificially low levels so urban dwellers could afford them, translating into severe disincentives at the farm level. Although agricultural growth figures were driven up by exports (cotton, rice, and sugar) produced on large and middle-sized farms in the *Oriente*, output of staples in the highlands continued to be meager.

From 1951 to the mid-1970s, Bolivia's unfavorable balance of trade in commercial food stemmed in part from adverse tariffs and the importation of agricultural products that could have been produced at home. Cariaga (1982) critically reports that with a total of 918,535 square kilometers of arable land, Bolivia had less than 2 percent of the area (28,794 square kilometers) in production.

Whitaker and Wennergren (1982, pp. 244–249) argue that, in addition to the credit and input-supply problems, agricultural output expanded slowly because of inadequate applied research combined with ineffective extension services. Moreover, there had been little investment in rural education, so *campesinos* in Bolivia were among the least schooled in Latin America. Beneficiary response to any new, technical, farming information was thus restrained.

In the 1980s, food output rose 9 percent (World Bank 1992b, Table 4, p. 224). Although the Bolivian economy was depressed for much of the decade, agriculture was somewhat more healthy, since it enjoyed the privileged treatment (freer trade, fewer urban consumer's subsidies on food) given to an export sector during structural adjustment.

Initially land reform brought peasant beneficiaries a higher level of living, which stabilized when credit and inputs to increase productivity were not forthcoming; eventually inflation eroded the gain.

ORIENTE AND REFORM

Since climate and soils are more favorable in the *Oriente* than in the traditional sector of the altiplano and high valleys with its severe weather and eroded soil, after land reform the government's attention quickly turned to commercial farming—in both the Santa Cruz area, the center of production for trade in Bolivia, and the Beni—as well as colonization schemes in the frontier of the vast *Oriente*. In its quest for growth, the government realized the potential of the lowlands for earning foreign exchange.

Sugar and rice production in the *Oriente* expanded, to be followed by cotton and livestock after the first highway opened to link the region with urban centers in the highlands. Most of this expansion took place on large holdings, some held by longtime residents, others by recent in-migrants. Few of these properties were subject to land reform because they were not *latifundios*; by law they were considered "commercial farms" because they were worked with "modern technology." The government-directed colonization in the area, moreover, settled a number of *campesinos* on smaller properties, where they provided a ready labor force for the commercial farms. Still, only about 5 percent of the agricultural population of the country works in the *Oriente*.

Although the political strength of the country remained in the highlands, economic power moved increasingly to the lowlands (for years this part of the country had been relatively isolated, with lowlanders feeling little allegiance to the altiplano). A demanding commercial upper class developed in the *Oriente*, whom the elites of the altiplano and upper valleys tried to neutralize. Some policy moves jeopardized altiplano beneficiaries, in that the Agricultural Bank of Bolivia (Banco Agricultura de Bolivia, BAB), reorganized after the reform purportedly to provide credit to beneficiaries, made rather large loans in the *Oriente*. Through the early 1970s, BAB loaned *campesinos* only 10 percent of its portfolio as it meted out the lion's share to the *Oriente*. Ladman and Tinnermeier (1979) argue that political, not economic, factors guided this pattern of credit distribution; marginal returns on investment in the *Oriente* were not that much higher than elsewhere in the country. Furthermore, they document how delinquency and default rates were extremely high in the lowlands and that loanable funds were frequently replenished with foreign aid, suggesting that the government conceived of this monetary transfer as a way to purchase the solidarity of *Oriente* elites.

Settlement of the *Oriente* proceeded rapidly in the 1970s when, under rather dubious interpretations of the Agrarian Reform Law, the military government granted land to large holders who were committed to ranching or commercial farming.[4] Presently, the modern sector of Bolivian agriculture in the eastern lowlands comprises farms of a median size—50 to 100 hectares; farms exceeding 1,000 hectares are not uncommon, however. A number of productive farms in the *Oriente* are held by foreigners (Barnes 1992, p. 3).

Hendrix (1992, p. 33) asserts that native groups claim up to one-half of the eastern lowlands, though the government recognizes a smaller area. Other land in the *Oriente* is set aside for concessions to loggers; once forests are cleared, opportunistic settlers move in. The relationship between indigenous groups and logging concessionaires is an uneasy one, as the Chimane forest incidents of the late 1980s and early 1990s illustrate.

Indigenous peoples living near the Chimane forest protested the government's 1986 logging concession around the Beni Biosphere Reserve. The central government thus conceded land on the forest fringe to the Indians, with lumber concessions left in the center of the territory. The indigenous peoples vehemently rejected this plan. In 1990, in a show of protest, more than 300 Indians walked the 400 miles from Trinidad (capital of the Beni) to La Paz, being joined by 400 more native people along the way. As a result of this highly publicized "March for Dignity and Territory," Bolivia's president signed executive decrees that complied with native territorial demands. Furthermore, Bolivia's president called for an "ecological pause" in 1990; no new logging concessions would be granted pending further study of forest reserves and forest policies (Campos-Dudley 1992; Jones 1990).

In addition to the "traditional" and "commercial" regions of agricultural production in Bolivia, Barnes (1992) calls attention to an intermediate, migratory sector in the Chapare area, along the base of the eastern and central mountain chains. Here institutions are flexible enough to accommodate new members; there is an "agricultural ladder" on which tenants may climb up from a bottom rung to a position of ownership as they save money to buy land. A sharecropping system called *partidaria* prevails. In return for maintaining crops (coca, bananas, urku, peanuts), share tenants receive half of the produce and hold some prospect of eventually owning land; outsiders may acquire land by paying off the existing debts of a landowner.

POSTSCRIPT TO THE REFORM

In contrast to the Mexican reforms, Bolivian agrarian reformers faced no opposition from the United States; indeed, Bolivia enjoyed an expanded postreform aid program.[5] A pattern of increasing commitment of U.S. funds for economic assistance to Bolivia began in 1954, continued through the Alliance for Progress era of the 1960s (Wilkie 1969, Appendix A, p. 48), and, with interruptions from time to time, continues today.

Since the revolution, however, the *campesino* class has not really entered politics in Bolivia. Patch, in writing about the new military government led by René Barrientos in 1965, recognized that the revolutionary days were over and something else was taking their place:

> [T]he vision of a new democracy, jubilantly expectant in 1952, brightly sustained in 1956, and still adhered to in 1960, had all but disappeared in 1964 with the disintegration of ... the MNR party and substitution of the personalism of Victor Paz Estenssoro for party and program. It remained for Paz's elected Vice-President ... to depose Paz in November 1964, establish a military government, and then profess the respect for free elections and democratic institutions common to unconstitutional governments in their first months of power (1965, p. 1).

The military government was not reformist, and Patch remarked, "Barrientos makes much of his *campesino* support; he is active in cultivating it and makes many statements meant for the edification of *campesinos* and workers. Still, while he may vaguely favor a better life for Bolivia's unfortunate masses, neither he himself nor the people surrounding him have the mentality for transforming what is essentially a fatherly feeling for his fellow countrymen into a program likely to help them" (1965, p. 6). Patch spoke of one administration; he could have been referring to several decades of governments that succeeded Barrientos.

A bill allowing for complete private titling of both indigenous and agrarian-reform community lands is currently circulating among legislators and public opinion leaders in Bolivia; it would introduce policies similar to those of President Salinas's modifications to Article 27 of the Mexican Constitution. If passed, the new law would provide for land to be legally cash-rented, sharecropped, parceled, mortgaged, and regrouped into larger farms via sale. The draft legislation also calls for administrative consolidation of colonization, agrarian reform, and forestry under the National Land Institute (Instituto Nacional de Tierra, INT), which registers and titles rural lands, compiles the national cadaster, and acquires properties for conservation purposes. A judicial branch of government would be created, including an agrarian court to rule on matters of agrarian justice (presently such matters fall to the executive branch for resolution).

Another bill would issue community titles to approximately 10,000 *campesino* and indigenous communities (understood to include both original groups and those created as a result of the agrarian reform). After the *comunidades* obtain legal personalities, they could then divide their properties into individual farms according to internal rules. If the decision is made to sell to outsiders, the communities could legally disband, with members acquiring individual, salable titles (conversation with Grenville Barnes, 10 November 1992).

An open land market would mean that small peasant plots could be combined into larger, more efficient farms better able to compete for credit and other inputs. As in Mexico, danger lies in the peasant displacement and landlessness that might be created. In a country with a dynamic labor market and an adequate public works program to employ or provide shelter to those displaced from the land, increasing rural landlessness is not as much of a problem as in Bolivia, which lacks both. In Bolivia, rural landlessness often means joblessness and destitution.

4

Early Revolutionary Reforms: Guatemala

The first agrarian reform in Central America seemed at the outset to be as revolutionary as those in Mexico and Bolivia. But in Guatemala, the reforms of the early 1950s clashed with violent counterrevolutionary forces (composed of landlords, members of the entrepreneurial middle class, and hierarchy of the Roman Catholic Church), which joined with the United Fruit Company and ultimately the U.S. government. This mighty alliance withered the reforms, which were quickly rolled back.

BACKGROUND TO THE REFORM

Guatemala's system of land tenure, as in much of Latin America, has roots in the Spanish conquest. Jonas put it well: "[Land was the] primary source of wealth, and one pillar of colonial society was the land tenure system" (1991, p. 14). Lacking mineral wealth, Guatemala, like most Central American countries, relied on agricultural exports during its early days as an independent nation. The area at first specialized in exporting cochineal and indigo, dyes used in the European textile industry.

Land was initially given as a reward for conquest and so tended to concentrate in the hands of a few. Parts of the indigenous population were forced or persuaded to become workers on estates of the elite; the rest were relegated to marginal land unsuited to growing export crops. The poor, however, grew the country's staples of corn and beans on small plots.

At first, Guatemala's rural work force consisted of the indigenous peoples, whose ancestors had created the great Mayan civilization. As in most Latin American countries, the colonial institution responsible for making Indian labor available to the emerging landlord class was the *encomienda*, a grant of jurisdiction over one or more villages ceded to conquistadors in rough proportion to their influence or valor. It enabled its recipients, the *encomenderos*, to collect labor and tribute from the inhabitants. As Creoles (those born in the region but of European ancestry) became dominant participants in agriculture, policies more invasive to the existing social structure were devised. Private estates were consciously established near populated areas; when necessary, land was granted to indigenous peoples to keep these potential laborers nearby. In time Ladinos (a mixture of Creole and Indian, called mestizos in some other Latin American countries) made up a large portion of the laboring class. Many Ladinos were neither landowners nor village dwellers, but free laborers. Most hacienda workers were Indians, however, who had small parcels of land, or *minifundios*, which they worked only in off-seasons or when the *hacendado* did not need them for other tasks.

Indian labor, though relatively plentiful in Guatemala compared to the rest of Mesoamerica, was not always compliant, and escape was common. Many indigenous people died of European diseases. Thus it became necessary to redesign institutions to safeguard landlords against a declining pool of workers; the agriculture of the time required little capital, but it needed plenty of labor. When *mandamiento* (another state-enforced institution that compelled people to work on agricultural estates) became offensive to mainstream opinion, new forms of labor-retentive organization evolved. In debt peonage, Indians were paid with chits from the company store in order to tempt less-than-prudent purchases and landlords often loaned money for fiestas. In both cases the family became indebted to the store and had to work to pay off financial obligations.

The resultant land-tenure pattern came to be known as the *latifundio-minifundio* system. The *minifundistas* worked for the landlord and, when not so occupied, could grow subsistence on their own small plots. This arrangement was practical for both parties and established an enduring social system: The small-plot operators had an assured crop to feed their families and so were not entirely dependent on wage work; the hacienda operator could command a nearby labor force needing seasonal supplementary employment.

In colonial and postcolonial days this paternalistic system was held together by a measure of mutual convenience and, more important, by coercion, racist ideology, and support from the Catholic Church (Jonas 1991). Yet the resistance of the indigenous population is legend: The huge number of Indians living today in Guatemala (they make up over half the population) is testament to the persistence of their struggle against assimilation—to live according to their own customs, to speak their own languages.

The endurance of institutions forged in the colonial period is remarkable; more than a century and a half after independence, a respected study of land tenure concluded that Guatemala remains characterized by striking inequalities in the distribution of land (Hough et al. 1982). Independence, diversification of exports over the years, militarism, economic growth, and guerrilla warfare have not brought much change to Guatemalan society: It is still polarized and ruled by a small and rich minority; although its middle class has grown recently, most people are extremely poor. As Hough et al. concluded, after independence "the government of the new republic seemed committed to exacerbating the inequalities which existed between Indians and Spanish settlers" (1982, p. 21). Their dedication to inegalitarianism lasted; despite occasional skirmishes and a brief period of agrarian reform and populism in the mid-twentieth century, the elites have always retained their control.

As in much of Latin America, independence in Guatemala brought a see-sawing of power between so-called Conservatives and Liberals. Liberals advocated Central American federalism, free trade, reduced church privileges, and private ownership of property (as opposed to communal land titles). Conservatives favored governmental centralism, the established church, and state-protected monopolies. Liberal party adherents included somewhat more progressive *latifundistas*, Ladino petty bourgeoisie, intellectuals, and pro-independence activists; the conservative group drew support from old-style *latifundistas*, the church, some merchants, and artisans. Rights of the Indian and Ladino populations were not a concern of either party; the country was governed as though the majority ethnic groups did not exist. Society was configured by and for the white Criollo class, which dominated both parties.

In 1825, Guatemala passed its first agrarian law; its purpose was to increase the amount of public-domain land transferred to private ownership. Some believed, even then, that "the small number of landowners is one of the causes of [Guatemalan] underdevelopment" (Hough et al. 1982, p. 21). The result, however, did not expand the ownership base. The Indian population lacked capital to buy the newly privatized holdings, which either served to enlarge existing estates or added a few new members to the landed class. Another idea that had currency in nineteenth-century Guatemala was that economic progress required the entrepreneurial capacities of newly immigrated Europeans. The Guatemalan elite came to view underdevelopment as a consequence of the predominance of tradition-bound Indians, whose influence needed to be counteracted by an infusion of hardworking Europeans. Early efforts to establish agricultural settlements with Swiss, Belgian, and Austrian settlers failed, however. German settlement did prove successful toward the end of the nineteenth century as a result of Guatemala's search for a commercial, export-oriented crop to replace indigo and cochineal, the market for which was destroyed by the manufacture of artificial dyes. After coffee, which is well suited in areas between 800 and 1,500 meters in altitude, was discovered, several entrepreneurial German families were granted appropriate hillside land. They quickly set the standard for a major coffee-exporting industry.

Although most of the labor for coffee could be hired seasonally from nearby *minifundios*, another labor institution was established to accommodate the year-round needs of the hacienda, which, as it intensified its production, came to be known by the less pretentious term, *finca*. The *finqueros* allotted some poorer-quality plots on their farms to laborers, who could use the land for subsistence crops but still had to be available for *finca* work when needed. The institution was called *colonato*; the worker, a *colono* or a *mozo colono*. During coffee harvesting, the *colono* work force was augmented by a large supplementary labor force, most of whom farmed their own *minifundios* in the off-season.

The Liberal General Justo Rufino Barrios came to power in 1871; government goals were to complete settlement of the highlands, establish incentives and infrastructure needed by coffee growers, and make strategic adjustments to land tenure. Again, the idea that Guatemala needed a class of yeoman farmers gained prominence, and a presidential decree was signed to provide for the sale of public-domain tracts of 45 to 225 hectares in the south coastal region. The plea for small, private farmsteads emerged in the wake of anticlerical sentiment, which surged through Latin America in the last three-quarters of the nineteenth century. In Guatemala, the liberal reforms removed the legal bases not only for massive landholdings of the church but also for communally held lands of Indian villages. Most church lands moved into the hands of the elite, whose numbers had been augmented by the new coffee growers. Much Indian land was also absorbed by landowners of substance, who were able to take advantage of individual titling to acquire Indian property. At altitudes suited for coffee, growers often forced Indian villages to relocate farther up the mountain on land too cold and marginal for the favored crop. By 1890, coffee made up 96 percent of Guatemala's exports. Meanwhile, the *campesino* sector stagnated, flagged by its consignment to ever-poorer land, and foodstuffs came to be imported.

When public-domain land on the south coast was offered for sale, highland growers took advantage of the opportunity to obtain property for diversifying into tropical crops. Some coffee farmers established a cropping pattern on the Pacific coast that would be complementary in terms of labor requirements to their highland enterprises; after the coffee was picked, able-bodied males were expected to leave to work in cotton on the coast. The large migratory stream from the highlands to the coast and back again is as much a feature of the contemporary rural labor market as it was late in the last century. And it is just as disruptive of Indian family life now as it was then, perhaps more so. As the property of Indian families came to be more subdivided with passing generations, *campesinos* found themselves ever-more dependent on wage labor.

Thus the Rufino Barrios period saw expansion of the elite class as more Ladinos acquired land and, along with the German coffee farmers, became locked in common cause with the old aristocracy to keep the majority group of Indian laborers from enlarging its precarious economic foothold. Coffee required a ready but seasonal labor force, one that could support itself when it was not in demand for picking, planting, and husbanding chores on *fincas*. The land-tenure system evolved to accommodate this need. Smith (1990, n. 10, p. 38) writes about the lengths planters went to assure their labor supply. She describes a system in El Quiche in which *fincas de mozos* or "serf farms" were created. Several diversified owners bought up Indian land and then permitted indigenous groups to continue to farm there provided they would work on the same landlord's south coast plantation land at reduced wages.

Although debt peonage was finally abolished in 1934, it was quickly replaced with antivagrancy legislation, which obliged workers to carry a notebook documenting days they had worked. Indians were required to toil between 100 and 150 days per year or face punishment by government authorities.

The government facilitated other coffee-farmer needs—legal access to highland property in the public domain and more infrastructure (railroads, port facilities, and the like). As Jonas wrote, the liberal ideology of government in practice meant "a more active role for the state in protecting and subsidizing (but never in regulating or restricting) private enterprise and in encouraging foreign investment. The political expressions of increased and more centralized state power were dictatorship and coercion, particularly in regard to the mobilization of Indian labor ... and to build public works" (1991, p. 18).

The practice of creating small peasant farms in locations where they were interspersed with *fincas* persisted so commercial agriculture would have a ready labor force. In 1929, colonization programs, based on establishing peasants on their own tiny farms, began in at least eight departments (provinces) that still had public-domain land. This program did not even dent the enormous landless problem. Moreover, if family farming had ever become a serious government goal, the landed class would have lost its ready supply of labor.

In 1901, the United Fruit Company (UFC) began operations in the lowland tropics of Guatemala, obtaining a foothold by providing mail service via its fleet of banana boats (it had established successful banana plantations in Costa Rica in the late nineteenth century). In 1904, the company's subsidiary, International Railways of Central America (IRCA), was asked to complete the trans-Guatemalan railroad. By 1924, the Guatemalan government had ceded large tracts of land for the company's use. In 1930, other properties in the Pacific lowlands were granted; concessions to UFC grew to nearly 190,000 hectares.

Once granted with either 25- or 99-year leases to land, the banana plantations virtually reigned in the country. For example, though the company paid a tiny tax on exports, its imports and most of its profits were exempt from Guatemalan taxes. UFC could remit unlimited profits to the United States and was not obliged to obey labor legislation of the Guatemalan government, rudimentary as it was. It often enticed the Guatemalan government to construct the infrastructure it needed. UFC operated almost as a sovereign within Guatemala, beholden only to the laws it drafted largely itself. The relationship between the banana company and the country's landed gentry became close and cooperative.

Jorge Ubico became dictator of Guatemala in 1931, inaugurating a long regime that would steer the country through the Great Depression and the major part of World War II. With the full support of the United States, Ubico came to power against more nationalistically minded candidates. Ubico's 1936 reelection occurred as contract revisions to bestow further privileges on UFC and IRCA were being prepared. While most of Latin America took advantage of the depression in the United States to lessen dependence on agriculture and to develop strategies of import-substituting industrialization, Ubico resolved to reinforce the status quo. Guatemala attempted to neither increase its manufacturing capacity nor diversify its farming sector. In rather blatant disregard of the dire condition of many of its poor, the country undertook no policies to alleviate unemployment or to establish more control over foreign corporations operating in the country.

Ubico did, however, enact a provision that would tax idle land in estates larger than 500 hectares, pronouncing that farms over 4,500 hectares were to be considered an "obstacle to agrarian development" (Hough et al. 1982, p. 23). The tax law was never enforced, however, and the legacy of Ubico in most Guatemalan minds is his distribution of large tracts of land to favored military officers.

The United States, becoming steadily disenchanted with Ubico's fascist tendencies, saw its alliance with Guatemala soften during the 1940s. At the same time, it became more preoccupied with the German economic interests in Guatemala. The new U.S. attitude weakened Ubico and strengthened his more nationalistic opponents. In response to popular pressure that fomented general strikes within Guatemala, Ubico saw the handwriting on the wall and resigned in 1945, but not before maneuvering to install a puppet regime. His ploy failed, however, and armed students and workers joined with dissident military officers to demand elections. The landmark election in 1945 of reformer Juan José Arévalo stands as a dramatic manifestation of nationalism and urban middle-class aversion to the dictator. Antagonism to U.S. dominance in the economy had fueled the opposition, anxious as it was for more diversification. Some disenchanted *campesinos*—most of them Ladinos—also were part of the reform movement; the more repressed and downtrodden Indian *campesinos* were not.

THE REVOLUTIONARY PERIOD

Without Arévalo's groundwork, later land reform might have been impossible. Arévalo, by establishing a new constitution, undertook the herculean task of making Guatemala a political democracy. With a vision and ideological orientation labeled "spiritual socialism," government targeted economic enfranchisement among the lower classes to expand the market and propel capitalist development forward. The government expanded male suffrage,[1] assured freedoms of speech and political organization (the exception being the Communist party), and affirmed university autonomy in an effort to decentralize the power that Ubico had concentrated. For the first time, Guatemala enacted labor legislation aimed at protecting rather than exploiting workers.[2] The government retained the right to recognize certain unions (while dissolving illegal ones) and arbitrate labor disputes.

In addition, Arévalo attempted to regulate foreign firms. In 1947, the government demanded that the UFC submit to arbitration of wage disputes, but the company resisted, eventually winning by lockout and suspended operations. In fact, Arévalo made little progress toward reining in the existing foreign fruit monopoly; his government needed foreign investment and felt that it could not attract a more diversified portfolio if it also imposed punitive measures on UFC. He did, however, regulate new private foreign investment somewhat more than in the past.

The agrarian issue was the most intransigent problem for the Arévalo government. A law prohibiting the eviction of renters at the caprice of owners was enacted. Another law provided that rented land in both the private sector and the public domain could continue to be leased by its present tenants for an additional two years, but only if the lessees could prove occupancy during the four years prior to the law's promulgation. Furthermore, under provisions of a law of "forced rentals," landowners were compelled to lease idle land and charge no more than 5 percent of the crop thereby obtained. German farms that had become state property during the war were rented out to individuals.

The new constitution declared it was the state's responsibility to develop agricultural activities and that benefits must go to those who worked the land. It also recognized the social responsibility of property—a concept established for Latin America by the Mexican Constitution in 1917—and prohibited *latifundios*. Although no farms were expropriated under Arévalo, a titling law (*Ley de Titulación Supletoria*) was passed providing that squatters who farmed land for ten years could obtain title to it. Paradoxically, this law legalized possession of much land onto which larger farmers had already encroached.

None of these measures really made the agrarian structure in Guatemala more egalitarian, but the legislation did lay the foundation for the action program that followed the election of Jacobo Arbenz in 1951. Arbenz vowed to convert Guatemala into a modern capitalist nation through an inclusive agrarian reform. He envisioned rural reforms that would widen the market so that simple manufacturing industries could capture economies of scale. Although he pledged to support existing industries and encourage the creation of new ones, he realized that a policy emphasis on manufacturing would have to await the inauguration of future administrations (Gleijeses 1991, p. 149).

Arbenz sternly warned of impending agrarian reforms in his inaugural address and, directing his pique particularly at UFC (which had made some installations but aggravated Guatemalans by forbidding host-country nationals from using them), called for a program of improved infrastructure.[3] However, details on both would wait a year while the new president focused on other matters. Arbenz soon learned that economic development, especially those parts that concerned social justice, was not high on the agenda of the Guatemalan elite. With the exception of the Communist party, whose honesty and disciplined working habits Arbenz openly admired, politicians feared the possibility of rising aspirations of the Ladino and indigenous poor. Presently, however, there was little pressure at the grassroots level for change in land-tenure arrangements; prospective beneficiaries were unorganized. Arbenz knew that, as soon as he pressed forward with agrarian reform, the United States would block him, especially since it was known that his friends in the Guatemalan Communist party were helping to formulate the legislation. If agrarian reform were to succeed, Arbenz concluded, it would have to disrupt agricultural production as little as possible.

In March 1952, Arbenz announced that within a year the Congress would receive the first draft of the proposed law (in fact, it was delivered the next month). The Asociación General de Agricultores (AGA) responded with fear and anger, asking Arbenz to consider their draft law. The church and most of the press urged Arbenz to accept the AGA's "reforms," which would have done little more than distribute generous credits to the association. Arbenz did not budge, able to sustain his position but only because he was a high-ranking military officer; agrarian reform had become an obsession with Arbenz. Gleijeses reports that some U.S. officials were opposed to the reform because it might hurt large landowners and UFC; others "were less biased, but on one point they all agreed: 'The law opened the way for a further extension of Communist influence'" (1989, p. 459). Congress approved the Agrarian Reform Law, Decree 900, on 17 June 1952.

THE AGRARIAN REFORM AND ITS DEMISE

The declared objectives of Decree 900 were to: (1) eliminate feudal estates; (2) obliterate all forms of indentured servitude; (3) provide land to the landless and land-poor; and (4) distribute credit and technical assistance to smallholders. The agrarian reform provided that all uncultivated land in private farms with more than 270 hectares would be expropriated. Idle land in estates of between 90 and 270 hectares would be expropriated only if less than two-thirds were under cultivation. Farms with fewer than 90 hectares would not be affected. The *Fincas Nacionales*, those farms taken from the Germans and from Ubico and his generals, would be parceled out. The reform was a moderate one; only uncultivated land could be expropriated and then only from large farms. Beneficiaries were to be any *colonos* on affected plantations and *fincas* as well as smallholders and rural wage workers. The amount of land distributed to each beneficiary was to depend on the present use of that property: If it were cultivated land, between 3.5 and 7 hectares were to be distributed; if uncultivated, between 10.5 and 17.5 hectares were allotted.

In the Petén, land could be held only in usufruct (*usufruct vitalicio*) in large farms (up to a maximum of 1,350 hectares). Land on the *Fincas Nacionales* was also granted on the basis of lifetime usufructuary rights, and 3 percent of the value of the harvested crop was to be paid to the government each year. These use rights could not be transferred from the original assignee, but land could be rented out.

Beneficiaries who received land expropriated from private owners were expected to pay for it by turning over 5 percent of the value of the crop each year for twenty-five years. Again, this land was not to be sold or otherwise alienated but could be rented out during the repayment period. Compensation to owners for expropriated private land was to be based on the value of land claimed by the owner for tax purposes in May 1952. The government reimbursed landlords in agrarian bonds yielding 3 percent interest.

The agrarian-reform decree was administered by the National Agrarian Department, whose director reported directly to the country's president. Presidential decisions were sought when disputes arose and could not be appealed to the courts.[4] A national agrarian council reviewed the expropriation decrees and a local agrarian committee helped determine which lands were subject to expropriation. The local committee consisted of one person named by the governor of the department, one named by the local municipality, and three named by the local peasant organization or workers' union.

Expropriation began on 5 January 1953 and ended on 16 June 1954. During that period the government issued 1,002 expropriation decrees affecting 603,615 hectares. Lifetime usufruct was granted on another 280,000 hectares, though some sources give higher figures (see Gleijeses 1989, p. 465). Estimates of beneficiaries also vary according to source—between 78,038 and 100,000 families; the number with lifetime usufruct ranges between 23,000 and 30,000. One-tenth of the population of the country benefited from the agrarian reform; concurrently, the highest number of workers in Guatemala's history were unionized (Simon 1988).

Credit to beneficiaries came from the government's National Agrarian Bank, created in July 1953, and loans to recipients represented one-sixth of the government's budget for the fiscal year beginning 1 July 1953. The government was also charged with providing technical assistance and inputs. Most contemporary agrarian reforms in Latin America have delivered land but not credit or technological assistance. This frequently meant that newly assigned land could not be entirely planted because beneficiaries were rarely equipped with working capital needed to purchase inputs.

Agricultural production held up well through the reforms, because the reform did not disturb cropped land. To avoid expropriation some landlords pressed idle land into use. Harvests of rice and cotton, crops grown on large estates, increased during the life of Decree 900, when exportable cotton became very profitable on the world market and underwent expansion on the Pacific lowlands in Nicaragua and El Salvador as well. Coffee also appeared unaffected by the agrarian reform even though about one-fourth of it was grown on the *Fincas*

Nacionales. When the *campesino* beneficiaries took over, they did not switch cropland from coffee into corn and beans, which had been widely predicted. Unlike in many reforms, the government made certain that input and product prices were favorable to farming. Rather than court the urban consumer with wage-good subsidies, the new government adopted farm-level price supports to stimulate production (Gleijeses 1989, pp. 468–470). Even the American embassy issued a spate of reports noting that production disturbances in the countryside were small, minor, and local.

Arbenz also put more emphasis on social programs. A literacy campaign was initiated in rural areas, and *campesinos* were encouraged to organize. Just before Arbenz was deposed, an income tax was nearly passed that would have made the reform government's social programs more fiscally responsible (Gleijeses 1989, pp. 478–479).

As problems neared solution in rural areas, urban difficulties multiplied with the rise in food prices. Emphasis on public works and agrarian reforms took the focus of government policy off urban areas, where real incomes stabilized and a housing crisis became severe.

The process of agrarian reform did not always go smoothly. Since the distribution process was rapid, laws were not followed to their letter. Landlords frequently retaliated against their *colonos* with violence, and on other occasions, peasants attacked their landlords. Sometimes *campesinos* took initiatives before the government was ready to act; land occupations by groups of peasants were commonplace. Sometimes would-be beneficiaries seized the holdings of their marginally better-off neighbors. At times, peasants claimed the same land and fought over it. In other cases, ancient feuds between farmer groups surfaced in the scramble to obtain land (Gleijeses 1989, p. 463). Also, beneficiaries who obtained land under lifetime usufruct grants complained that they had merely switched from working for a private owner to working for the state.

Gleijeses explained how violence in the countryside increased in the last weeks of the Arbenz administration:

[T]he conclusion of Neale Pearson, the foremost American authority on Decree 900, is unimpeachable. There were cases, he wrote, "in which the peasant illegally occupied lands and a few in which they burned pasture or crops in order to have land declared uncultivated and subject to expropriation. But these cases were isolated and limited in number." Moreover, the peasants' attacks against landlords were often acts of self-defense.... On several occasions, particularly in the early months of Decree 900, the landowners' violence was condoned by the local authorities. Police officers, other officials and even some governors of departments found it difficult to curb their sympathy for the "genteel" elite that knew how to reward favors. This was the time-honored response of a world that Arévalo had hardly disturbed. But now, under Arbenz, unprecedented orders emanated from the capital ... "Put an end to such abuses immediately" (1991, pp. 162–163).

The loudest complaint came from the huge, multinational UFC, which had come to be known as *El Pulpo* (the Octopus), the country's largest private landowner (Schlesinger and Kinzer 1982). At the time of reform, the company was working only 15 percent of its holdings. UFC argued that it needed large reserves so the crop could be frequently moved to another area in order to combat the banana disease that was then plaguing the Guatemalan crop. Even in contemporary times, it is common for the banana companies not to farm their entire concession; idle land is fully planted only when market conditions warrant. Nonetheless, the government would have been inconsistent had it not applied the law to UFC. It was difficult to justify the maintenance of idle land when so many farmers lacked use rights.

Of UFC's 222,580 hectares, the agrarian reform expropriated 146,000 and offered just under US$1.2 million in compensation (as in other expropriations, the valuation was that on which the company had paid its taxes). The UFC claimed that the Pacific coast holdings alone were worth US$16 million and "enlisted the aid of two close contacts, U.S. Secretary of State John Foster Dulles and his brother, CIA director Allen Dulles, and the U.S. State Department embarked on destabilization campaign and propaganda blitz to convince the public that President Arbenz was a Soviet sympathizer" (Simon 1988, p. 21).

Gleijeses commented on the economic situation:

Despite UFCO's furious complaints that the government was strangling it and would force it to leave the country, 1953 saw the highest level of banana exports since 1948, thanks mainly to favorable weather conditions and to a diminution of labor conflicts. Decree 900 had precipitated capital flight, but this loss was amply offset by high coffee prices—in this regard luck truly blessed Arbenz. As a result the government's foreign currency reserves were sound.... The funds needed for the agricultural credits provided by the government and for the public works program came mainly through indirect taxation. The rising value of Guatemala's foreign trade brought higher receipts from existing import and export duties. The authorities also sought to tighten collection and began, in late 1952, to raise taxes and duties. These measures hit the well-off hardest, but the urban poor were not unaffected (1991, pp. 167–168).

Although it appeared that the reform was on sound economic footing and that Arbenz was politically popular, disaster was not far away.

On 18 June 1954, Carlos Castillo Armas, with a tiny mercenary force of fewer than 200 men, invaded Guatemala from Honduras. Airplanes, believed to belong to the CIA, began bombing and strafing the country's major cities. The chiefs of the armed services urged Arbenz to resign, which he did on June 27. Castillo Armas flew into Guatemala City on a U.S. embassy plane to claim the presidency. Had the United States been acting single-handedly, the counterrevolution would not have succeeded. Opposition to Arbenz came not only from landlords, but also from the nonlanded bourgeoisie in cities, the Catholic Church, and the

Guatemalan military. The United States, fresh from the McCarthy hearings, justified its actions on the basis of "fighting communism" and used a shipment of arms from Czechoslovakia that had arrived in Puerto Barrios on board a Swedish ship as a pretext for invasion.

Castillo Armas reversed the reform quickly, often with flagrant disregard for human rights. Some estimate that 9,000 persons were imprisoned, many of them tortured. The UFC union and the labor unionization movement were destroyed. Over 99 percent of the land distributed in the agrarian reform was returned to its owners, including that of the United Fruit Company (though the UFC did return some 40,500 hectares to the government and agreed to pay a 30 percent tax on profits). Even the literacy programs were stopped on the grounds that they were tools of communist indoctrination. In the ensuing years, little was done to ameliorate the plight of peasants in Guatemala. Tragically, many of the same social and economic problems of the prereform *campesinos* remain today. Guatemala had its day in the reformist sun, but nightfall came quickly.

AFTER REFORM

From 1960 to 1980, according to Nairn, "the Guatemalan gross national product grew more than 5 percent annually, yet ... peasants' living standards declined" (1983). Progress toward social goals and the incorporation of the Indian peasant population into mainstream life in Guatemala was thwarted by the conservative military governments that followed the Castillo Armas administration. Since 1954, the Guatemalan "capitalist class"—understood to include the traditional agro-exporting class and those committed to diversifying agro-export production in Guatemala along with their urban complements—has been known for its unity. The left wing, on the contrary, became deeply divided by ideology and lack of organization. Given this political constellation, the agricultural strategy since Arbenz can be characterized as the promotion of "growth without distribution." With the exception of the decade beginning with 1944, as Schweigert has concluded, "Perhaps more than any other country in the world, economic policy in Guatemala for half a century, from 1930 to 1980, followed a nineteenth century liberal laissez-faire course" (1990, p. 528). The only exceptions to government noninterventionism that Schweigert encountered were "the various mechanisms of *mandamiento*, debt peonage and the vagrancy laws through which campesinos in general and indigenous ones in particular, were coerced into the plantation workforce" (Schweigert 1990, p. 528).

Two economic growth strategies were attempted in the postreform period; both omitted the peasantry. One emphasized export diversification, the other promotion of the Central American Common Market (CACM). It was understood that social issues were not to be addressed, though some felt that this would be remedied by the election of Christian Democrat Venicio Cerezo Arévalo in the mid-1980s, only the second civilian president since 1954. Although Cerezo frequently spoke of redress for the large and intransigent class of poor as a "social debt" that needed to be paid, he was not able to return agrarian reform to the political agenda as had other Christian Democrat leaders in Latin America, most notably Eduardo Frei in Chile and Napoleón Duarte in El Salvador. Some (see Smith 1990) attributed this muzzling to the military, which exacted this price for allowing Cerezo to take office. Threatened by a number of warning coups, by the end of his electoral period Cerezo had stopped referring to the "social debt."[5]

Meanwhile, a social "report card," funded in part by the chastened Catholic Church in Guatemala and released in August 1987 (LARR 1987a), gave failing marks to Cerezo and enumerated several issues responsible for the country's poverty:

1. *Unequal development*—during each recent period of measurement, the poor received progressively less of the country's wealth. On the other hand, the richest 20 percent of the population received 47 percent of national income in 1970, 55 percent in 1978, and 57 percent in 1984. Social expenditures were low because taxation generated few revenues.[6]
2. *Low wages with high unemployment*—in the forty months prior to September 1986, labor's purchasing power fell by 46 percent, a drop without precedent in Guatemalan history. More than a third of that loss took place in the first year of the Cerezo administration. In 1985, more than 40 percent of the adult population was without a permanent job.
3. *Within agriculture, food production and nutrition suffered*—growth in staples between 1950 and 1980[7] averaged a rate below that of population increase, whereas export crops thrived. From 1965 to 1975, the number of children suffering from malnutrition rose by 50 percent.

The report (LARR 1987a) proposed agrarian reform and cited Agency for International Development (the U.S. government's bilateral foreign aid-giving organization) figures showing that 1.2 million hectares of private, high-quality agricultural land were idle, which, at 7 hectares each, could benefit 171,000 families. Public land appropriate for farming could benefit another 53,000 families. Altogether, this land could all but eliminate land hunger in the country. The report (LARR 1987a) also suggested the need for tax, foreign trade, and banking reforms. Another document (LARR 1987b), issued somewhat later, showed that 83 percent of rural dwellers lived in poverty, 81 percent of all children in the country were malnourished, 66 percent of homes lacked drinking water, over 50 percent of the population was illiterate, and 49 percent of all children died before age 9. This latter figure seems so high as to be unthinkable, but it was derived from official sources. Manning (1990, p. 57) notes that 13 out of 100 Guatemalan children die before age 5.

While social problems festered, agriculture overall continued to grow and change. As in other Central American republics, cotton was a popular crop in

Guatemala in the 1950s largely because of the thriving international market during
the Korean war. Sugar was added to the list of exports after the Cuban Revolution
redistributed sugar quotas throughout the region. The growth of fast food in the
United States made livestock farming profitable. Schweigert noted: "The 5.1%
average annual growth rate of agricultural output from 1965 to 1980 was one
of the highest in the world" (1990, p. 530); its dynamism came from the
production of primary commodities for export. But even the work force for export
crops did not benefit from the farm-export boom since wage hikes only
compensated for inflation; in real terms, according to Schweigert, wages were
"set" at the amount of corn workers could purchase: "The real agricultural 'corn'
wage on the South Coast has for decades been in the vicinity of 30 pounds of
corn per day. The average productivity of labor in the subsistence agriculture
of the highlands, characterized by labor surplus, has for at least half a century
been in the vicinity of 30 pounds of corn per day" (1990, p. 538).

Meanwhile, Guatemala's land-tenure structure became more dualistic. Between
1964 and 1979, farms with fewer than 0.7 hectares almost tripled in number
(expanding from 20 to 40 percent of all farm households as the average holding
size dropped from 0.4 to 0.3 hectare) while total farm acreage in Guatemala
expanded by 20 percent (Barham et al. 1992, p. 3).

As diversification proceeded, Guatemala came to depend more on its rich south
coast, first opened in the late nineteenth century. Clearing land in the area had
environmental as well as production consequences, however. This tropical lowland
was not favored for settlement until DDT made it possible to control malarial
anopheles mosquitoes. But by the 1960s, the area was thriving. Schweigert
concluded that in three decades the south coast was transformed at the enormous
environmental expense of virgin woodlands: "In 1950, 39 percent of the area
was still covered by forest; by 1979, this figure had dropped to 6 percent" (1990,
p. 97). During that period, forest went from being the most important use of
farmland to being the least important. While forest shrank by 84 percent, land
in permanent crops, annual crops, and pasture increased by 152 percent, 126
percent, and 27 percent, respectively.

Increasingly diversified exports helped Guatemala weather the long-run drop
in coffee prices after the mid-1950s, but they could not assure the country's safe
passage through the dark 1980s when the growth rate slowed markedly as the
region became enmeshed in debt crisis (which afflicted so many Latin American
countries). President Ronald Reagan's Caribbean Initiative and President George
Bush's Enterprise for the Americas were largely without substance for Guatemala,
but the two policies did revive the idea of diversifying agro-exports to more "nontraditional" products. Throughout the 1980s, Guatemala gave life to its economy
by targeting nontraditionals, that is, fruits, flowers, and vegetables for marketing
in the U.S. winter. During the 1980s, especially in Mexico and Central America,
debate continued over whether or not economic development should come to rely
more on nontraditional exports. One school of thought (Bulmer-Thomas 1987;

Sanderson 1986; Weeks 1985; Williams 1986) charges that agro-exports displace staples on the country's best land. Since these crops may continue to be grown on large holdings by the elite and foreigners, there are few multiplier effects for the peasants. For their part, *campesinos* producing domestically consumed crops face controlled prices since staples make up a large percentage of the wage goods of urban workers. Meanwhile, most agro-exports can effectively restrict the translation of these profits into higher wages (a fact that Schweigert's 1990 study seems to confirm), and mechanized operations on large holdings may even entirely displace some labor-intensive activities.

The other side of the argument holds that, since small countries do not have an adequate domestic market, growth of their economies must depend on expansion of exports. Options are few, and any that present themselves—even given their shortcomings for multiplier effects benefiting the peasantry—need to be utilized. Eventually, as the core of activities around exports widens, so will the domestic market; ultimately, incomes will rise. It is even conceivable that peasants can produce exportables if granted adequate assistance. Even if not, more labor will be needed since vegetables, fruits, and flowers are not amenable to mechanical husbandry. The current government in Guatemala has opted for this argument.[8]

Traditional agricultural exports showed lackluster performance in the 1980s. After three years of negative growth and four of less than 1.6 percent, the farm sector recovered and grew at an average rate of over 3.5 percent from 1987 to 1992, according to the Inter-American Development Bank (IDB 1993, p. 97). Nontraditional exports were an important factor in this expansion. IDB claimed: "The trade balance improved further in 1990. The value of exports grew by 7.5 percent, primarily because of an important expansion in nontraditional products.... Nontraditional exports—mainly chemicals, vegetables, flowers and fruits—were very strong as their sales expanded by an estimated 24 percent [in 1990].... The performance of traditional products was uneven" (1991, p. 93). In 1992, the IDB report noted, "The trade balance deteriorated substantially during 1991. The value of exports increased only slightly, as expansion of nontraditional products barely offset the sharp contraction in sales of traditional products. Nontraditional exports, vegetables and other agricultural products continued to register rapid growth" (1992, p. 22). However, by 1993, "Agriculture grew some 2.9 percent.... This growth occurred despite ... a slump in nontraditional agricultural products" (IDB 1993, p. 94).

Export booms in Guatemala have historically benefited large commercial farms and displaced small farmers. The recent experience in the western highlands of Guatemala gives more reason for optimism in that it appears that small-scale production of broccoli, cauliflower, and snow peas is more efficient than large-scale production for export. Although these crops are riskier than corn and beans, they have a high value per land unit. Use of family labor means that crops can be supervised closely and disease and insect problems caught early. Also, the crops are labor intensive and the work of many family members can be usefully absorbed. In their field studies, Barham et al. found that "small farms are participating in the production of the new exports. Farms as small as 2.5 acres are estimated to have a 75 percent probability of growing at least some non-traditionals" (1992, p. 22). The study tempered its optimism by showing that the amount of land devoted to these exports levels off at about 0.8 acres and does not increase as farm size increases from 4 to 11 acres, probably due to capital constraints. As farms exceed 11 acres in size, however, percent of land area planted to nontraditionals rises again. Barham et al. (1992) also find a group of non-*campesino* producers with more than 25 acres who are accumulating land through rental to grow nontraditionals. Whether peasants will substantially gain from growing nontraditionals is still an open question; a new worry in 1993 was their possible exclusion by U.S. port authorities because of high pesticide content.

CONTINUING RURAL UNREST

Beginning in 1962 and continuing to the 1990s, left-wing insurgency and the militarization of the Guatemalan society proceed unabated, with severe human rights abuses being one outcome. The increase in defense expenditures per member in the armed forces between 1955 and 1965 was greater in Guatemala than in any other Latin American country. Official expenses for defense and internal security reached 17 percent of government spending (as compared to 2 percent for the university). Jonas concluded, "in a very real sense, the military became a leading force in Guatemalan politics. At a deeper level, however, the political power of the armed forces was an expression of the class *alliance* underlying the counterrevolution. The militarization of politics permitted the Guatemalan bourgeoisie and foreign investors to rule indirectly" (1991, p. 62). Meanwhile, workers and *campesinos* bore the brunt of the terror of the military, especially where guerrilla activity was intense. Jonas (1991, p. 63) sets the number of peasant deaths from 1966 to 1970 at 8,000. For their part, *finqueros* and foreign enterprises were no longer troubled by union activity. By 1962, only 1.2 percent of the country's labor force was still unionized. Landholders today rely on the army or the police to get rid of troublesome organizers and to dislodge peasants who invade *fincas*. Smith concluded that by the mid-1960s, the Guatemalan military was "the strongest, most fully institutionalized, and most nationalistic military force in Central America.... After facing down the threat from small insurgent groups in the 1960s with assistance supplied by the United States, Guatemala's military moved from simple seizure of high office to the establishment of a political security apparatus, which today penetrates all levels of society" (1990, p. 9).

Still, Weeks (1985) judges that *campesinos* in Guatemala were more land-poor than landless. He shows that in both Guatemala and El Salvador, 2 percent of the farms contain about 65 percent of all land in farms. In these countries, Weeks (1985) infers that the great majority of peasants fall into the *minifundio* category, cultivating less than 10 acres of land (61 percent for El Salvador and 57 percent for Guatemala). Considering the size of holding and the condition of landlessness together, Weeks (1985, Table 34, p. 112) calculates that 83.9 percent of Guatemala's rural people are either landless or near-landless. Among the Central American countries, land concentration increased most markedly between the 1950s and the 1970s in Guatemala. Weeks concluded that for the second half of the 1960s and the 1970s, "Guatemala experienced a government-fostered process of marginalization of the peasantry to a degree perhaps unique in Latin America in such a short period of time" (1985, pp. 117–118); and Jonas thinks that the "major tendency in recent decades has been expropriation of minifundia, leaving an increasing proportion of the agricultural work force with no land or insufficient land to subsist" (1991, p. 96). This process, Weeks noted, "goes far to explain the seething rebellion in the Guatemalan countryside" (1985, p. 117).

Popular movements with substantial Indian support reemerged in the 1970s, stimulated by attempts on the part of landowners to dispossess indigenous farmers and convert their operations to more modern capitalist enterprises. In the process, class conflict ignited between landlords and highland Indians who migrated to plantations on the south coast on a seasonal basis. Jonas (1991) believes migration occurred as peasants were deprived of their highland parcels and were not fully absorbed by the agriculture of the coast. They fought as guerrillas because they lost their "stake" in society. The fact that they were an oppressed ethnic group exacerbated the problem as did the fact that they were denied any participation in the government (Guatemala had not legalized party politics to represent the interests of the poor since 1954; taking up arms was not a preference but a last resort for this group [Jonas 1991, pp. 133–134]).

In the 1960s and 1970s, it was considered subversive to even speak of land reform, but in the economically depressed 1980s, as civil war deepened and violence escalated, there came renewed public calls for structural agrarian changes.[9] As Manning wrote: "Ten years ago, talk about improving the lot of the poor could attract a visit from the death squad. Today, even middle of the road politicians speak lovingly of the campesino. It's not hard to see why: three quarters of all Guatemalans live in the countryside and anyone wanting to get elected must appeal to them for their votes" (1990, p. 57). And Jonas concluded: "As we enter the 1990s, Guatemala is still embattled, rent asunder by the crises and legacies of past decades. Reconciliation between the two Guatemalas will be virtually impossible without addressing the interests of the 87 percent majority and of the Indian majority. At some level there will have to be a real sharing of power ... if the war there continues, the Guatemalan tinderbox could become an open threat to Central American peace" (1991, p. 240). She speculates on what might have happened if the 1954 reforms had been allowed to stand and concluded the result would have been "not communism, but capitalist industrialization and modernization. Land reform had to be part of that process, but it would have served to rationalize Guatemalan capitalism, to stabilize the country by bringing its dispossessed majority into the economy" (Jonas 1991, p. 240).

5

Reforms of the Alliance for
Progress Era: Chile

Nineteen Latin American countries enacted land-reform laws as a result of the Alliance for Progress, which originated in the 1961 Charter of Punta del Este of the Organization of American States (Dorner 1992, p. 33). The Alliance proposed to reflect the compassion of the John F. Kennedy government for Latin America and to head off the possible occurrence of more "Cubas" in the hemisphere; the general idea was that if countries carried out agrarian and other reforms to rectify maldistribution of income and resources and to promote economic growth (both of which would likely make countries less susceptible to the blandishments of communism), they would qualify for U.S. economic assistance. Most of the ensuing reforms in Latin America were minor efforts having little domestic impact, but in each country they generated considerable debate over the wisdom of such laws and the philosophy motivating them.[8]

Many of the Alliance reforms involved some colonization of public lands. Only later did countries realize that as a result of settlements in fragile, tropical areas, ecologically damaging despoliation of natural resources occurred. The original hope was that colonization of the frontier would deflect the pressure for land from private property, thus postponing conflict between peasants and landowners. For the same reason, the government agency charged with enacting agrarian reform would sometimes purchase idle farms for subdivision and sell them to *campesinos*. In cases of escheat or donation, governments may already have held some properties that were ultimately used for agrarian reform.

Countries like Colombia, Venezuela, Brazil, and Paraguay fall into the category of "minimalist" reforms. Others, like the Dominican Republic (Stanfield 1989; Dorner 1992, pp. 40–41; Meyer 1989), Honduras (Stringer 1989; Pino and Thorpe 1992; Ruben 1989), and Ecuador (Haney and Haney 1989; Forster 1989; Dorner 1992, pp. 35–37), sponsored somewhat more ambitious efforts.

Two of the agrarian reforms with widest impact occurred in Chile, treated in this chapter, and Peru.[9] Although starting out as rather insignificant events, they grew to become quite important; some would say that they were watershed events in both countries.

From its earliest days, the bulk of the land in Chile with highest productivity and greatest potential was owned as large estates, which were both large properties and large enterprises. The eminent chronicler of early Chile, Benjamín Subercaseaux, wrote of the importance of land distribution in shaping early colonization in Chile: "The *encomienda* and the *hacienda* built up an aristocracy that, once the government of Spain was overthrown, stepped into the place vacated by the representatives of the crown and set up a new government in harmony with the existing social order. The common people took virtually no part" (1943, p. 125). In Chile, the land question had been high on the social agenda for decades when reforms were finally seriously addressed in the 1960s. The debate over entailed estates (the practice of limiting the inheritance of farms to a specific line of heirs),[3] for example, divided a generation of the country's leaders in the early nineteenth century. Bernardo O'Higgins, the man whom most Chileans would name as their "primary historic patriot," favored the abolition of entails, a heretical idea for which he was overthrown and permanently exiled in 1828 (Falcoff 1989, p. 87). As Falcoff put it, "O'Higgins had believed ... that a change in the structure of ownership would radically transform Chilean society, replacing an aristocratic republic of landowners with a Jeffersonian commonwealth of yeoman farmers" (1989, p. 87).

Over a half-century ago, McBride revealed his prescience in writing a classic study of land tenure relations in Chile: "No superficial reforms can long retard the movement. Only a fundamental modification of the hacienda ... system seems capable of saving the country ... change is inevitable" (1936, pp. 379, 385). In 1945, Ellsworth added, "The chief obstacle [to agricultural development] appears to be the influence of the easy-going tradition of the hacienda.... This obstacle is gradually being worn down.... Progress, however is very slow and it is doubtful if it can become sufficiently rapid without great changes in Chile's landholding system" (1945, p. 156).

HISTORICAL BACKGROUND

Before the land reforms of the 1960s and early 1970s, the structure of land tenure in Chile was like that in most Latin American countries: a small number of large farms and a large number of smallholdings harboring an ample and expanding population of landless workers. Chile's *latifundios* can be traced, as in so many countries described here, to the system of *encomienda*, or trusts over Indian communities given by the crown to favored local subjects. *Mercedes* or direct grants of land were also given. The Spanish colonists had no intention of farming personally, so land grants without Indian labor were nearly worthless to them. For that reason land grants were usually near *encomiendas*; alternatively, Indian communities were transferred to *mercedes*. The indigenous groups were obligated to supply a certain amount of each year's produce and labor in mines or agriculture. For their part, *encomenderos* had to pay taxes, maintain irrigation canals and roads in their domain, care for the religious training of the Indians, and provide protection for their subjects. Although *encomiendas* were not meant to be land grants, *encomenderos* in time came to think that they owned not only the Indian community, but the land on which the native population farmed.

In 1603 the crown attempted to rectify the growing feeling of proprietorship of *encomenderos* and other abuses of this system by sending authorities, including a surveyor, to Chile. Those owning too much territory were to return the excess to the Indian communities. The crown also attempted to regulate the working condition of the native population, which worsened as demand for labor increased while progressively more indigenous natives fled into the southern frontier. However, these humanitarian efforts from Spain failed: working conditions got worse, and land was not returned to the indigenous population. Landless labor was already an integral part of the system.

Although fewer in number, the Araucanian Indians (also called Mapuche, the language they speak), who occupied the southern part of middle Chile, were much more hostile to Spanish incursions than other tribes to the north. For 100 years after Pedro de Valdivia founded Santiago in 1541, the Spanish and the Araucanians were at war. Violent attacks frequently broke out after that, even though a treaty had been signed that established the Bío-Bío River, at the southern extreme of the Central Valley, as the northern limit of Mapuche territory.

Furthermore, most of the indigenous groups of central Chile, unlike most of the Indians of northern South America, did not dwell in permanent villages. They lived in temporary shelters, farmed a piece of land until it was depleted, and moved on. Extracting labor and tribute from a group with a nomadic lifestyle became increasingly difficult as sedentary economic activities gained importance to the colony. Thus the low number of Indians in the central zone, their belligerence, and their penchant to flight meant that the *encomienda* did not work as well in Chile as in many other Latin American countries. When the crown abolished the *encomienda* in 1791, there were few left in Chile; the hacienda and its subdivision known as the *fundo* had already evolved from colonial institutions.[4] At that point, primogeniture (*mayorazgo*, or the practice of entailing estates to the eldest son) kept large estates intact. Primogeniture was finally removed from statute with laws passed in 1852 and 1857. Still, the large estate predominated in Chile, and Sternberg noted that in 1880 "the concentration of land, in one sense, was at maximum, that is, fewer people owned the land of Chile than ever before or since" (1962, p. 25). By the 1930s, "[i]n respect to landholding, Chile [was] far from making substantial progress. In 1928 some 513 persons, less than one half of one percent of all landholders, were reported to own 60 percent of the land in private hands; two and one half percent of all landed proprietors possessed 78 percent of the arable land" (Cox 1963, pp. 401–402).

After 1875 and through the first third of the twentieth century, acreage used for agriculture doubled and irrigated acreage tripled in response to increasing demand for agricultural products from expanding international trade as well as mining centers in northern Chile and growing domestic commercial centers.

The hacienda and the *fundo* showed a fair degree of adaptability to changing market stimuli as the products in demand were "land extensive and required a modest technical competence" (Felix 1961, p. 291). Since untilled land was still available for colonizers, agricultural expansion in the nineteenth century was relatively easy as population spilled into the heretofore forested region south of the Bío-Bío and European colonists entered the area around Valdivia. These movements were facilitated after the War of the Pacific (in which Chile earned many of its northern mineral riches); in 1883 soldiers were sent from the north finally to pacify the southern indigenous groups. Expansion of agriculture in this manner was not accompanied by much increase in production per acre. Grain prices turned sharply downward between 1873 and 1896; concurrently, the scope for farm expansion into the frontier was beginning to disappear. Rather than increasing per-acre yields on land already planted in grain, pastures were converted to cultivated fields. By the first decade of the twentieth century, the size of herds leveled off. Crop acreage doubled between 1910 and the mid-1930s, when it ceased expanding. Production per acre overall dropped 20 percent in that period because of a relatively constant yield in the rich parts of the Central Valley and markedly falling figures in the formerly forested southern Central Valley, where cultivation quickly caused leaching and severe erosion (Felix 1961, p. 294).

Even so, agricultural production per capita rose moderately until 1930, and net agricultural exports showed only a slight downward trend. Intensification of livestock through artificial pasture spread slowly, and viniculture expanded until the 1930s, when growers established a licensing system for land on which grapes were to be grown for wine. In the main, however, a more mixed agriculture did not change the dominant pattern of grain and cattle farming. Before the 1930s, copper and nitrate booms sheltered the agricultural sector by paying taxes needed to expand farm infrastructure (like irrigation). (Chile's Central Valley has fertile land, but since rain and snow come only in winter, irrigation is essential for all farms there, with few exceptions, above the Bío-Bío River.) With the mineral-boom collapse during the Great Depression, the true state of agriculture was revealed. Between the mid-1930s and the mid-1950s, production per land unit rose by 20 percent, but this was insufficient to support a higher population growth rate. (The rate of population increase between 1930 and 1964 was 2.2 percent annually whereas the rate of growth of the agricultural sector was only 1.8 percent.) As a result, farm imports steadily increased, and by the mid-1960s, they were absorbing one-fifth of the country's foreign exchange earnings. As a result, discussions within Chile on problems of the agricultural sector turned to debates, becoming increasingly heated and politicized. Two lines of reasoning were presented.

The "agrarian structuralists" placed the blame for faulty farm production on the institutional organization of Chilean agriculture (Chonchol 1971; CIDA 1966; Barraclough 1973; Dorner 1971; Barraclough and Domike 1966), which allowed *fundo* owners to idle farmland or work it extensively. Land was not significantly taxed, so it could be held as speculation against inflation; existing taxes were not proportional to soil quality, a feature that would have charged the best farmland at a greater rate in order to encourage *fundo* owners to use land for its highest and best use. Also, the argument went, the system did not give sufficient incentives to the efforts of farm laborers who produced the food. Under this formulation, the landed class was severely criticized. Aníbal Pinto Santa Cruz asserted: "the demand of the landlords, like that of other upper class groups, is geared to luxury imports.... The market for consumers' goods is already narrow. Demanding luxury goods coupled with the slowness of growth of the agricultural sector ... puts a barrier in the path of the growth of domestic industries" (1962, p. 88). Kaldor (1959) claimed that if the upper-income groups had the same consumption pattern as their counterparts in developed countries, the savings rate could be doubled.

In contrast, the "rate of return" school of thought blamed the price system and macroeconomic policies, arguing that they were urban-biased and favored import-substituting industries while discriminating against farming. The result was a rate of return in farming that was too low for farmers to invest (Mamalakis 1969; Crosson 1970; Bray 1962). While both positions in the debate harbored partial truth, the passionate arguments at the time seemed to require that each combatant pick a side.

The heart of the agrarian structuralist argument, which assumed prominence in the 1960s and early 1970s, was that the inequality in land and water distribution led to a lack of competition in the land and capital markets and a resultant inefficiency in the allocation of resources. As Kay put it, "While the minifundia had too much labour and too little land the reverse was true of the latifundia" (1992a, p. 103). Even so, the hacienda system in Chile was hardly a static institution during the period. Mechanization, for example, increased by 7 percent between 1945 and 1955. Labor productivity in agriculture grew at about 2.2 percent annually between 1940 and 1964 (a rate only slightly below that of manufacturing). Area cultivated in fruit doubled between 1930 and 1964, and many more technical inputs came to be used as the green revolution made itself felt toward the end of the 1960s and into the 1970s. Most *fundos*, according to Kay (1992a, p. 104), had converted their farms to capitalistic enterprises by the mid-1960s.

The rate-of-return adherents maintained that governmental policy discriminated against agriculture. Kay observed, "the government did fix or control prices of some essential agricultural commodities but it did not turn the commodity (or net barter) terms of trade against agriculture" (1992a, p. 104). Furthermore, the price index of agricultural output when compared to the price index of agricultural inputs remained more or less the same. The state's credit policy also favored agriculture; in addition to public subsidies given routinely to agricultural borrowing, in 1951 and 1960, agriculture received, respectively, 28 percent and 34 percent of credit (agriculture's share of GDP was only 13 percent).

There were some compelling arguments in favor of the rate-of-return school when the trade sector is examined, however. The government manipulated the multiple exchange rate so that protection for many key agricultural products was negative. With food products subsidized for urban consumers, producers faced unfair competition from imports into the local markets. Also, agricultural exports were discriminated against through the foreign exchange mechanism. Furthermore, prices of some local industrial farm inputs were higher than international prices for the same products because of high tariffs around local manufactures (Kay 1992a, pp. 105–106).

Kay argues that, on balance, government policy did result in "discrimination against, or at least neglect of, the agricultural sector" (1992a, p. 106). As elsewhere in Latin America, the import-substituting nature of the industrialization policy in Chile created some bias against agriculture. At the same time, "if government policy did not particularly favour agriculture, it did not squeeze it of investment funds [which came from mining or industry itself].... The fundamental problem of agriculture ... was its inadequate land tenure structure. In this sense government policy was not so much 'urban biased' as biased against the implementation of an agrarian reform and was thus 'landlord biased'" (Kay 1992a, p. 106).

GRASSROOTS *FUNDO* ORGANIZATION

Slow division of properties occurred in the last part of the nineteenth and the beginning of the twentieth century, but most important, in terms of numbers, was that small pieces of marginal *fundo* land were hived off and sold to farmworkers. Upon transfer of these properties, *fundo* owners assured themselves of a more or less permanent labor supply for which they would have few direct maintenance responsibilities (Thiesenhusen 1966, p. 15). Of course, some peasants had received their small plots years before.

In addition to these *minifundistas*, who served large landlords when they needed wage labor, Chile's traditional agrarian structure was composed of a number of other types of rural laborers with varying tenure status. In the 1960s, it was estimated that the working class in Chilean agriculture made up about 87 percent of the active agricultural population and received 34 percent of the income from farming.

In rural Chile, when the *fundo* structure was still very much in dominance, the laboring class was made up of wage laborers or *afuerinos*, who did not live on the *fundo*, resident farm laborers or *inquilinos*, who did live on the *fundo*, and sharecroppers or *medieros*, who may or may not have lived on the farm where they worked. *Inquilinos* had a status higher than *afuerinos*, but were on the lowest rung of the class ladder of residents on the *fundo*.

The term "inquilino," although it means "renter" in Spanish, has a special meaning in Chile. An *inquilino* received a small cash wage for his labor and was given the use of his house and garden plot or *cerco* near it; the *inquilino* family may also have been allowed to grow corn, beans, and squash collectively on a parcel, called *chacra*. The family may have received other perquisites (*regalias*), in lieu of a cash wage, which might include bread, a plate of cooked beans at noon, pasturage (*talaje*) for a given number of animals, and permission to collect firewood on a certain part of the farm. In return, *inquilinos* were expected to work six days a week for the *patrón* (landlord) on the *fundo*'s demesne. When sons of *inquilinos* (*voluntarios*) worked, they usually received a higher percentage of their pay in cash. The *inquilino* was called the *obligado* and was responsible for performing the work himself or, if the landlord allowed, he could send a substitute.

It appears that *inquilinos* were not the lineal descendants of the *encomienda* system. After an extensive study of early Jesuit records and archives of the *Real Audiencia* and the *Capitania General* as well as other documents, Góngora (1960) traces the *inquilino* to a group of "poor Spaniards," itinerant Indians from the north (*yanaconas*), and others who arrived with the conquerors. After winning middle Chile for the crown, some of them became hired workers on the estates. Since land was nearly a free good, they could establish themselves on "loaned" hacienda land. They were welcomed by *patrones* because they could guard property boundaries. Once railroad construction and work in the mines offered wages sufficient to draw workers from agriculture in the late nineteenth century, landowners expressed the need "to root" (*arraigar*) their *inquilinos* to the estates by offering more *regalias*. They saw the need to keep labor at hand for chores throughout the year. Given the prevailing structure of agriculture, with the best land and irrigation facilities being controlled by a few landowners, some peasants actively sought *inquilino* positions on large estates as secure employment alternatives. For the owners' part, as long as land was cheap relative to wages they would otherwise have to pay, landholders attempted to attract *inquilinos* (Bauer 1992, p. 27).

As irrigation expanded in the early part of the twentieth century, demand for labor and *inquilinos* increased. Land was added to production during this period, but when this annexation stopped around 1930, the *inquilino* system began its slow disappearance. Mechanization became more and more profitable, a trend that accelerated in the 1950s. Throughout much of this period, an overvalued exchange rate made mechanizing relatively inexpensive as land prices rose. Thus some *inquilinos* became wage laborers; those who remained saw their *regalias* diminish and money wages increase. In the mid-1950s, it was legislated that 25 percent of the wage had to be paid in cash; by 1965, it was 75 percent. The cash-based system was supposed to make relations more businesslike (and less "feudal") between *inquilinos* and landowners. But in fact more cash meant *inquilinos* were less protected from inflation. In 1955, *inquilinos* occupied about one-fifth of *fundo* land and produced about 25 percent of hacienda production; by 1965, *inquilinos* controlled only one-seventh of hacienda land and contributed about 20 percent of total *fundo* output. Concomitantly, a few lucky, displaced *inquilinos* became sharecroppers (*medieros*). Most, however, became wage workers and made up an increasingly larger part of the *fundo*'s labor system (Kay 1992b, pp. 43–45). Former *inquilinos* thus had to compete with *voluntarios* and *afuerinos*. Kay (1992b, pp. 49–52) calculates that beginning in about 1965 the cost of hiring an *inquilino* was higher than contracting with an *afuerino* or a *voluntario*. This increased the landlords' incentives for the proletarianization of the *inquilinos*.

Bauer (1992) argues that the political justification for *inquilinaje* was perhaps as important as its economic rationale. *Inquilinos* were relied on to cast their votes for landlord causes and candidates, handing rural property holders a dominance in government policymaking out of proportion to their numbers. Landowners' power thus stemmed not only from their control over land but also from their control over people (Bauer 1992, p. 28). In 1874, a new law permitted universal suffrage to literate males (ability to write one's name was a sufficient test for this). Thus landlords could pack *inquilinos* into vehicles and send them to the polls on election day with the assurance they would vote for the *patrón*'s candidate in a nonsecret ballot. As Bauer (1992) shows, more members of parliament had landlord connections in 1900 than in 1850, and the countryside remained solidly conservative into the 1960s. Bauer (1992, p. 30) also feels that personal service and the deference to landlords accorded by *inquilinos* were further reasons for landlords to keep the system intact. Toward the end of the eighteenth century in Chile, the term *inquilino* separated meaning from its synonym, *arrendatario* (which came to mean only cash renter).

Fundos may also have employed *medieros* or sharecroppers, who often farmed a different part of the *fundo* each year. The *mediero* usually contributed all of the labor and half of the remaining operating costs. The *patrón* provided the tilled land, the remainder of the inputs, and the operating credit (and sometimes living expenses) until the crop was harvested. Produce was then divided 50-50 so that the *mediero* could either sell his product or keep it for his own use. There were many variants of *mediería*, however, some of which melded *inquilinaje* and *mediería*.

LAND AND LABOR REFORMS

Before the Chilean agrarian reform, some safeguards for *fundo* workers made their situations somewhat better than the prereform periods in other countries. *Inquilinos* retained full juridical freedom in the latter half of the nineteenth century, though debt peonage in the prerevolutionary Mexican sense was never widespread. Although *patrones* did not always pay it, a minimum wage was set by the government. An unsatisfactory *inquilino* could be discharged with two-month notice. Also, a weak social-security system was in place, as was the custom of paying workers for seven days if they worked six (*semana corrida*). Still, access to education and health facilities for rural workers was limited, and in 1960, even though city-based labor unions were common, only about 1 percent of agricultural laborers were organized. Restrictive legislation included provisions that rural labor could unionize only if all members lived on one *fundo* and then only if the property had more than twenty workers; no federation of farm unions was allowed. These provisions prevented the organization of labor unions on 96 percent of Chilean *fundos* (Troncoso 1957).

Proscription against labor's organizing in rural areas finds its historical roots in the election of 1920 that put Arturo Alessandri in the presidency: "With the election of 1920 ... political power in the nation as a whole passed from the rural landlords to the city. However, Alessandri was only allowed to come into office as the result of a tacit agreement that the landlords be left untouched. This meant that there would be no attempt at agrarian reform, and that the government would not allow the organization of agricultural workers into unions" (Alexander 1962, p. 238).

Until the position favoring change was translated into political terms, little progress was made toward concrete agrarian and labor law reforms. In the presidential elections of 1958, however, there was a rebellion of the country's peasants, who voted for the candidate of the left, Salvador Allende. This became possible only after President Carlos Ibañez del Campo (1952–1958) had introduced the secret ballot into rural elections. With a stroke, the issue of Chile's *latifundios* was transformed into a political problem (Keller R. 1963, pp. 14–15).[5] Although Jorge Alessandri (Arturo's son) beat Allende by a narrow margin, the fragmented urban political parties learned in the process that the mass rural electorate could help them in highly contentious elections. Several years later, the effects of the Alliance for Progress, coalitions of "popular" left-wing parties, and progressive ideas emanating from the Roman Catholic Church of Pope John XXIII converged in favor of land reforms (Thiesenhusen 1966, pp. 58–65). A definitive end to the hacienda's sway over Chilean politics was in view.

Even so, the agricultural unionization law, designed to rectify archaic unionization provisions and put rural and urban unions on par with one another, did not pass until 1967, making good on Eduardo Frei's presidential platform promise to "repeal or leave without effect, the present agricultural trade union law and establish legislation which promotes free regional and national unions..." (PDC 1964, p. 23). Chile's agrarian reform came on the heels of the labor legislation, and it differed from reforms in Bolivia, Mexico, Guatemala, and Nicaragua in that it did not come about through a revolution; it was legislated.

There were important precursory events and certain institutions that set the stage for the 1967 Agrarian Reform Law, however. As early as 1925, the constitution provided that "[t]he state will promote the convenient division of land into private property." This was the basis for the founding of the Caja de Colonización Agrícola in 1928. Ironically, the first work of the Caja was to establish forty-three German families on a subdivided *fundo* near Santiago in January 1929. As in Guatemala, it was commonly thought at the time that Europeans could bring a lacking entrepreneurial element to agriculture. In fact, the Caja purchased few *fundos* and benefited more professionals, soldiers, and civil servants than peasants (Thiesenhusen 1966, pp. 33–36, 174–194).

In 1962, the Caja became the Corporación de la Reforma Agraria (CORA), organized to shape and administer the agrarian program of President Jorge Alessandri. The law to make this possible was Chile's response to the Alliance for Progress and was designed to be an unimaginative and underfunded colonization program, different in name only from the Caja. The law (No. 15,020) was as complex as it was full of loopholes, a 104-article behemoth. Although it recognized the social duty of landlords to use their land for agricultural production purposes, it did not permit deferred payment for expropriated land; the Constitution of 1925 had provided for the "inviolability of all property." This was interpreted to mean that expropriated land must be paid for in cash at the market value at sale, a provision that resulted in a stillborn reform; Chile could not afford one that did not provide for delayed payment. (After much public debate and growing trepidation among Chilean landlords, a constitutional amendment on this matter was finally passed in July 1967, permitting indemnification of landlords at 20 percent in cash, with the balance paid over a minimum of ten years at 4 percent interest with annual readjustments for inflation.) The most notable effect of Law No. 15,020, derisively called "flower-pot reform" (*reforma de macetero*) by some Chileans, was not what it did to settle *campesinos* on farms of their own; the few peasants who received land under its provisions were mostly located prominently on one mammoth farm with land on both sides of the Pan-American highway south of Santiago.[6] Rather, Law No. 15,020 sent a signal to landowners, who began to divide their *fundos* into fractions, called *hijuelas*, often among relatives so they could retain control. Some prescient landowners, recognizing that targets of land reform would be overly large farms and idle land, were motivated to make sure that all tracts that comprised their former *fundos* showed increased production. Indeed, the effort resulted in cropping of fields that had been fallow for years. While the reform was being discussed interminably with little to show, the activity occurring in traditional farming tended to be over-looked.

Christian Democrat Eduardo Frei, whose presidential election platform contained a strong land-reform plank, submitted replacement legislation to Law No. 15,020 in November 1965; after arduous debate in the Chilean congress, it finally passed as Law No. 16,640 in 1967. Between his inauguration and enactment of the new legislation, the Frei administration installed reform on land that the government had purchased from willing sellers, having assured former owners of more favorable terms of exchange than they would get after the law had passed (nearly 500 farms totaling 1 million hectares were acquired in this manner). Thome (1989) records several reasons for the prominence of land reform in Frei's policy agenda. In the first place, available data on the concentration of land and water resources in the hands of a few showed that not much had changed since Cox (1963) wrote in 1934: 2.2 percent of farm units, each over 2,000 acres, still controlled nearly 69 percent of total agricultural land whereas 185,000 rural families owned no land whatsoever and 117,000 had only tiny, uneconomic, *minifundio* plots representing 78 percent of farms and only 5 percent of total farmland. According to the Christian Democrats, this amount of land concentration resulted in low productivity and an increasingly unfavorable balance of agricultural trade (Thome 1989, pp. 192–193). Furthermore, a growing current of Roman Catholic thought supported agrarian reform. In this manner peasants, who began to feel their newfound potency as a political force, became an electorate to be reckoned with.[7]

The agrarian reform was viewed differently by factions within the Christian Democratic party itself. The *oficialistas*, whom Frei represented, believed in the primacy of economic growth and inflation control and favored individual farming in cases of reform. The left wing of the party was more preoccupied with equity; for it, production cooperatives worked by groups of beneficiary members on the undivided *fundo* became an organizing principle of agrarian reform. In the first part of the Frei period, left-wing elements were prominent; by 1968, the *oficialista* faction dominated.

Law No. 16,640 empowered CORA to transform certain public land and to acquire privately owned land for redistribution to *campesinos*. Parcels that had been titled to the government over the years through escheat and donation were transferred to CORA for distribution. Private land could be expropriated by CORA for reason of large farm size, deficient land use, abandonment, unauthorized subdivision of farms (to evade the large-farm provisions of Law No. 16,640), corporate land ownership, lack of compliance with the liberalized labor laws (passed just before the agrarian reforms), and public infrastructural use. CORA could also continue to buy properties from willing sellers; some landlords, made skittish by endless public discussion of reforms, were anxious by this time for an escape route from farming and were quick to sell.

Because most reasons for legal expropriation were ambiguous, difficult to use, and often promised litigation, CORA decided to focus upon excess size and voluntary transfers, which combined for 70 percent of the Frei transfers into the reform sector (Thome 1989, pp. 194–196). The excess-size provision was easiest to implement. It established that on large farms, areas greater than the allowed 80 basic irrigated hectares (BIH) could be expropriated regardless of productivity. The standardized unit referred to land in one of the richest and most highly irrigated parts of Chile; the law provided a conversion table showing exactly what 80 BIH equated to in other regions of the country. On well-irrigated farms, actual area was less than 80 hectares; in the dryland north, it was much larger. The landlord's retained segment was called a *reserva*; its location on the expropriated *fundo* was at the owner's discretion (invariably the best land, including the infrastructure, was picked).

Expropriation on the basis of deficient or unproductive land use increased toward the end of the Frei presidency as the availability of lands ripe for size-based expropriation shrank. The rate of expropriation slowed markedly and landlord-reimbursement expenses per hectare dropped: Indemnification payments to landlords were smaller when this method was used.

Landlord compensation was limited to the amount of the current appraisal of the land for property-tax purposes plus the market value of improvements. A 30-day period from the date of the expropriation decree was allowed for appeal to the agrarian tribunal. Chile's endemic inflation accentuated the fact that long-term fixed-price bonds were the poorest form of indemnification. Upon expropriation due to excess size, landlords were given 10 percent of their payment in cash and the remainder in 25-year bonds; if the land was shown to be abandoned or poorly used, then from 1 to 5 percent was paid in cash and the remainder in 30-year bonds. A percentage of each bond was adjusted for inflation.

The agrarian tribunals constituted a special court system to hear cases of conflict over expropriation and its terms. The Frei reforms in fact brought few court cases, but the numbers were considerably higher during the term of Salvador Allende (1970–1973), when the government used more ambiguous reasons to expropriate. The goal was for CORA to take quick possession of a farm, declare it an agrarian-reform settlement, and argue the case later so no production need be lost; this laudable goal was never fully realized.

Frei incorporated about 1,319 properties—organized into about 1,000 *asenta-mientos* (group farming settlements) on about 3.5 million hectares, representing 13 percent of the farmland in Chile—into the reform sector. Most of the farms were in the country's Central Valley, where the richest farmland is located. While Frei's goal was to vest 100,000 families with land, his government benefited only about 28,000 families or 5–10 percent of peasant families in the country.

ORGANIZATION UNDER THE REFORM

Under the agrarian reform, resident farm workers (*inquilinos*) of an expropriated *fundo* would constitute themselves as an *asentamiento*, becoming *asentados* or *socios* (agrarian-reform beneficiaries or members) in the process. The *asentamiento* was organized like a production cooperative. On the usual *asentamiento*, the physical layout of the *fundo* was not changed; large fields continued to be operated intact. Work was accomplished in "field crew" fashion, much as it was before the reform. But now the former owner and his on-farm representative, the administrator, had left. Many field foremen (*capatazes* or *mayordomos*) also elected not to take part in the reform.

For their part, settlers elected a five-member settlement committee, which entered a contract with CORA that formally established the *asentamiento* organization. Supplemented by a technician or two from CORA, a prime function of the committee was to plan the new community's farming program and make management decisions. For their part, settler-beneficiaries agreed to live on the farm, carry a workload as directed by the settlement committee, not cede their rights to another, and market all crops through the *asentamiento*. Crops grown individually and privately owned animals, for which each member was granted some free grazing rights on common pastures, were exempted from prescribed marketing provisions, however. During the year, *campesinos* were advanced a lump sum (the *anticipo*) each month from CORA as living expenses; if assigned jobs meant that beneficiaries would have some special skill (like driving a tractor), the *anticipo* was somewhat larger. At the end of the year, the farm's net income (after *anticipos* were subtracted as an operating expense and investment capital and administrative expenses were set aside) was divided among members as a dividend according to days worked or some other agreed-upon formula.

Under this system, productive inputs for the farming program were supplied by the government (though they were charged to the production cooperative as an operating cost). A team of extension specialists inspected progress frequently. CORA also suggested investment programs for the *asentamientos* but did not try to impose them.

According to the compromise made by the left wing of the Christian Democrats and the *oficialistas*, the *asentamiento* was to last from three to five years; if members then wished to divide property, they could vote for that option in a membership referendum. The *asentamiento* was seen by some as a period of management tutelage for new owners, during which the production structure of the old *fundo* was to be changed as little as possible. The settlement committee replaced the *patrón*; the rest of the farming procedure would change little for *campesino* beneficiaries, who were expected to be motivated to diligent effort by potential dividends that came with harvest. Toward the end of the Frei period, it appeared that *asentamiento* membership throughout the country would favor individual parcels while grazing lands would continue to be held as restricted-access commons. But since CORA felt that most *asentados* were not ready for individual farming, few land divisions actually took place. Allende's later penchant for communal work continued the production-cooperative organization.

Under the *asentamiento*, beneficiaries were expected to pay off their land debt (which would be adjusted for inflation each year by the percentage rise in the price of wheat) in thirty years. Initial value was reckoned to total the tax-assessed value of the land in the year of assignment, CORA's infrastructural investment, plus a 2 percent administrative fee. A three-year grace period was offered on the land, but a small down payment was required. There was no moratorium on the payments required for livestock and machinery, which CORA may also have brokered.

This kind of postreform agriculture was part of a philosophical quest throughout Latin America to find its own path to development and not to embrace the capitalism of the United States and Europe or the communism of the Soviet Union. So in a range of social and economic endeavors in Chile at the time, the principle of "communitarianism" was espoused, of which the *asentamiento* was an example. A value judgment often made by the more radical wing of the Latin American Christian Democrats was also important: it was better for society at large to have farm people working together toward a common goal rather than toiling in isolation on individual farms. In welfare terms, an *asentamiento* entitlement could be thought of as a sort of safety net or insurance policy protecting the weak members through income rewards not too different from those of the strong.

But there were more practical considerations for the *asentamiento*. It would have been costly to divide the old *fundos*, adapted as they were to the intricate system of gravity-flow irrigation from the mountains. Also, roads would have to be cut all over the *fundo* to new houses, which were built if the hacienda was divided into individual farms (on the *asentamiento*, old *inquilino* housing could continue to be used). This says nothing about the electrical grids needed to connect houses and the fences required to avoid constant bickering over property rights between the new owners. In the end, the *asentamiento* was an institutional arrangement that met key economic as well as ideological goals.

The *asentamiento* also had shortcomings: Major among them was the free rider, the *asentado* who reasoned he could obtain essentially the same income if he showed up for work and labored diligently or merely appeared for work and shirked or malingered. This practice surely cut into *asentamiento* profits. Also, since each cooperative member had a private plot, the matter of time allocation came to be crucial. Steenland (1977, p. 121) noted that in one production cooperative he studied in the Allende period the peasants made more income from private production than from cash advances. Since members could influence how much they produced but got the same cash advance regardless of effort, they spent more time than contractually permitted on their individual miniparcels.

Passage of the rural unionization law (though Frei's government permitted *campesino* organization prior to the law's enactment) and agrarian reform in 1967 both served to heighten *campesino* expectations. On the matter of rural labor unions, Almino Affonso noted, "When the peasants form a union they stop asking: they demand their rights.... By the mere fact that peasants represent themselves, verticality ... may not survive.... The boss is no longer *Señor*, [he] loses his mythical character and shrinks to the true dimension of an employer" (in Gomez 1981, p. 11). Consequently, an increasing number of strikes and *fundo* invasions (*tomas*) took place.

Fundos that spawned rural union activity tended to be the first reformed, but because those who petitioned together for land kept working together on the *asentamiento*, *campesinos* did not abandon their esprit de corps and organizational activity after the land was granted. Not understanding the new organization very well (or perhaps understanding it very well), *campesinos* began to bargain with CORA for higher *anticipos*. Remarkably, many were successful, and as a result there was usually no income to divide among *asentamiento* beneficiaries at the end of any year. An added complication was accounting, which was to be done centrally; it became complex very quickly and CORA was unprepared to handle the enormous volume of bookkeeping that hundreds of *asentamientos* required. Accounts soon became so hopelessly tangled and delayed in this precomputer age that some disastrous economic outcomes were not known until the same compounding errors were made during the next agricultural year. When notified of overruns, beneficiaries became dispirited. They were somewhat mollified by the *anticipo* issue, however, which by default redounded to their benefit. Since CORA made no effort to collect overbargained advances, an activity that probably would have been fruitless anyhow, higher *anticipos* meant that *asentados* enjoyed an inadvertent subsidy. Subsidizing the few is not a trivial matter in a country beleaguered with rural poverty; it added to the privilege that *asentados* already possessed as new landholders and detracted from the broadly based "fairness" and "equity" that the government aimed for. It was no less onerous under Allende than under Frei. In 1972, agricultural credit to beneficiaries was shifted from CORA to the Banco del Estado, but CORA still bailed out *asentamientos* unable to show a profit.

Another difficulty was the crucial matter of labor absorption. A major goal of land reform was to create more rural employment; not only were urban endeavors insufficiently labor intensive to occupy all in-migrants from the countryside with wage work, but mechanization was steadily making agriculture itself less labor-absorptive.

Once again, organization assisted beneficiaries in resisting government pressure to admit more members. The original beneficiaries were *inquilinos* who had lived on the *fundo* prior to reform; once the land was turned over to them, they did not wish to permit interlopers. For its part, the government favored admission

of *afuerinos*. Thus *asentado* groups often mechanized farms as rapidly as possible
to eliminate the need for day laborers, who, *asentados* reasoned, might be tempted
to make land claims. Indeed, even when the *asentados* needed to contract day
labor, they tended to pay more poorly than had the old *patrones*. The land-reform
beneficiaries aimed to keep whatever claim on income they could for their own
use and guard whatever extra labor-absorptive capacity the farm might have for
the eventual use of their own children. These exclusionary tactics worked to the
benefit of the cooperative members. Even under Salvador Allende's Popular Unity
government, *asentamiento* membership did not spread much wider than the
original *inquilino* group.

As Kay commented:

> The *asentamiento* was a system which maintained and even increased economic
> and social inequity among rural labourers.... The *inquilinos* kept their rights of
> usufruct over a plot of land and pasture, while the *voluntarios* remained with no,
> or only minor, access to production fringe benefits [*regalias*]. Furthermore, the
> *inquilinos*, now *asentados*, enjoyed full rights in the administrative council of the
> *asentamiento*, whereas the *voluntarios*, now *socios* (partners), had only the right
> of voice but not of vote.... A third category of labourers ... were left out complete-
> ly.... In some cases the *asentados* continued to employ these *afuerinos* for a
> traditional wage, thus transforming themselves into "*nuevos patrones*" (1992c,
> p. 138).

Kay noted that "the Christian Democrats were forming a privileged group
of peasants, the *asentados*, who would eventually become a petty bourgeoisie
and act as a buffer for the social tensions resulting from the conflicts between
the rural bourgeoisie and the proletariat" (1992c, p. 141). He also cited case
studies that showed the growing political conservatism of the *asentados* as they
came to share common cause with landowners (Kay 1992c, p. 141).

PRODUCTION RESULTS OF THE REFORM

The Frei agrarian reforms did not cause the agricultural production problems
that many had forecast, given the rather considerable structural change that was
occurring. Setting the 1961–1965 index of agricultural production at 100, by 1970
the index had risen to 121; in the 1966–1970 period, the lowest annual index
recorded was 114. Most microstudies of *asentamientos* show that production after
reforms held its own, not a bad commentary given that landlords were permitted
to remove working capital to land they retained. Landowners had also claimed
the central core of their farm as their reserve. Most reserves seemed to be farmed
more intensively after the reform; there is evidence that, once assured that no
more land would be taken, landlords considerably intensified their operations
so that postreform income would be maximized. At least some unaffected

landlords also increased their production to lessen the pressures of expropriation that would likely be leveled at them as reform continued, though they surely did not make many long-term investments. Brown (1989, pp. 216–239), with J.D. Stanfield and S.M. Smith, studied 105 large haciendas, selected randomly in the Central Valley, that were prime candidates for expropriation at the beginning and end of Frei's term. In 1965, they were *fundos*; by 1971, virtually all had been affected by agrarian reform, and 73 percent of the study area had undergone some land-tenure change. The 105 properties in 1965 had become 215 farms by 1970. This period also saw the adoption of many yield-increasing inputs; in 1965, only 15 of the 105 *fundos* used "improved" corn and wheat seeds; by 1970, a time of intense "green revolution" activity in the region, only 4 farms out of the 215 did not use improved seeds. Also, natural pastures dwindled over the period and cultivated crops, like vegetables, increased, especially on farms with tenure changes. Intensity of land use on those properties remaining as *fundos* hardly changed.

Brown's (1989) study calculated value of production on 44,283 BIH in 1965/1966 and on the same land in 1970/1971. He demonstrates that on the latter date, 42 percent of the land had been assigned to reform beneficiaries, 26 percent had been subdivided into smaller plots (*hijuelas*) by landlords (to evade the reform's impact), 5 percent had been retained by original owners as reserves, and 27 percent remained unaffected. All of this land showed positive change in production "value added per BIH" between the first and last year of the Frei presidency. The greatest amount of value added per BIH accrued to reserves of old landlords, 4,192 Chilean escudos (E) of 1971; E2,822 accrued to *hijuelas*; E1,702 to the *asentamiento* land; and E431 to the unaffected *fundo* land (Brown 1989, pp. 227 and 233).

ALLENDE AND HIS REFORMS

When Allende took over as president in 1970, he pledged "to eliminate the hacienda, nationalize foreign mining interests, and expropriate the largest industrial and commercial enterprises" (Loveman 1976, p. 263). To that end, Allende decided not to write new agrarian-reform legislation, but to use the existing law, pushing it harder and faster than Frei had done. In fact, Allende's hand was stayed by a congress not likely to pass a more liberal law, at least not until after local elections scheduled for March 1973.

Allende aimed to expropriate all of the remaining 2,000 farms over 80 basic irrigated hectares in Chile within two and a half years. In the short run, he wanted to expropriate 1,000 farms before June 1971 so they could be ready under the new organizational regime for spring planting in September. His progress was remarkable. With Jacques Chonchol (1970, p. 159, who advocated agrarian reforms that were "massive, rapid, and drastic") working the helm of the Ministry of Agriculture and David Baytelman heading CORA, the organization reformed almost as many farms during Allende's first year in office as during Frei's entire six-year term.

The Popular Unity government, unlike that of the Christian Democrats, attempted to focus reform in one geographic region at a time, the idea being that this would make possible better planning and create agrarian-reform centers (*centros de reforma agraria*, CERAs), which were to group several nearby (former) *fundos* to take advantage of supposed economies of scale and thus to correct one overriding, perceived defect of the *asentamiento*. In a hard-fought campaign, the Unidad Popular had bitterly criticized the *asentamiento* and, after Allende took power, he could ill afford to adopt it without substantial innovation. In fact, CERAs appeared little different from the Frei *asentamientos*, for *fundo* agglomeration was locally resisted; only the nomenclature differed. When one happened upon a farm reformed in Frei's time, it was called an *asentamiento*; if beneficiaries were granted land during Allende's presidency, the organization was called a CERA or a pre-CERA.

Officially, the CERA was to be a more inclusive organization than the *asentamiento*, incorporating more service functions and neighboring landless workers. Popular Unity hoped that the larger, multiple-*fundo* composition of the CERA would make machinery pooling more common (thus leading to more efficient use), cause nearby landless labor to be finally accepted into membership, extend membership to all *asentado* family members older than 18, control product marketing, and so forth.

Clearly it was the intent of the Popular Unity government to promote "class solidarity" with the CERA. But the *campesino* community in Chile was not sympathetic to this idea, differentiated as it was between *inquilinos*, *afuerinos*, sharecroppers, indigenous community members, *minifundistas*, and so on. *Campesinos* in Chile were highly class conscious, *inquilinos* regarding themselves as hardly in league with the totally rural landless. As Brown noted,

> The self-perceived social identity and the concrete economic and political interests of *inquilinos* were rarely, if ever, identical to those of *minifundistas* (subsistence farmers), *afuerinos* (temporary workers), and *Mapuches* (indigenous groups). Failure to recognize this fact was probably responsible for unrealistic expectations on the part of both social scientists and political activists in Chile. Unfounded expectations of "*campesino* solidarity" were especially salient during the Allende years (1989, p. 220).

There was also a preoccupation on the part of beneficiaries that, as the production structure got larger, members might lose control of it to bureaucrats (as had happened in socialist countries). As it was, even firm control of the input and output markets was impossible in the Chilean milieu. The opposition soon seized upon the CERA, calling it Chile's entrance into the world of the state farm, thus feeding on the already palpable fears of the peasantry that their hard-won land rights might be lost to the capricious whims of a socializing state. Even some left-wing Christian Democrats had by this time conveniently discovered the virtue of individual private properties and accused Popular Unity of seeking to merge all land into a system of state farms. In the cold war milieu of the times, according to Falcoff, this was "a message which met with considerable resonance not only among *asentados* but *minifundistas* as well" (1989, p. 105). Another preoccupation among CERA members was that long-term property disposition under the Allende organization was never clear. With the Frei-established *asentamientos, campesinos* were promised that they could vote whether to continue in group farming or divide the property; whether this individual-farm option even existed under CERAs remained opaque. The CERA soon became an end in itself, as Allende vetoed a bill that would have assured beneficiaries title to their land in two years (Falcoff 1989, p. 106).

From this rather flammable caldron of ideologies there emerged a spillover of peasant requests for the Allende government to expropriate land on their behalf. Indeed, the Allende years tested the resilience of the law and, when his government toppled, gave the new regime ample cause to declare key expropriations as "illegal."

It was the so-called "overlooked provision" in the new Labor Law of 1967, Law No. 16,640, ARTICLE 171, that made it possible to acquire land in the event of labor disputes. Allende used it amply (Falcoff 1989, p. 102). The ultra-Left (not included in the Popular Unity) and even some of the far-Left within the coalition made certain there were enough labor conflicts to fuel expropriation demands. CORA even took farms smaller than 80 BIH when labor conflict was alleged. Socio-politics thus came to play a key role as a legal reason for expropriation whereas size and land-use were relegated to minor roles. Thus farms as small as 40 BIH having labor unrest were expropriated, provided there was also at least some evidence of poor land use, abandonment, or the like. Landlords had to accept fewer than 80 BIH as their reserves because, although the law specified that no landlord could retain more than 80 BIH, it did not include a minimum holding size.

During 1971, 1,278 farms were invaded or occupied, mostly in harvest months (Thome 1989, p. 203). The conflict that brought this about was so intense that the Ministry of Agriculture physically moved for two months from Santiago to the southern province of Cautín, where the conflict was greatest (Steenland 1977, esp. pp. 106–120). Instead of the usual practice of calling on the police to remove *fundo* invaders, CORA simply expropriated the farms or ordered them intervened. (Farms or factories having labor conflicts in Chile often were "intervened" under order of a decree/law passed in 1932: A government representative took over and enforced existing labor legislation so that no production would be lost. This technique could form the basis for repression of the labor movement and break a labor-management conflict. In this case the provision was used to facilitate government takeover of private property.)

Tomas often involved more than one estate, and rural laborers who were not resident laborers of the seized estate increasingly participated. "This helped to overcome traditional cleavages and fragmentation between peasants, as the experience of the *toma* brought various groups together for mutual help in carrying out the occupation. It particularly brought *afuerinos* into the picture" (Kay 1992c, p. 149).

For a time public order seemed to completely dissolve in the Chilean country-side, and often it was difficult to discern whether *campesinos* were at the leading edge of reform or whether government actions were at the forefront with peasant pressure merely being utilized as a prod by the government. Whichever the case, landlords increasingly sought redress in an overloaded court system. The resulting unrest halted new investment in agriculture and many landlords fled their land and the country, taking what capital they could; some were so fearful of confisca-tion that they drove their cattle over the border into Argentina.

As expropriations became more frequent, *tomas* diminished. In 1972, an additional 2,170 farms were affected for a two-year total of 5.5 million hectares. By July 1972, 35 percent of the farmland in Chile was in the reform sector. Of this, 40 percent was expropriated in the Frei period and 60 percent in the first year and a half of the Allende period. By June 1972, there were only 200 farms in the entire country with more than 80 BIH. But the expropriated land benefited only 75,000 families, still less than 20 percent of the total number of peasant families in Chile (Thome 1989, p. 204).

The Allende period was characterized by expanded reform; little attention was given to production of food and marketing of output. Imports of foodstuffs quickly doubled in value terms and were distributed at highly subsidized prices. Rather strict price controls were also extended to food produced in Chile, fostering scarcity, arousing consumer annoyance, and reinforcing the land-reform beneficiaries' practice of spending more time on their house plots, production from which could then be sold at high prices on the black market.

The matter of production under the Allende reform is a controversial issue. Official data show that agricultural production declined in all three years of the Allende presidency, but the source of that decline is in doubt. Brown concluded, "The 'chaos hypothesis' does not square with our observations..." (1989, pp. 236–237). Brown doubted that the major issues during the Allende period were production problems; he felt the problems lay elsewhere in the system:

> The 1972 truckers' strike certainly delayed input deliveries and very probably affected wheat yields in the south-central region. And the black market definitely diverted farm products from the conventional channels in which they could be easily counted by the statisticians who kept track of national accounts. On-farm consump-tion also increased. Scarcities in major cities were highly visible and very problem-

atic, especially for people who could not pay black market prices.... Reports of abandoned fields, corruption, and chaos on the *asentamientos* (indeed, in the entire rural sector) were greatly exaggerated. There is little hard evidence and little reason to conclude that production per se fell significantly (Brown 1989, p. 237).

The distribution of income in rural Chile was probably only marginally improved, because under the Allende and Frei reforms the richest group of peasants in the traditional system obtained land rights on *asentamientos*; these better-off *campesinos* then restricted entry on the *asentamientos* or CERAs. As a result, numbers of *campesinos* reached by reform were smaller than the capacity of the farms to provide full-time employment. Also, *asentamientos* paid day labor less than did the old *fundo* (Bloom 1973) while mechanization of farming increased. Dependence of private agriculture on *inquilinos* or other permanent resident labor decreased sharply as this nonreformed sector came to prefer temporary, seasonal labor (Dorsey 1984). Unlike *asentamientos*, which did not pay prescribed minimum wages if they could avoid doing so, Ringlein's (1971) sample of private farms showed that in the 1963/1964 to 1968/1969 period, workers' real wages, including payments in-kind, nearly doubled (in some cases, this was probably in response to worker scarcity; in others, a desire to comply with labor legislation to avoid expropriation). Loveman concluded, "It may be the irony of the Chilean land-reform process that a growing emphasis on collective and cooperative enterprises produced ever more efficient private farms in which the rural labor force obtained an increasingly important share of income in the rural enterprise" (1976, p. 280).

With reform and the green revolution, which were occurring almost simultaneously, came a more intensive pattern of farming with greater amounts of productive inputs per hectare and smaller amounts of natural pasture, fallow, and wasteland. But in the later Allende period, uncertainty led to disinvestment in farming, especially as macroeconomic conditions deteriorated, food shortages developed, and inflation spread uncontrollably.

INFLATION AND ECONOMIC POPULISM

Inflation had plagued Chile for years and was cited by Allende in his presidential campaign as one of three major economic ills that he proposed to tackle. The other two were unequal income distribution and unemployment. Upon taking power, Popular Unity faced a stagnant economy with a manageable inflation rate of 35 percent in 1970. Meanwhile, the trade sector was healthy; the balance of payments experienced substantial surpluses during all but one of the Frei years, and Allende entered office with significant international reserves (Dornbusch and Edwards 1989, p. 11).

Believing there was substantial excess capacity in manufacturing and in the economy generally, Allende proceeded with nationalization and a set of policies often referred to as "economic populism." Assuming excess capacity, the Allende team of economists felt that many firms faced decreasing costs in the immediate future and that fiscal deficits would not lead to more inflation. Allende believed that if income were redistributed to poor groups (through faster agrarian-reform and welfare measures), demand and output would expand. Because foreign reserves were available, this rising demand would not meet foreign-exchange constraints. Since earnings went to lower-income people under Allende's policies, the demand structure would change to include more simple consumer goods. Achievement of significant growth with a lower level of investment would be possible because luxury goods, which the economy had traditionally produced and which required high capital/labor ratios, would no longer be produced. Employment would grow rapidly in the favored set of labor-intensive industries. Even though the goal of Allende's government was to diversify exports, economic policies disregarded monetary and financial management and the exchange rate except to eliminate the possibility of devaluation. To Allende's peril, as Dornbusch and Edwards noted, "This view ... ignored many of the key principles of traditional economic theory" (1989, p. 18).

The first year brought a burst of public spending to pay for the agrarian reform, the beginning of a nationalization program, and increased salaries among workers in the lower echelons of the public sector. Higher public expenditures were also made for construction and social security. Bringing euphoria to the government, real GDP boomed in 1971, growing at 7.7 percent while aggregate consumption grew at 13.2 percent and the rate of unemployment dipped below 4 percent (Dornbusch and Edwards 1989, p. 20). Allende felt that this result affirmed his economic prescription; what was not seen clearly was the fact that the rapid growth of GDP rested on a 40 percent increase in the importation of intermediate goods to propel the domestic manufacturing sector.

Plummeting foreign exchange reserves were not the only danger signal, however. By the end of 1971, inflation plus price controls had brought increasing scarcity in some consumption goods; productivity of nationalized firms began to drop, and they ended the year with losses (Dornbusch and Edwards 1989, p. 22). As the fiscal deficit grew in the artificial atmosphere of controlled prices, the underground economy expanded rapidly. Because the informal economy paid no taxes, public revenue fell, and inflation spiraled to 217 percent in 1972. Although the government could have put on the economic brakes, it was unwilling to devalue and enact a stabilization program, for this would erode support from its traditional middle- and lower-class constituency (Dornbusch and Edwards 1989, p. 25). Because the state had completely lost control over wages (which paralleled its inability to govern increases in *anticipos* in the growing CERA sector), ever-more rampant inflation ensued. The third year of the Allende government only exacerbated these negative trends. Popular Unity was faced with either enacting a stabilization program or broadening price controls; it opted for the latter, a choice that led to alienation of the middle class, scarcity of basic necessities, and street demonstrations. In the March 1973 elections, the opposition parties prevailed. Inflation rose to 606 percent in 1973. While the Chilean military readied its response, no assistance was forthcoming from foreign sources; the United States had long since imposed economic sanctions and had convinced multilateral funding agencies not to grant relief to Allende.

AFTER ALLENDE: THE MILITARY REGIME

After the coup that ended in Allende's death in September 1973, the military government acted quickly to undo much of what the previous government had effected. Indeed, in an extraordinarily conservative backlash, the military government decided that dismantling past agrarian reform would be one of its first priorities, under the rationale that would end the food scarcity and check the crippling inflation engulfing the country. Urban Chile attributed both maladies to Allende's agrarian reform. To gain middle-class legitimacy as it engaged in unspeakable repression, the military government annulled the land-reform law and demoted CORA to a transitory agency charged with returning as much agrarian-reform land as possible to private hands. The institution that provided credit and technical assistance to small farmers and land-reform beneficiaries, the Instituto de Desarrollo Agropecuario (INDAP), was likewise debilitated by having its staff and portfolio sharply reduced.

The military government completely banned rural worker organization, to say nothing of invasions of farms and rural worker strikes. Landlords, in turn, regained their prominence in government decision-making circles; *campesinos* completely lost the voice in governmental affairs they had so recently acquired.

When the military took over, much land was still in the expropriation process; a separate fraction was under litigation as landlords had increasingly protested Allende's swift expropriations under somewhat dubious legal authority (Jarvis 1989, p. 244). The new government began by returning land slated for expropriation to its original owners. It disbanded *asentamientos* and CERAs, dividing land among selected land-reform beneficiaries. Land was given to *campesino* beneficiaries who could make the best case that they had lived and worked on the farm prior to expropriation, were a head of a household, and had nothing to do with the illegal strikes and invasions of the Frei or Allende governmental periods. This assured that land went to older, less-educated *asentados* and left landlords feeling that they had settled old scores with their former rebellious *inquilinos*. The *asentados* who did not qualify under the criteria set forth by the military government joined the ranks of the landless (Jarvis 1989, pp. 244–246).

Members of the old landlord class were firm allies of the new regime; to cement these ties, many former owners demanded return of their farms. As a result, some 1,649 farms were wholly returned to their former owners and another 2,174 were partially restored. Restitutions were made on three grounds: (1) that the Allende expropriations and interventions were illegal; (2) that the government wished to cut its expenditures on both interest on bonds that the old owners were given and beneficiary subsidies; and (3) that agricultural production needed to be raised and the way to do that was to put land back into the hands of "experienced" agriculturalists.

Jarvis (1989, p. 245) shows that, of the land originally expropriated, 57 percent in value terms remained in the reform sector, 28 percent was returned to the original owner, 5 percent was auctioned, and 10 percent went to the public sector (this latter mainly to be afforested and then sold to individuals). Of those who received *asentamiento* rights under Frei and Allende, roughly half got a parcel under the military government. Nearly all of the 15,000 adult single males who worked on the *asentamientos* for wages (most of them sons of *asentados*) were denied property.

Allende and Frei beneficiaries who received parcels of farmland under the military government paid about 50 percent of its market value; it was financed with 30-year loans, the principal adjusted according to the cost-of-living index plus 6 percent real interest. Loans from the past (from the Frei and Allende governments) were totaled and charged pro rata to the new *parceleros*. In addition to having no operating capital, most *parceleros* began their lives as independent producers without machinery or livestock, which was sold from *asentamientos* to pay back as much of the past due credit bill as possible. Jarvis (1989, p. 249) calculates that by 1977/1978, the net income for beneficiaries was about twice the minimum agricultural wage but less than that of a *minifundista* with a similarly sized parcel. Incomes varied widely around this mean, with 42 percent having less than one-third of the mean and 18 percent having negative incomes. Jarvis concluded, "This government neglect of the beneficiary sector often appeared to be land-reform-sector sabotage" (1989, p. 250). Continuing, Jarvis notes, "The vast literature on land reform efforts throughout the world has long shown that beneficiaries are likely to develop successfully only if they receive support during the first decade or so after land receipt. The Chilean government chose to ignore such lessons..." (1989, p. 252). As a result, many *campesinos* who got land found that they had to sell it, and land transactions in the late 1970s and 1980s burgeoned.

Jarvis (1989, p. 257) estimates that in 1986, the mean size of all farms over 80 BIH in the country was about 125 BIH whereas before the reform it averaged 235 BIH. At an enormous price, Chile had achieved a land distribution considerably more equal than before Frei began his presidency. In 1976, for example, the area controlled by farms exceeding 80 BIH was shown to have been reduced by half while the area controlled by farms having from 5 to 20 BIH was tripled. "The change was less marked than had been intended by reformers, but the net effect of the reform was that some 50,000 new farms had been created; this left about half of Chile's agricultural land in the hands of small farmers and *minifun-*

distas" (Jarvis 1989, p. 253). Part of this size reduction took place because of the division of properties into *hijuelas* by landlords who feared reform as well as some postcoup division of *asentamientos* into individual farms. Small farms (as opposed to middle-sized properties) grew in number and became weaker as the government discriminated against them. Carter and Mesbah concluded, "The number of transactions in *parcelero* holdings have been startling numerous in the relatively brief period since the mid-1970s" (1992, p. 4). The most recent study on *parcelero* land sales estimated that 57 percent of the original *parcelero* grantees sold their property (Echenique and Rolando, no date). Summing up the agrarian-reform efforts in Chile, Solon Barraclough noted:

> Notwithstanding this counter-reform, a decade of land reform, together with greatly accelerated private sub-division of large estates, has profoundly modified Chile's bi-modal structure. The very large estates have practically disappeared ... and small holders hold over one-third of the land in contrast to only one-tenth a decade earlier.... Land and labor have become market commodities. Rural poverty was still widespread in the 1980s, but less so than before.... [A]gricultural exports prospered and commercial farmers became extremely sensitive to price incentives in shifting their production priorities. This was in no small measure due to the structural changes accompanying land reform (1991, p. 110).

THE LATE-MILITARY AND THE POSTMILITARY PERIOD

Whereas the agrarian reforms and peasant unionization movements of the 1960s and early 1970s were aimed at increasing peasant participation and raising *campesino* incomes by making them integral parts of the agricultural economy, the commercial agriculture of the later 1970s, the 1980s, and the early 1990s expelled *campesinos* from the system. Recent evidence shows that the poor within Chilean agriculture are still doing badly. Jarvis (1985), who assesses this matter from the perspective of 1979, showed that agricultural unemployment and underemployment was high, job-specific agricultural wage rates had declined to their 1965 levels, and the structure of agricultural employment had shifted toward fewer permanent and more temporary jobs. Although the official statistics showed that agriculture grew by 5 percent annually between 1974 and 1980, Jarvis (1985) states that the correct figure was about 1.7 percent.

In contrast, the rate of agricultural growth was extremely rapid after 1983 as middle-sized and some capitalized small farms in Chile's Central Valley commercialized (with large amounts of international borrowing), specializing in fruits to export to North America and Europe during their winter months. Chilean agriculture grew by an average of nearly 6 percent annually in the last six years of the 1980s. Some economists feel that this economic growth has generated many more jobs in agriculture and believe that during the long harvest season there is almost complete employment of men, women, and teenaged children of peasant stock (though this more optimistic assessment lacks a convincing database). Others worry about the increased rootlessness of peasants who harvest the fruit (*temporeros*). Many students of Chile are concerned that the rural poor are once again bypassed—even by this heady economic activity.

Total area under fruit cultivation nearly tripled in the 1974–1990 period, and the current dollar value of the agroforestry exports in 1990 was more than ten times as large as that of 1974. Of Chile's success with nontraditional exports, Carter et al. note, "This sustained agro-export growth is the success story of the neo-liberal economic strategy and has garnered widespread admiration for the Chilean policy model" (1993, p. A-1).

The sector has indeed modernized, assisted by the neoliberal policies of the military government, to which the present government is also committed. Nonetheless, the repression that the military government visited upon the rural poor today remains the reality for Chilean peasants. Kay and Silva noted, "Despite the restoration of democratic rule in March 1990, the rural population still views the future with some apprehension" (1992, p. 291). A striking aspect of Chilean agriculture is "the co-existence of a marked process of productive and technological modernisation in the countryside and the extreme poverty suffered by thousands of rural families" (Kay and Silva 1992, p. 293). Kay and Silva (1992, p. 294) also note that the rate of extreme poverty in the countryside in 1980 stood at an alarming 56 percent of rural families, whereas in 1970, the first year of Allende's government, the figure was only 25 percent. The former figure proves the persistence of poverty; "extreme poverty" in the countryside in 1990, after a decade of "export boom," afflicted 55 percent of rural households. The Christian Democratic government of Patricio Aylwin, which came to power in 1990, pledged to achieve sustainable growth with equity, but in fact it changed few of the military government's economic policies. Given the importance of low labor costs to achieving the profit level needed to keep horticultural exports competitive, helping the *temporeros* is not an easy task.

In addition to improving the situation of the *temporeros*, the government must also improve the living conditions of peasants (the sector referred to as *pequeña agricultura*), 250,000 families who control almost one-third of the agricultural land in the country and represent 10 percent of the Chilean work force. Assisting this group implies providing some degree of technical and credit assistance and perhaps supporting the nongovernmental organizations (NGOs) that already work in this sector.

The neoliberal model has produced new kinds of status differentiation among Chile's peasantry. In general, there are two main agro-exporting zones in the country. One is the Bío-Bío region in the central-southern coastal strip, where the main export is forest products; the other is the horticultural central zone. These areas have produced new and fairly low-wage jobs, but "in the rest of the country ... the demand for wage labour is much more restricted and the main tendency is towards forms of peasant survival and pauperism" (Cruz 1992, p. 251).

Cruz noted that rural *pobladores*, shack dwellers arranged cheek-by-jowl in an unfamiliar urban area, are an "expression of a new and concrete social reality which represents one of the most despicable characteristics of neo-liberal capitalist expansion. As a new social sector, the rural pobladores have lost all their roots: housing, employment, landlord, forms of organization, familiar spaces and boundaries, and skills acquired from childhood" (1992, p. 247). In explaining the rise of the rural *pobladores*, Cruz noted, "An important characteristic of this form of uneven capitalist expansion has been the massive expulsion of permanent workers from their old houses and places of employment to new marginal settlements located in rural areas or in towns and cities of agrarian zones" (1992, p. 251). Unlike the *inquilino*, who had a plot on which some household necessities could be grown and an old but quite serviceable house, the *poblador* lives in a shack (*mediagua*) and has no land for subsistence. She relates the appearance of these rural *pobladores* to: (1) the disintegration of the agrarian-reform communities (some of the *campesinos* who lost their land became *pobladores*); (2) the marked change in agricultural employment (commercial enterprises try to reduce costs when they can and permanent labor is discharged first); (3) the bulk of the labor force in the fruit sector is needed in the tending, harvesting, selecting, and packing season from October to March (seasonality has meant that workers are thrown to their own devices after the fruit is shipped); and (4) urban unemployment is more serious than rural unemployment (thus instead of migrating to cities, workers remain in the countryside as *pobladores*) (Cruz 1992, pp. 251–253).

In 1965, capitalist enterprises in the central part of Chile employed an average of 7.7 permanent workers; by 1976, that number had fallen to 3.6 workers, and is even lower today (Cruz 1992, p. 255). In addition to quality of life, the major problem for the *pobladores* is obtaining a livelihood during the parts of the year they are unemployed. The *afuerinos* often returned to their *minifundios* when there was no work and the *inquilinos* had assigned *fundo* plots; the *pobladores* have no way to make ends meet when they are is not working except in the rare case when wages are high enough to permit some savings. Also, while *afuerinos* and *inquilinos* (*obligados*) were usually men, the *pobladores* who work in fruit production are often women (*temporeras*). This brings an additional complication since, including the Frei and Allende years (when women were excluded as beneficiaries of agrarian reform), Chile has never had a policy that recognized women workers (Lago 1992, p. 263).

The peculiarities of orchard production seem to mitigate peasant ownership: "Shifting production to fruit plantations and forestry is a long term process that requires large initial capital investments with no return over a long gestation period. Export crops also require standardized production and packaging, necessitating large quantities of working capital and access to additional investment funds. In Chile, exporter credit was available for such production but most smallholders and *parceleros* could not borrow" (Carter et al. 1993, p. A-l). From samples taken in a fruit-growing area and in a more traditional farming area, Carter et al. (1993, p. A-1) found that export crops were more predominant among larger farmers. As crops that small farmers grew became steadily less profitable, pressure on these peasants to sell their land to fruit producers mounted. With evidence to supplement that of other studies, Carter et al. (1993, p. A-1) show that the rate of sale of small producer's land in the fruit-exporting zone of Chile is greater than in a traditional area examined; the faster the rate of expansion of fruit production, the faster the rate of parcel sale (Carter et al. 1993, p. A-2).

Thus, the type of agriculture fostered by the military reforms (which individualized *asentamiento* property) is, according to Carter and Mesbah, "exclusionary" in that "peasant access to land and stable employment have diminished with the rapid concentration of land ownership and the increasing seasonality of labor demand which has accompanied that growth" (1992, p. 1). They generalized that this reality "dampens expectations ... that non-distortionary, laissez faire agricultural policy suffices to link growth with poverty reduction" and demonstrated that "policies to remedy exclusion by using the land market to improve peasant access to land are quietly finding their way onto that country's democratized political agenda" (Carter and Mesbah 1992, p. 1). Carter and Mesbah grappled with the question, "Can a more interventionist group of policies modify the exclusionary aspects of agro-exporting in Chile?" They conclude that tackling imperfections in the factor markets through organization of cooperatives and mutual-responsibility borrowing groups would help to alleviate the marginalized position of the rural poor. Neoliberalism may be an indispensable policy to fostering economic growth, but if rural poverty is to be adequately addressed, a penchant for laissez faire needs to be supplemented with government policies that help to make it possible.

6

Reforms of the 1980s: Nicaragua

The insurrection that toppled Anastasio Somoza Debayle in 1979 and sparked Sandinista agrarian reform was precipitated by events that occurred earlier in the decade but was also rooted in the pattern of economic and social development of the preceding century. Toward the end of the 1800s and during most of the 1900s, Nicaragua was transformed from a country offering little but rural subsistence into an agro-export economy producing coffee, cotton, sugar, and beef for the world market (Gilbert 1986). This process created social strains as the well-to-do and landed became extraordinarily wealthy while the poorest were systematically omitted from Nicaragua's economic progress. Although economic growth was stimulated by trade, for many *campesinos* this movement toward an export economy meant increased landlessness, intermittent employment, inadequate nutrition, and sometimes even falling wages.

The dictatorship of the elder Somoza, followed by the rule of his two sons, firmly established a growth-without-redistribution development pattern. As *campesinos* were repressed, wealth increasingly accumulated in the hands of the Somoza in power and his cronies. The Somozas' ruin, orchestrated by a coalition of political forces reminiscent of those that toppled the *porfiriato*, was instigated by the frustrations of facing a regime that became more illegitimate and corrupt with each passing year. The beginning of the end of the Somozas is frequently traced to the earthquake in 1972, which captured the sympathy of the world and inspired many in the United States and Europe to send relief, much of which was pocketed by the dictatorship.

BACKGROUND TO THE REFORM

Even before independence from Spain, Liberals and Conservatives battled over policy. Their argument was so bitter that it resulted in militarism, *caudillismo*, and political violence costing thousands of lives.

The Conservatives were aristocratic landowners, cattle ranchers, and large merchants—"descendants of the colonial military and bureaucratic elites, backed by the Church hierarchy." On the other hand, the Liberals, small landowners and artisans who were less influential than their counterparts in the rest of Central America, were "part of a regional wave of Liberalism influenced by English notions of free trade, which had sought briefly and ineffectively to create a Central American Federation which would break with colonial stagnation and develop wider export markets" (Black 1981, pp. 4–5). The persistence of these two political groups together with their geographic focuses—the Conservatives located in Granada and the Liberals in León—helped to prevent the development of a strongly unified elite in Nicaragua.

Indeed, geography is a key to understanding those early days. The advantageous means of transit across the isthmus via Nicaragua's river and lake system in the south made early foreign interference easier than in other places in the region. Like most of Central America in its early days, Nicaragua depended on trade. Its exports were agricultural—first cacao, then dyes and livestock—all of which suffered extreme price fluctuations. Maldistribution of resources (especially land, which concentrated further as commerce developed) was influential in determining the country's future.

Early Liberal-Conservative rifts reflected not only a difference of ideology, but also a controversy over which faction would dominate the colony and the new country. The Liberals wanted free trade, infrastructural development (roads, over which to ship their products, and especially port facilities), and an end to the privileged position of the Roman Catholic Church. For Conservatives, who had benefited richly from earlier and more restricted transactions, additional trade meant unwanted competition and higher taxes. León and Granada developed mutual animosities that shaped the history of the time and led to bitter, even ferocious clashes. The Mexican empire (after it had separated from Spain in 1821) granted Nicaragua independence in 1823, which made divisions between the two elite groups sharper and discussion more vitriolic. Civil war soon destroyed a postindependence Central American federation and Conservatives emerged victorious. In 1838, Nicaragua became a republic, beginning its independent history in deep depression.

Status in the early days of European settlement reflected ethnic origin. Creoles dominated resources and were the significant landowners. Ladinos became artisans, professionals, and petty traders, sometimes engaging in small-scale agriculture, but were excluded from the elite. Indians were hard hit by European diseases, dislocations (Creole and Ladino encroachment onto their property was a continuing fact of life), and attempts at their extermination. Meanwhile, Liberal-Conservative battles ebbed and flowed.[1]

Creole landowners raised cattle whereas Ladino smallholders more often produced dyes and subsistence crops. Coffee appeared in 1850, becoming an important commercial product in the 1870s. To support this new export after

1875, Conservative President Pedro Joaquín Chamorro introduced "liberal" reforms similar in time and substance to those proposed by Rufino Barrios in Guatemala: The indigenous *ejido* was individualized; the amount of land in church hands was reduced; coffee production was stimulated, with immigrants recruited to grow it; infrastructure was developed to easily transport coffee to market on the more accessible Pacific coast; and a credit system was established. By 1890, coffee was king in Nicaragua; between 1920 and 1940, it provided half of the country's export earnings. As coffee growers steadily expanded production, they augmented cultivated areas by encroaching on the lands of *minifundistas*, continuing a cycle that began in the 1870s and 1880s. As Black claimed, "Capitalist expansion meant, paradoxically, turning the clock back to impose semi-feudal social relations between the landowner and the rural workforce, relations which remained the norm in much of the Nicaraguan countryside until the 1979 Revolution" (1981, p. 11). After land was taken from *campesinos*, plantation owners needed a work force for their property, so "workers were partly salaried and partly paid in kind, and given small subsistence plots to work. The combination left them tied to the land and the *patrón* for life" (Black 1981, p. 11). Liberal-sanctioned intrusions on church lands and indigenous communities also permitted the production of more coffee.

Ultimately coffee brought new members into the national elite as some of the holders of formerly middle-sized estates acquired more land and, where climate and geography were favorable, planted coffee. Some enterprising bureaucrats also took advantage of government subsidies to become *cafetaleros*. Expatriate Germans and British immigrants used these subventions and the growth in demand for coffee to establish themselves as cultivators. As in Guatemala, foreigners eventually gained control of coffee exporting and the credit market.

Systems to keep labor close at hand resembled Guatemalan institutions designed for the same end; debt peonage and antivagrancy laws were common. But labor in Nicaragua was more scarce than in Guatemala. In some cases, therefore, *minifundistas* were prohibited from growing subsistence crops and were required instead to work off "taxes" by laboring for nearby landlords. To escape from this growing oppression, rural labor often fled to the Atlantic jungle, mountainous regions, and cities.

With coffee as Nicaragua's principal export, a small middle class composed of those who were employed in the input and product markets and in processing started to appear. Also, a new group of middle-class bureaucrats emerged as government grew to assume the principal role of promoting coffee exports. Whereas coffee planters constituted a rather homogeneous ruling class in El Salvador and Guatemala, they complemented, but did not displace, the livestock farmers in Nicaragua to make up the country's elite. This social bifurcation made it progressively more difficult for Conservatives to cling to power.

Liberals gained control again in 1893. President Roberto Sacasa, a Conservative, was defeated in his bid for reelection, and Liberal José Santos Zelaya assumed office. Zelaya was supported by the rising middle class, intellectuals, and coffee producers and exporters. By that time Nicaragua had diversified its agricultural exports by adding tobacco, cotton, rubber, cacao, and sugar to coffee and livestock. Zelaya escalated foreign investment, established a system of primary education, encouraged exports, expedited infrastructural development, increased the role of government, assuaged the animosity between León and Granada, reduced the economic power of the church, built a national army, and expanded the communications network in the country. Zelaya incorporated the eastern coast much more meaningfully, including the immense department (province) that still bears his name. His goal was to integrate Nicaragua more fully, enabling it to compete in the world economy. But the income benefits of this development went largely to the elite, especially to Zelaya's supporters. Zelaya also had his own businesses, and since he speculated in commodities, his government in the end elevated the cost of subsistence for the urban poor. In his zeal to export from the sparsely settled country, Zelaya tied more *campesinos* to plantations by instituting draconian labor-draft methods; he also continued the process of individualization of communal lands.

Meanwhile, the Conservatives—that is, large holders and cattlemen—resented their displacement from power and the rise of a middle class. Their efforts at popular resistance resulted in Zelaya's increasing use of repressive measures. Although the United States was eager to invest in Nicaragua, Zelaya was determined to control the way this foreign capital was used. In U.S. eyes, Zelaya's reactions were tantamount to "meddling" with foreign investment. Eventually this uncooperative attitude was a prime consideration in the U.S. decision to build the trans-isthmus canal through Panama rather than Nicaragua. Furious at losing this transportation boon, Zelaya asked Japan and Germany to build a Nicaraguan canal, a move that infuriated the Conservatives, the British, and the United States. After the Zelaya government collapsed, the United States sent an envoy to reestablish concessions for U.S. investors. In 1911, Conservative President Adolfo Díaz accepted U.S. protectorate status for Nicaragua, and when opposition to this interventionism grew in Nicaragua, President William Howard Taft landed the U.S. Marines to "protect U.S. lives and property." According to Booth, this unrest ushered in "twenty-five years of chaos" (1985, p. 24). Although neither party was willing to admit it, by this time differences between the Liberals and Conservatives had blurred—both had prospered from the policies set in place by Zelaya. But Zelaya's Conservative opponents recognized that they alone could not defeat him, so they aligned with foreigners; the United States, Britain, and the Conservatives thus conspired to oust the Liberal government. During the subsequent unstable period, much of what Zelaya had done to promote economic development was destroyed. The civil war that followed led the United States to prop up the Conservatives by physical occupation. The United States retreated from supporting the Conservatives in 1927 and, in an anomalous move, switched sides to champion the locally stronger Liberals. The Liberals, it turned out, had assured the United States that they did not desire a "Mexican solution"; they did not aspire, that is, to a "socialist" revolution. The United States found this an auspicious time to demand that the Nicaraguan government organize a truly nonpartisan national guard to take over police and military functions, thus allowing U.S. forces to withdraw. In fact, when the United States reached its accord with the group of Liberal generals, only one, Augusto César Sandino, did not sign the agreement.[2]

THE RISE AND FALL OF SANDINO

Sandino, son of a smallholder, worked as a mechanic, laborer, and merchant. He received "political training" by living for various periods in Honduras (working for the United Fruit Company), Guatemala, and Mexico. Sandino's experience in postrevolutionary Mexico shaped his destiny in Nicaragua. His ideology was populist and reformist, not Marxist. When Sandino returned to Nicaragua, he joined a Liberal uprising in 1926. Under Zelaya, Sandino saw church and national lands sold while squatters and small- and medium-sized farmers were expelled in a single-minded drive for agricultural commercialization.[3] Abetted by threats from Sandino, who had by that time acquired a ragtag group of followers, the government, for a time at least, returned some land to peasants in the late 1920s and early 1930s (Brockett 1990, p. 26). Sandino vowed, "I will not abandon my struggle while my people have one right yet to win. My cause is the cause of the people, the cause of America, the cause of all oppressed peoples" (Queister Morales and Vanden 1985, p. 467). He began to recruit for the Liberal cause and, when rebuffed by a major Liberal leader, came to direct his own troops under a black-and-red flag. After defeats in various skirmishes, Sandino and his 300 men adopted guerrilla tactics. Adding to Sandino's pique was the perceived Liberal "sellout" to the United States in 1927.

Guerrilla battles between the guard and the renegade Sandino troops continued as Sandino proclaimed that he would be neither victimized nor cowed into submission by the United States. From mid-1927 until 1933, Sandino fought from the hills, many troops returning to their farms during the day and fighting at night. Increasingly an irritant to both the Nicaraguan government and the United States, Sandino would not be put down. The National Guard and its 2,000 or so U.S. Marine tutors were frustrated by his irregular method of fighting and often responded with individual acts of terrorism. When the U.S. Marines pulled back, Nicaragua replaced them with a reorganized National Guard, set in place in time to supervise the 1928 elections (which brought the Liberal José María Moncada to power).

The Sandino maneuvers cost the Nicaraguan government dearly: In 1929, a depression year, one-fourth of the national budget went to the National Guard. Even so, the Moncada government did little but hold its ground against the insurgents. As the depression deepened, support for Sandino seemed to increase with the level of his invective. Sandino spoke of the Marines as "pirates" and the Nicaraguan politicians who hosted the North Americans as "political mongrels who fight to grovel under the invader's whip" (Booth 1985, p. 45). In 1932, Sandino's army struck in the western part of the country, a heretofore immune zone; the disheveled troop registered 176 military encounters with American forces in the course of the year.

Since monoproduct economies are especially vulnerable to world price fluctuations, the depression of the 1930s was particularly hard on Nicaragua. Coffee prices plummeted from US$458 per ton in 1926 to US$142 per ton in 1938. To compensate, planters tried to maintain profits by cutting wages, a move that refueled the discontent.

For Sandino, the land problem was paramount in this period; he came to favor a "state within a state" in which he and his followers would control a new department stretching from Las Segovias eastward to the Atlantic coast. Sandino believed that the land he controlled on the banks of the Río Coco could be organized into agricultural cooperatives that would eventually produce the subsistence crops that Nicaragua imported. His dream was dashed as it conflicted with land-ownership patterns of the region's dominant classes, which had already been antagonized by his earlier effort to deliver some coffee land to peasants in the area he commanded (Black 1981, pp. 15–27).

As the list of Marine casualties in Nicaragua grew, so did opposition by large groups of the U.S. public. North American opinion was aroused by the liberal press, some vocal Democratic members of Congress, and labor unions. Congress was especially incensed over the unilateral executive decision to intervene in Nicaragua. Meanwhile, an increasing number of opponents speculated about whether it was wise to dissipate the country's energy in Nicaragua when the Soviet Union, Germany, and Japan were more formidable threats. Soon after taking office, Franklin D. Roosevelt pulled out the Marines as part of his Good Neighbor Policy. Between the decision and the departure itself in 1933, however, there was a short interim period meant to give North Americans in Nicaragua time to put the National Guard in the hands of compliant leadership. With the ascension of Juan Bautista Sacasa to the presidency, the guard's command fell to his nephew, General Anastasio Somoza Garcia. Although the United States had insisted on an apolitical National Guard, no such fetters bound Somoza; to replenish the positions vacated by the departing North American soldiers, Liberals Sacasa and Somoza filled the ranks with soldiers of their political persuasion.

Soon after the departure of the Marines, Sacasa and Sandino arrived at a cease-fire: complete amnesty for the insurgents, disarmament of all but 100 of Sandino's men (this group acting as a guard for Sandino), and cession to Sandino and his men of some land in the Río Coco region for farming. Peace in Nicaragua accompanied the depression, during which coffee, sugar, and banana prices continued to plummet. Political problems then dissolved into economic afflictions—defaulted loans, low profits, reduced wages, unemployment.

The truce between Sandino and Sacasa proved ephemeral, however, and the National Guard and Sandino's troops resumed fighting. On 23 February 1934, Sandino was called to the presidential palace to discuss violation of the cease-fire with President Sacasa. After their meeting, Sandino and two of his generals were detained by a National Guard vehicle and, on orders from Somoza, were slain. In a coordinated action on the same night, guard members shot Sandino's brother and, at his northern headquarters, killed several hundred of the first Sandinistas.

THE RISE OF SOMOZA

Somoza felt that he could overcome his background as a business failure and petty criminal by dominating the National Guard. As Booth notes, "Somoza was apparently backed inexorably into the assassination plot in his effort to keep control of the Guard" (1985, p. 53). With bravura, Somoza lied to his guard conspirators, telling them that the U.S. embassy in Managua supported the assassination plot.

Politically fortified by his murder of Sandino, Somoza set about attaining the presidency by undermining his uncle. In 1935, Somoza announced his presidential political intentions, picking up some key Conservative support from congresspersons who saw him as someone who would contain labor unrest in the country and steer it toward a business and commercial agriculture point of view. In late May 1936, Somoza's troops surrounded the presidential palace and secured the stronghold of Sacasa loyalists in León. After a prudent lapse of time, Somoza took over as Nicaragua's dictator.

For twenty years thereafter, the National Guard was the Somozan power base. Despite numerous plots against Anastasio, he proved to be a consummate but sinister politician capable of any treachery when aboveboard tactics failed. Under his guidance the National Guard took over some critical government functions, such as the postal service, the national radio and other communications, and the immigration service. These activities foreshadowed the graft that characterized much of the reign of the three Somozas. Without much delay, the Somoza sons occupied positions of responsibility within the guard so they could inform on disloyalty plots against their father. A warm relationship between Somoza and the United States brought Nicaragua a great deal of materiel with which to prop up the dictatorship. Augmenting the pay of the National Guard and threatening tribunal action were the first of Somoza's efforts to increase the guard's loyalty to him.

World War II made it impossible for Roosevelt to keep Somoza in check. In 1939, in a flare of publicity, Somoza pledged to support the antifascist Western allies. Strongman rule in El Salvador and Guatemala receded after the war, but

Somoza clung tenaciously to power. By denying Somoza the arms he wished, the United States indicated opposition to his reelection; in response, Somoza installed a puppet president, Leonardo Argûello, and continued in fact to rule from his National Guard post. When Argûello tried to oust Somoza from the guard, Somoza swiftly removed him and reclaimed the presidency. After World War II, U.S. President Harry S Truman demanded a pledge of anticommunism from countries that the United States recognized (he was less concerned that they be democratic); for his part President Dwight Eisenhower, exercised over Jacobo Arbenz in Guatemala, attempted to contain any "red" threat by backing Conservative governments elsewhere in Central America. Always in tune with the times, Somoza included a peppering of anticommunist rhetoric in his speeches and helped the United States rid Guatemala of Arbenz. Throughout this period U.S. friendship with Somoza increased, and when Somoza was shot in 1956, it was a U.S. plane that took him to a military hospital in the Canal Zone.

The elder Somoza's rule was characterized by repression and terror, in which "the Nicaraguan government and the law became the personal domain of the dictator. Crooked elections supplied a pliant Congress that legislated and appointed judges according to Somoza's whim" (Booth 1985, p. 61). The landed class, Liberals and Conservatives alike, had been frightened by Sandino and the *campesino* organization of the 1930s. Landlords felt that workers' parties were solidifying under Sacasa and believed that only Somoza would have the gall needed to break rural unionization. As cronies were allowed to take bribes and embezzle money, the political process all but ceased to exist. Meanwhile, by cleverly manipulating policies and grasping opportunities Somoza was acquiring more and more economic premiums for himself as were others in the elite of the country.[4] Somoza purchased or acquired immense acreages in coffee by dispossessing *campesinos* as commercialization in agriculture advanced. Although agricultural modernization brought wage work to the newly landless, it was only seasonal and *campesinos* were unemployed for much of the year (Weeks 1985). Still, one of the landlords' most acutely felt problems was insufficient labor. What they lacked, in fact, was labor at peak times, during the harvest of coffee and cotton. A major problem in agro-exporting, in Nicaragua labor needs for picking coffee and cotton crested in a short, several-month season, after which unemployment reappeared with a vengeance. Consequently, Salvadorans were regularly brought in to augment local labor forces during the harvest period.

As cotton production expanded during the Korean War boom, the elite continued to appropriate *campesino* land. The country's cotton land was located on the Pacific coast, and production rose 120-fold between 1949 and 1955, coming to occupy 40 percent of the country's farmland. The seasonal jobs it created did not compensate for the more secure, year-round, peasant livelihoods that were lost in the conversion. In increasing numbers displaced peasants migrated to cities and to the northern and eastern frontiers.

By 1944, Somoza was the owner of fifty-one cattle ranches and forty-six coffee plantations; he was the largest coffee producer in the country.[5] In addition, the Somoza family invested in sugar, cement, insurance, electricity, rental properties, the media, the merchant marine, the national airline, and textiles. By virtue of its position the family could modify the market to its own gain. After the Somozas were well established in a particular line, the dictator played to the rules of monopolistic competition to squeeze out more profits.[6]

THE NEW SOMOZAS

In 1956, Somoza García died—of an assassin's bullet—in the Canal Zone hospital to which he had been taken. Pedro Joachín Chamorro, editor of opposition newspaper *La Prensa*, was questioned and tortured as a possible coconspirator in the murder; Chamorro was exiled, but most of the other suspects arrested at the time were tried in a kangaroo court and jailed or shot. From then on, Luis and the young Anastasio Somoza Debayle ruled together; the former, personable, the latter, an abusive enforcer.[7] Luis was president from 1956 to 1963, when unrest caused the brothers to pass the office to several puppets. In 1967, after Luis died, Anastasio Jr., ruled until unrest forced him to cede executive power to a three-person junta in 1971. He resumed the presidency after the 1972 earthquake and ruled until the Sandinista victory deposed him in 1979. The young Somozas faced increasing opposition. Nevertheless, for two decades after the elder Somoza was murdered, U.S. support was forthcoming in the form of economic assistance coupled with military training in counterinsurgency.[8]

The Somoza dynasty generally treated *campesinos* with cruel repression, but during the Alliance for Progress period of the early 1960s an effort was made to settle a few of them on abandoned farms, which were subdivided to accommodate families on land parcels. This "agrarian reform" was widely publicized as government compassion for its poor rural citizens. Its real purpose, however, was to obtain aid from the United States, which during the Kennedy presidency was extended upon the condition of reforms. It also helped to quiet internal protests from Nicaraguans who had come to despise the Somozas and who sympathized with the plight of the poor.

Meanwhile, the Nicaraguan economy ebbed and flowed with world market prices. Coffee and cotton prices fell toward the end of the 1950s, precipitating a recession. This slump ended in the 1960s, when prices improved again. Simultaneously, the inception of the Central American Common Market and growing U.S. economic assistance had salutary effects on the economy. The Nicaraguan government wisely used the boom years of the 1960s to construct badly needed infrastructure. Among other projects, the road to Rama—into the eastern jungle and close enough to the Atlantic coast to permit passage to Bluefields on the navigable river system—was completed, binding east and west

Nicaragua together (Taylor 1968).[9] Industrial projects were also initiated throughout the country. All in all, as with much of Central America, the 1960s and early 1970s were a period of heady if inequitable economic growth. Booth's (1985, p. 78) calculations show GDP more than doubled between 1960 and 1975. In 1960, the manufacturing sector generated only 15.6 percent of GDP; by 1976, it produced more than 23 percent despite losing 10,000 jobs in the 1972 earthquake. International commodity prices once again rose in the early 1970s after another bust in the late 1960s.

Outsiders viewed the rather large growth figures that resulted from increasing farm exports during the 1960s and early 1970s as healthy economic indicators. But this wave of progress left the poor far behind. Social legislation was not passed nor was unionization allowed to provide succor for the land-poor and the landless; underemployment kept advancing. The numbers of *campesinos* whom economic growth bypassed rose with the soaring population growth rate (about 3.5 percent).

Even after the 1972 earthquake, a reconstruction boom based on foreign borrowing "benefitted the upper class by further concentrating wealth and ownership of production" (Booth 1985, p. 78). The ensuing inflation adversely affected labor (which became progressively more agitated) as well as others in the middle and lower classes. As the civil war began toward the end of the 1970s, investments and the economy's overall growth declined further. Those who enjoyed rising incomes in the mid-1970s were people who held resources: the old-line Liberal and Conservative landholders; the new industrialists benefiting from the nascent CACM; the investors in real estate and construction; and the Somoza group. Reduced tariff barriers propelled capital into more interregional commerce than before—meat packing, tobacco products, fishing, domestic construction, mass media, automobile importing, shoes, data processing. The Somoza group's power surpassed that of other parts of the Nicaraguan elite because it had an additional advantage: It controlled the public exchequer and the regulation of commerce, which it could use to private gain. At the time of the revolution, the Somoza family dynasty owned over 25 percent of the agricultural land in the country and 147 commercial entities, ranging from the country's Mercedes Benz dealership to a cement factory (Colburn 1986, p. 31).

In the years after the earthquake, Somoza and his cronies reprogrammed their investment pattern somewhat, taking advantage of the calamity to invest in earth-moving equipment, concrete, metal buildings, heavy equipment, construction materials, and the like. Weeks noted that "bilateral and multilateral aid for reconstruction flowed in great quantities and was treated as personal revenue by the Somozas" (1985, p. 155). Booth claimed that "his greed and his willingness to take advantage of his compatriots' suffering seemed boundless" (1985, p. 81).

Through it all an emerging middle class was stimulated by the needs of the elite for such services as processing, marketing, assembly, and other product transformations and for managers, sales people, clerical workers, and government bureaucrats to backstop manufacturing and farming. The new middle class and the lower-class majority were increasingly afflicted by unemployment and underemployment in the 1970s. Protests erupted, bringing more student support for those whom the system was disenfranchising. Stridency, in turn, led to vigorous government repression. In the countryside, where conditions of employment were worse than in town, there were more land invasions and strikes. Meanwhile, migration, especially to Managua, resulted in the growth of marginal settlements on the outskirts of the cities and on lots rendered vacant by the earthquake. Finally, the Association of Rural Workers (Asociación de Trabajadores del Campo, ATC) was founded by a long-established underground group, the Sandinista National Liberation front (Frente Sandinista de Liberación Nacional, FSLN).

THE REVOLUTION

Although the distinctions between Conservatives and Liberals had all but disappeared by the 1960s, Pedro Joachín Chamorro tried to regain legitimacy for his Conservative party when he returned from exile. He beguiled yet another Somoza in 1967 by leading a demonstration against the "election" of Anastasio Jr. Forty thousand people turned up; Somoza's troops fired into the crowd to disburse them, killing 300 and wounding another 100, and jailed the leaders. Several years after the march in Managua, a deal with Somoza guaranteed a predetermined share of the congress and the public service sector to the Conservative party. The young Conservative movement, which had emerged in the 1950s to protest what it saw as an increasing convergence of philosophies between the two major parties, interpreted this as a sellout and shifted its ideology to the radical left.

The FSLN originated in and was nurtured by anti-Somoza student movements of 1944–1948 and 1959–1961. With the victory of Fidel Castro in Cuba interpreted by Nicaraguan radicals as a vindication of the ideas of Sandino, the FSLN was formally founded in 1961 by Carlos Fonseca Amador, Tomás Borge Martínez, and Silvio Mayorga. It laid low during the Alliance for Progress and the period of rapid economic growth in the 1960s. When Luis Somoza died in 1967 and the presidency passed to his more ruthless brother, the movement regenerated.

In 1967, FSLN planned and executed a campaign east of Matagalpa, but the National Guard acted efficiently and many Sandinistas were killed, including Silvio Mayorga. According to leaders, the FSLN's 1970 Zinica campaign, which involved raids on National Guard outposts in the north-central region, was successful because, "[w]e found a way to recruit the campesino" (Booth 1985, p. 140). The FSLN renewed operations after the 1972 earthquake, now having stronger organization in both cities and countryside in addition to a military arm. In 1974, FSLN took over a party at the home of José Maria Castillo Quant, former minister of agriculture and a cotton exporter. Quant was killed and the remaining guests were held hostage, including some of Nicaragua's oligarchy and foreign visitors. Somoza, on his way to Spain, quickly returned to the country to negotiate with the front, with mediation supplied by Archbishop Miguel Obando y Bravo. In the end, FSLN won many of its demands and attained a symbolic victory.

The press, especially *La Prensa* and editor Chamorro, proved a continuing irritant to Somoza. When Chamorro published a less-than-flattering story about the dictator's son in 1978, Somoza had him shot. This blatant retaliation inflamed most Nicaraguans. *La Prensa* and the widow, Violeta Barrios de Chamorro, helped mobilize the massive protest demonstrations that followed.

By 1976, FSLN had split into three philosophically distinct—and often antagonistic—factions. Contact between them was maintained, however. Eventually their rising common opposition to Somoza inspired détente between the groups. Meanwhile, non-Sandinista opposition to Somoza rallied to a group of businesspeople, professionals, and intellectuals known as "The Twelve" (Las Doce). They allied with the Sandinistas in September 1978, after Chamorro's death, under a provisional government based in Costa Rica.

Booth (1985, p. 85) documents that at the eve of the revolution, half of Nicaraguan income earners received 15 percent of total income whereas the top 5 percent received 30 percent; only 49 percent of the population could read and write (25 percent in rural areas); half of the country's homes (80 percent in rural areas) lacked plumbing; the average Nicaraguan lived to only 53 years of age, the lowest life expectancy in Central America; and lack of potable water led to one-fifth of all deaths in the nation. Also, Nicaragua had the highest rate of alcoholism among Central American countries, spent the least on health and education, and had the highest murder rate. Booth concluded, "Nicaragua had the classical ingredients for unrest among important sectors of the populace, especially from the early 1970s on—rising expectations contrasted with increased insecurity or diminishing rewards.... [T]he intensifying frustration engendered unrest and demands for change" (1985, p. 85).

When civil war began, the largest farms (those over 350 hectares) were held by only 0.6 percent of the landowners and occupied 41 percent of the total land area; poor peasants, who made up 58 percent of all farmers, possessed 2 percent of the land. These inequities were compounded because smallholders—who literally fed the country by producing the staples of corn and beans—did not get enough credit and inputs to efficiently operate their meager plots. By the late 1970s, only about 13 percent of the economically active population had sufficient access to land to meet subsistence requirements. Close to 40 percent of the work force consisted of landless wage earners, most of whom could obtain only seasonal work.

The poor had been systematically bypassed in a drive to increase exports. By the late 1970s, the amount of land devoted to the leading export crops had increased 219 percent from the post–World War II period, whereas land devoted to the major subsistence crops had grown by only 92 percent. Accordingly, per capita production of the leading food crops declined by 13 percent from 1948/1952 to 1976/1978. Brockett (1990, p. 166) notes that the average daily caloric intake of half of the population was only 79 percent of the U.N.-FAO (United Nations Food and Agriculture Organization) recommendation.

By the time revolution started in 1979, Somoza was all but isolated from the sources of power that traditionally supported him; landowners, the Liberal party that he led, and the country's bourgeoisie refused to stand by him. At the end his government was held together with nothing but the brute military force that he still controlled. Even the National Guard repudiated him. The dénouement came when the United States suggested that Somoza leave Nicaragua; he spent his last months in Paraguay.

The destruction to the economy caused by the war was immense: 35,000 Nicaraguans died in the insurrection; 10,000 nationals were seriously injured; and 50,000 children were orphaned. If per capita GDP in 1977 is indexed at a baseline of 100, the 1979 figure is 65, the 1980 figure 70. During the conflict, the Somoza holdings were abandoned by managers and production fell. Output of beans and corn, traditionally peasant-grown crops, plummeted after the revolution. According to Booth (1985, p. 241), the revolution saw sugar production drop by 14 percent; milk, by an estimated 50 percent; and cotton, by 82 percent. In agriculture, if total product is indexed at 100 for 1977, the 1979 figure is 94, and the 1980 figure is 86. Weeks (1985, p. 163) estimates that the pattern of destruction, in which urban areas suffered more than rural regions, resulted in a rate of unemployment (largely urban) three times what it had been in the mid-1970s. Nearly a half-billion dollars worth of damage was done to Nicaragua's infrastructure (Weeks 1985, p. 158). The Economic Commission for Latin America (see Colburn 1986, p. 121) calculates that, in 1979, production levels had fallen to what they were in 1962; Nicaragua's foreign debt of $1.64 billion was the highest per capita debt of any Latin American country (Colburn 1986, p. 121).

The novelty of a "people's government" in Managua attracted a great deal of support from Europe, the Eastern bloc, the rest of Latin America, and private groups in the United States. Indeed, between 1979 until early in 1982, the Sandinista government received about $950 million in foreign credits and $250 million more in donations. In 1983, the country received an additional $624 million in credits and $76 million in donations (Colburn 1986, pp. 121–122). Reconstruction was but one of the many formidable tasks of the new government. Economic problems inherited from the Somoza regime and exacerbated by the war were: (1) dependence on the agro-export sector; (2) a pattern of financing deficits through foreign borrowing; and (3) enormous infrastructural damage.

The new government intended to rebuild the devastated economy, redistribute income, influence, and wealth toward the lower classes (thus ameliorating enormous inequities), dismantle the economic base of the old regime, and foster economic growth.

Nationalization by the Sandinistas increased the public share of gross national product (GNP) from 15 percent in 1978 to 41 percent in 1980 and 45 percent in 1984. State-ownership activities mostly affected natural resources, construction, manufacturing, banking, insurance, transportation, and agriculture. Enterprises declared to be "people's property" included 120 firms and 2,000 farms encompassing 800,000 hectares. Much of this property was taken over directly from Somoza and his cronies when they fled the country. In 1979 and 1980, tax revenues increased and, together with a general reduction in graft, public revenues ran ahead of expenditures.

U.S. government pressure on Nicaragua intensified when Ronald Reagan became president in 1981[10]; $15 million of the $75 million aid package that had been negotiated under President Jimmy Carter was suspended.[11] Similarly, wheat shipments were delayed. Early in the Reagan administration the Inter-American Development Bank and the World Bank were persuaded to interrupt lending programs to Nicaragua (Booth 1985, p. 240). In reaction, the new government in Nicaragua attempted to concentrate its strength by centralizing its administrative apparatus and increasing its spending on defense; inflation and shortages of basic wage goods soon appeared.

Once the war was over, the Sandinistas determined to induce economic growth and fulfill their promise to distribute resources and income more equitably. They knew agro-export production would have to be resuscitated to encourage growth and foreign exchange earnings; this meant giving assurances to the private sector. The conflict between the two goals was significant: the private sector had to be encouraged even as the government redistributed formerly private property to landless *campesinos*.

However, the new government was lucky at this early stage of land reform. Although agrarian reforms typically rely on expropriation and purchase from the private sector, the government obtained title to the best farms in the country by taking over those abandoned by Somoza and his cronies.[12] In the words of Thome and Kaimowitz, "The extent and nature of this confiscatory process was almost unique among agrarian reform processes.... [I]t was virtually costless, in political as well as fiscal terms" (1985, p. 300). Representing somewhat less than one-fourth of the country's agricultural property, these farms were to be operated mainly by the government as state farms. The new regime reasoned that the Somoza properties should not be subdivided because of economies of size in agro-export crop production. A centralized method of operation would also ensure that *campesinos* did not shift the cropping pattern to corn and beans, the traditional staples most often grown on peasant farms. The Ministry of Agricultural Development and Agrarian Reform (Ministerio de Desarrollo

Agropecuario y Reforma Agraria, MIDINRA) was set up to administer the land reform. Meanwhile, in order to promote production, the Sandinistas assured private-sector farmers that expropriation would not occur unless individual owners flouted the labor laws or left the land idle.

From 1979 to 1981, services to *campesinos* expanded markedly, both on and off state farms. *Minifundistas*, at last, got production credit and technical assistance; health clinics opened throughout the country. *Campesinos* were allowed to openly organize, and by mid-1980 the ATC had over 100,000 members. Production, marketing, and service cooperatives were also organized. In these heady times, a national crusade reduced illiteracy in the country from 50 to 13 percent. By 1980, when 59 percent of the reformed land was used for domestic staples (up from only 33 percent in 1977 when cropland was in the hands of Somoza and his supporters), better nutrition was reaching the poor (Brockett 1990, p. 171). After the revolution real wages in rural areas sharply increased. The government also issued decrees that lowered land rents and increased tenant security.

Although subsistence crops were now granted credit, the difficulties of smallholders persisted. The new bureaucracy was far from perfect, and in some cases late credit arrival, limited technical assistance,[13] and poor marketing facilities left farmers with scant production and high levels of default. In the meantime, despite repeated assurances by the Sandinistas, the private sector remained unconvinced that the new government would adequately attend to its interests; farm investment and agricultural production decreased. In 1981, middle- and large-sized farmers established the Union of Nicaraguan Agricultural Producers (Unión de Productores Agropecuarios Nicaragüense, UPANIC). As UPANIC took on the ATC, it became an overt counterforce to government. Despite rental legislation designed to discourage tenant expulsion, angry owners evicted tenants nonetheless.

The peasant sector did not remain tranquil for long. *Campesinos*, dissatisfied with the government's emphasis on state farms, which prevented them from obtaining land of their own, began to invade private holdings, undermining Sandinista policy. *Campesinos* felt that they should receive land because they had loyally supported the insurgents during the war. But just as the government had both to distribute landed assets and to reassure private producers, it also had to mediate between popular pressure for land distribution and its own ideological and economic preference for agro-export- and foreign-exchange–generating state farms.

The latter concern was addressed in a second reform period, beginning in 1981 and running through 1983, in which the emphasis was shifted from state farms to production cooperatives. In 1981, the ATC split, with the original organization serving agricultural workers and its offshoot, the National Union of Farmers and Ranchers (Unión Nacional de Agricultores y Ganaderos, UNAG), uniting small-

and medium-sized producers.[14] Also in 1981, a new law extended agrarian reform to property not formerly connected with Somoza. Although well-farmed lands were exempt, the new legislation made it possible for the government to expropriate land in excess of 750 hectares in the Pacific littoral and 1,750 hectares in the central region if owners "underutilized" the land or abandoned their property. Some 400 properties were expropriated by 1985, the majority on the basis of underutilization; others were taken due to abandonment. Agrarian courts were founded to adjudicate the law. Under the legislation, landlords were to be compensated with agrarian bonds (with property values based on the landlords' self-declarations for tax purposes); beneficiaries were prohibited by covenant from selling their property or subdividing it. In 1982, MIDINRA decentralized operations, establishing sixteen regional offices, thereby giving peasants better access to its programs. Eighty percent of the 294,000 hectares expropriated were organized into production cooperatives that had better access to credit and inputs than those few created during the first reform period. These cooperatives were also larger, having an average of 34 members and a per capita area of 14 hectares. The government hoped that this reform, which preserved economies of scale, would augment output by pressing idle land into use and satisfy peasant demands for more participation. It believed that the rural poor, who had not benefited much (except through higher wages) from the state-farm orientation of the first stage, would now feel more directly advantaged.

The third period of Nicaragua's agrarian reform began in late 1983 and early 1984, when individual properties became favored over both state farms and production cooperatives. This move corresponded to increasing *campesino* demand for individual family farming as well as stepped-up attacks by the counterrevolutionary (*contra*) forces. (For its part, the government had reluctantly come to believe that *campesinos* would defend their own land better than they would the property of a production cooperative in which they held membership.)

Moreover, nearly 30,000 squatter families received title to land they farmed during the 1984/1985 period. Augmenting its pressure, UNAG was assured by government that new land would be distributed as individual farms as it became available.[15] Some land on the Pacific coast was not subject to the expropriation legislation, so the government bought from landlords and, in a few cases, exchanged properties. The government also lowered the ceiling somewhat on land exempt from expropriation (Brockett 1990, p. 173). In addition, technical assistance and credit were distributed to homesteading farmers. Peasants benefited as price controls were removed from corn and beans. Concurrently, however, thousands of peasants were relocated against their wishes from the north-central war region. Of the reform, Booth concluded: "The reforms [after four years] had not made Nicaraguan peasants rich, but they appeared to have laid the groundwork for eventual real improvements in living conditions for the rural poor" (1985, p. 245).

By the mid-1980s, the counterrevolution was raging. To execute the war with more attention to local details and to better coordinate military movements, maneuvers were administered from the regional offices originally designed to decentralize the agrarian reform (Kaimowitz 1989, pp. 391 et seq.).[16] The unfortunate upshot of this association was that agrarian-reform sites frequently became *contra* targets.

Close to 40 percent of the agricultural land in Nicaragua had been confiscated or expropriated by 1989 when reform stopped, swamped by inflation, counterrevolution, and economic malaise. The amount of land held in the large estates over 850 hectares was only one-third of what it had been under prerevolutionary conditions. The quantity of land in the very smallest holdings had also been cut in half. Almost 77,500 families, or about 10 percent of the population of the country, had benefited from the agrarian-reform program (Enríquez 1991, p. 91).[17]

PRODUCTION AND EQUITY UNDER THE REFORM

A combination of continuing conflict; shortage of labor, markets, and investment; and conspicuous mismanagement fostered production problems during the 1980s. Cotton fiber output dropped by two-thirds; coffee output gradually declined, with output reaching 89 percent of 1977/1978 levels by 1984/1985. By the end of the 1980s, coffee production had dropped by one-third. Sugarcane, the other major agricultural export, reached 95 percent of 1977/1978 production by 1984/1985, but was higher than before by 1991. The revolution precipitated a massive slaughter of livestock; by mid-decade, production was 80 percent of what it had been in the late 1970s; by 1991, livestock output was only about half of its previous level. Using 100 as the index number for 1977/1978, corn production dropped to 80 in 1979/1980 but crept up during the 1980s, with harvests in 1989, 1990, and 1991 well exceeding those of the late 1970s.[18]

Scholars attribute Nicaragua's production difficulties during the 1980s to a variety of obstacles. Utting (1987) writes that problems related to reinvigorating cotton and cattle production after the revolution stemmed primarily from the insecurity of property relations introduced by the reforms, lack of investment, and distrust of Sandinista policies by the propertied class.[19] He determines that corn production on smallholdings did not rise in the early 1980s, even though prices were guaranteed and credit and technical assistance were forthcoming, because of inept communication with far-flung small-scale farmers. Further, Utting (1987) believes that these communication problems were exacerbated because the government did not attempt to differentiate its message to accommodate the varying information needs of peasant farms, plantation-like farms, and cooperative and state farms.[20] Also, guaranteed prices for cotton were set too low; although meant to protect farmers from price fluctuations, they acted instead as deterrents to production. Utting (1987) also shows that, during the reforms, internal terms of trade turned sharply against peasants who grew corn. In 1978, producers had to spend the equivalent of 0.5 quintal of corn for each machete and pair of work trousers; by 1984, these items cost 1.2 and 5.5 quintals, respectively, leading corn farmers to seek more profitable crop combinations. Other problems of cereal-producing small farmers included rising transportation costs and broken exchange relationships with traditional moneylenders (before new credit arrangements were complete). Moreover, there was a time lag before the Sandinistas were able to establish a functioning marketing service, manifesting a situation not atypical of revolutionary countries: "A time lag very often arises between the disarticulation of the old structure and the consolidation of the new. Experience has shown that it is much easier to displace agents than it is to replace those necessary functions that they performed" (Utting 1987, p. 134). With the acceleration of the counterrevolution after 1983, markets deteriorated further, disrupting distribution systems, destroying infrastructure, and promoting labor migration. Furthermore, before the revolution, corn farmers had often used the grain itself as a store of value to protect against inflation, selling their production only when cash was needed. In the past, corn was sold for cordobas when children had to see a doctor; free health-care service obviated growing and storing grain for this purpose.

Martinez (1993) believes that a fundamental problem in Sandinista agrarian-reform policy, which led to both economic and political problems, was faulty information on the type of peasantry in Nicaragua. Early in the reform period, especially, the government consistently overestimated the number of rural wage workers and understated peasant cultivators (who actually produced 80 percent of basic grains and even some export crops), a defect that was never completely remedied by what was otherwise a pragmatic policy toward agriculture. He concluded that "[t]his strategy placed [peasant cultivators] at the lowest priority for distribution of benefits from agrarian reform policy" (Martinez 1993, p. 484).

Despite this, from 1985 until reform was officially declared complete in February 1989, establishing peasant cultivators and servicing existing ones became an enunciated government priority. Individual parcels were distributed (in 1985 at a rate three times that realized over the previous six years). Prior to mid-decade, peasant squatters were granted title, a move that did not alter social relations in the countryside very much. As the counterrevolution raged, the government became solicitous toward established peasant producers: It raised producer prices, cut food imports, canceled urban subsidies on staples, and gave out additional credit for farm inputs. Martinez (1993) believes the reason for these policies, which eventually turned the internal terms of trade in favor of these producers for a time, was the tactical need to build up peasant allegiance to government. At the same time, the Sandinistas also found it necessary to capture the support of the ethnic minorities on the Atlantic coast who had become *contra* sympathizers. According to Martinez, favoring the peasant cultivators there "brought negotiated peace and stability to the [Atlantic] coast years ahead of the rest of the country" (1993, p. 481). Even so, Martinez argued that government support of peasant-cultivator policies did not represent a "shift in strategy ... with regards to the peasantry. Rather, peasants were lured toward supporting the revolution through a package of *ad hoc* incentives, often poorly timed or focussed" (1993, p. 481). He claimed, "It is possible that a conscious, strategic change at an earlier period would have increased both peasant support and peasant production to a great enough degree to have significantly lessened the political and economic pressures" (Martinez 1993, p. 484).

Enríquez (1991) believes that lack of wage labor after agrarian reform was responsible for production shortfalls. She argued that, as *campesinos* became land-reform beneficiaries, they grew less willing to accept wage labor: "As the *campesinos'* standard of living improved, they increasingly chose *campesinización* [conversion of peasant households to petty agricultural producers] over participation in the agro-export labor force.... The labor shortage threatened the very essence of agroexport production" (Enríquez 1991, p. 147).

Adding to labor scarcity, many workers migrated to cities during the revolution to be far from the war and close to social infrastructure. For a time, the revolutionary government permitted migrants to settle on vacant lots in Managua. Later, increasing differentials appeared between earnings of farmers and incomes of traders, particularly those dealing in contraband goods, the black market, and the informal sector. Due to its sparse population, Nicaragua had always depended on in-migration of workers from other Central American countries during peak harvesting seasons. This migratory stream diminished as war continued in El Salvador and a right-wing government in Honduras became increasingly at odds with Managua. In addition, between 70,000 and 100,000 persons were involved in the war in Nicaragua, and so a decreasing proportion of the population was available to produce food.

To counteract production shortfalls, Nicaragua expanded foreign purchases early during the postrevolutionary period. Imports of food products and raw materials were valued at $23.8 million in 1978; they rose sixfold by 1981. As export revenue dropped, this advance was unsustainable, and the country soon acquired a huge trade deficit. The proportion of exports required to service the foreign debt rose from 7 percent in 1977 to 33 percent in 1982. Other aspects of Nicaragua's food system, largely the legacy of the prerevolutionary period, made the country more dependent on trade (Utting 1987). For example, flour-based products could be baked, but the flour itself had to be imported. Similarly, milk needed to be imported for some dairy processing plants. This dependency made the food industries especially trade-sensitive.

For most foods, large consumption increases were recorded for the 1980/1982 period, an advance that decelerated with inflation, the foreign exchange crisis, and war (Utting 1987). Despite this slowdown, in mid-decade most food items were consumed in greater quantities than before the revolution because of the government's redistributive policies: More credit to the poor increased purchasing power, and subsidized food was available in stores at low prices. Utting (1987) calculates that these consumer subventions eventually rose to 6.3 percent of government spending by 1985, when subsidy reductions began.

It is tempting to blame the United States for the ultimate economic failure of Sandinista agriculture. As Collins et al. claimed early in the conflict, "the most powerful single obstacle facing Nicaragua today is the unrelenting hostility of the United States government" (1982, p. 147). Blasier summarized:

> The Reagan administration imposed a wide range of sanctions on Nicaragua: (1) terminating the $15 million balance of the aid approved under Carter; (2) seeking to block credits from international financial institutions; (3) turning its information services against the Sandinistas; (4) organizing and financing a counterrevolutionary force for military action against the Sandinistas, including the mining of harbors; and (5) holding large naval, military, and air force exercises around Nicaragua (1985, p. 292).

Colburn (1986, p. 38) points out that the Sandinistas created viable local institutions among the dispossessed city people and the peasants while strengthening local participation by channeling government services through the new organizations. He also argued that "just as Marx wrote that the French revolution cleared away lots of 'Medieval rubbish,' so have recent revolutions in the developing countries cleared away colonial or neocolonial relics. These relics are not only despotic and unjust, but are also obstacles to broad-based development" (Colburn 1986, p. 22).

Colburn (1986) concludes, however, that the Nicaraguan Revolution was not able to deliver on its economic promises and would not have been able to do so even had the United States not intervened. He claims that, in 1979, the new regime in Managua had a great deal of material support while most of the fighting occurred far from the Pacific coast where most agricultural production took place, and contends that Nicaragua's economy foundered because public spending was not matched by increased revenue. Well before the U.S. embargo, expanded imports confronted a stagnant export sector, a grave problem in a country where foreign trade occupies so paramount a position. Weeks (1985, p. 166) also shows that, in the early postrevolutionary period, export capacity was 30 percent lower than before the war; the unease of the private sector had been translated into a lack of investment and falling export production. Later, to prevent a cotton collapse, the government channeled scarce resources to plantation owners, held down wage increases, and established price concessions for landowners (initially this meant using a 15:1 exchange rate instead of the official 10:1 rate), policies that were inflationary. Cotton farmers perceived the government giving with one hand, taking away with the other. For their part, the *campesinos* and urban poor experienced a rise in income immediately after the revolution but soon saw real earnings stabilize and then sharply decline.

Colburn (1986) argues that the revolution did not change real power relations much except to insert the state as a new member of the agro-export business community. As an illustration, that part of the agricultural community most despised by the poor—the cotton exporters—ironically received enormous concessions from the revolutionary government, simply because it was they who controlled the commodity considered most apt to earn the needed foreign exchange (Colburn 1986, p. 128). In retaliation, the rural poor defaulted on short-term production credit, shortened hours worked on the new state farms, and, later, retreated into subsistence farming in the face of poor producer prices. The failure of the revolutionaries to match rhetoric with deeds was exploited by the increasingly well-funded *contra* movement (Colburn 1986, Table 17, p. 130).

Although many accounts of the Sandinistas are more favorable than Colburn's (1986), most agree they did not manage the economy very well. Weeks wrote that the Sandinistas wished fervently to help the poor: "On two issues they were firmly united: (1) that Nicaraguan independence was not negotiable, and (2) the revolution should primarily benefit the peasantry, working class, and middle class—not the wealthy" (1985, p. 170). But Weeks also shows that the Sandinistas regularly held down real wages and that the government's reliance on agro-exports meant extending incentives to the private sector. Through it all, the private sector warily regarded the Sandinista determination to shift the base of power to the disenfranchised, a radical and unprecedented change from policies under Somoza, when trade unions were illegal and workers could be fired at will. With the shift in power, "private employers could not treat labor relations in the old way.... In the broader context, private capital perceived itself as caught in a process of mass awakening and radicalization" (Weeks 1985, p. 172).

Weeks (1985) feels that, because of the war, the Sandinistas were forced to abandon key philosophic principles and that programs directed to the rural poor constantly had to be recast. Although in the early 1980s the government attempted to minimize the impact of the conflict on the poor, later in the decade this stance became impossible (Weeks 1985). Ultimately the local-based literacy and health programs were halted in favor of augmenting the military budget.

The final assessment of Nicaragua under the Sandinistas reveals modest social gains and enormous economic losses. Even so, enduring gains of the revolution include better organization and a larger voice for the poor.[21]

By the time the Sandinistas lost the 1990 election to Violeta Barrios de Chamorro, the electorate was no longer able to bear falling incomes and rising price levels. Inflation in Nicaragua had eroded purchasing power by 90 percent between 1981 and late 1990. When war finally ended, there was little doubt that it, together with the U.S. embargo and Sandinista inattention to economic realities, had crippled the nation. More than 70 percent of the population lived in "extreme poverty." As the Chamorro government took over, unemployment was estimated at about 40 percent, with thousands of soldiers crowding the job market when the armed services were disbanded (Gasperini 1990). The *Financial Times* of London noted that economics was the decisive factor behind the Chamorro win:

> Ravaged by the war with the U.S.-backed Contra guerillas and by inflation, the economy has taken a battering. Internal mismanagement has been compounded by U.S. economic sanctions and a drying-up of international lines of credit. Exports fell sharply, creating a vicious circle: The drop led to foreign-exchange shortages of imported raw materials, which affected output and, in turn, potential exports. To finance the war against the Contras, the government printed money, fuelling hyperinflation. In 1988, prices rose at an annual rate of more than 30,000 percent (Coone 1990, p. 22).

As Chamorro took over, exports were running at less than half the 1978 level. While regional (Central American and Panamanian) per capita growth of GDP during the 1980s declined by 10 percent, Nicaragua's per capita income in 1990 was over 40 percent lower than in 1981. External debt was 125 percent of GDP in 1979; it was 825 percent in 1990 (Hull 1991b).

THE CHAMORRO GOVERNMENT AND LAND RIGHTS

The Chamorro government inherited a chaotic land-tenure situation fraught with incomplete records and overlapping claims. Few of the demobilized troops who had been promised land were actually assigned property, often trading their uniforms for unemployment. A lack of security, which hampered investment, pervaded the agricultural sector. In some cases disputes over land were so vitriolic that crops were not planted for fear the land would be confiscated before harvest time. Although Chamorro promised that the agrarian reform would not be rolled back, she had no funds to mollify the former landowners or to supply the credit that beneficiaries needed to survive. The priority for the Chamorro government was privatizing state farms. Of some 305,000 hectares on 600 former state farms, 30 percent was returned to former owners, 38 percent was assigned to former soldiers (Nicaraguan army and insurgents), and 32 percent was allocated to former workers (Stanfield 1992, pp. 11–12).

Stanfield (1992) documents that the Sandinista government had acquired at least 5,362 properties (or about 1.75 million hectares) for purposes of agrarian reform. The fact that 70 percent of redistributed land was neither retitled nor reregistered to reflect new ownership presented the Chamorro government with a massive tangle of claims and counterclaims. As Hendrix argued, "the Sandinista government never thought it would be removed by the electorate. Therefore, not sensing any urgency, it was slow in proceeding with the legal formalization of confiscations and expropriations" (1992b, p. 14). Some of the former landowners whose land went through a legal registration process now argued that the property should be returned since it was taken under duress. Stanfield (1992, p. 20) estimates that 40 percent of the households in the country found themselves in actual or potential conflict over land rights.

To cope with the problem, Chamorro appointed a commission to review the land-acquisition policy of the Sandinista government and to determine whether some properties ought to revert (Hendrix 1992b, p. 17). The commission found that, even in cases where ownership was not in dispute, many properties could not be registered because boundaries were unclear. Moreover, the past government had given out a number of titles to joint owners of a production cooperative. Although membership at the time of land delivery was indisputable, the beneficiary group changed as some members died and left heirs and others dropped out and were replaced. The government did not know whether to title members of the original or the current group or to allow the property to return to its precooperative owner.[22] The 76,500 hectares that the Sandinistas took over after they lost the election and before the new government was inaugurated (called, colloquially, the *piñata*) created even more animosity and confusion.

The national commission received some 4,000 requests from previous farm owners for property reversion. Over 2,000 decisions subsequently ordered the return of properties to the original owners, but when land-reform beneficiaries sensed their land in peril, they protested vehemently; the Supreme Court declared much of the commission's work unconstitutional. In some cases, negotiation between the former and the present owner and/or the use of force produced a de facto solution.

Several decrees put the Chamorro government on record as promising to pay an indemnity to past owners more or less automatically while respecting the rights of those who received property in the agrarian reforms. The method of compensation was tax value paid in twenty-year bonds at 3 percent interest (indexed to the local exchange rate). This was not a favorable arrangement for former landlords (Hendrix 1992b, p. 19). To be compensated at all, former owners had to present proof of their land ownership.[23]

Stanfield listed three more complications with which the Chamorro government had to struggle:

1. When the government did not assign much newly available land to former combatants, invasions of existing agrarian-reform settlements and other properties ensued.
2. Agrarian commissions, conceived by the Chamorro administration to resolve land conflicts, were to decide on conflicting land claims at the departmental (state) and municipal levels of government, but their legitimacy was questioned in practice.
3. Indigenous communities were resurging as cohesive ethnic groups, and their claims for land sometimes conflicted with those of other communities. Compounding the matter was the fact that, although indigenous land could

not legally be bought and sold, it was frequently rented out (with multiple-year leases) to nonindigenous peoples (1992, pp. 9 and 13).

Adding to these difficult land-tenure problems, the Chamorro government allowed some peasants to settle on the frontier, thus reenergizing the process of converting forests to fields. (Settlers had to demonstrate the seriousness of their claim by clearing and farming the property.) Concern in Nicaragua mounted over the considerable environmental damage this represented.

The debate over land continues to rage in Nicaragua, and no one is certain when the final chapter will be written. An uneasy peace is challenged by a classic case of land-rights problems, a situation that also hampers sustainable economic development. No clear solution is in sight.

7

Reforms of the 1980s: El Salvador

El Salvador, in contrast to Nicaragua, is a land-scarce, heavily settled country with the highest population density in the region (even Haiti has fewer people per square mile). The smallest country in Central America, El Salvador is the size of Massachusetts, containing about as many people (5.2 million) but lacking the industrial base. Fifty-six percent of the Salvadoran population lives in rural areas, which are still dominated by export-oriented farms. Perhaps it was inevitable that land reform and civil war were prominent features of El Salvador's history over most of the 1980s and early 1990s: It has one of the largest and poorest work forces and one of the most intransigent landowning classes of Central America. Whether the prolonged and tragic war has substantially modified this social situation remains to be seen.

Of all Central American countries, El Salvador has the most serious problems with rural landlessness. The agricultural census of 1971 showed that 65 percent of the rural population was landless or land-poor—owning less than 0.7 hectares. As the civil war ended and after a land reform that incorporated one-fifth of the total land area of the country and 10 percent of El Salvador's population, sample surveys indicate that approximately 54 percent of the agricultural work force is still landless, land-poor, or unemployed (Seligson et al. 1993). If the land promised under the 1992 peace accords to 12,500 former combatants and 25,000 squatters (*tenedores*), who spent much of the war in the combat zone, is eventually granted, this figure should drop to 40 percent. About half of the country's peasant landholders are renters (Seligson et al. 1993).

BACKGROUND TO THE REFORM

As in much of Central America in the first part of the twentieth century, coffee production dominated the economy of El Salvador. If the price of coffee on the world market dropped, El Salvador had a bad year; if not, it was successful. Coffee had first replaced cocoa and then indigo as the major trading crop early in the twentieth century and by 1931 constituted 95.5 percent of the country's exports. The planters proved themselves efficient producers; their coffee yields were among the highest in the world. Even today coffee makes up 60 to 70 percent of Salvadoran agricultural exports.

As the consummate agro-exporting country, El Salvador also trades in sugar, cotton, and cattle on the international market;[1] as such, its economic growth is largely determined by conditions in the developed countries that receive its exports. El Salvador practiced some import substitution during the depression of the 1930s and World War II, when trade was stifled and foreign exchange was especially scarce. In the 1960s, import-substituting industrialization in the country was associated with growth of the Central American Common Market, which promoted regional trade, usually in simple consumer goods. As is the case with neoliberalism today, ISI orientation served to invigorate the economy; tariff-protected industries thrived in the prewar period in El Salvador, known by Central American legend as having an especially work-oriented, entrepreneurial population.

Meanwhile, agriculture fell from about 46 percent of GDP in 1929 to about 29 percent in 1965; it fell to about 11 percent of GDP by 1990 (Bulmer-Thomas 1987, Table 12.2, p. 271; World Bank 1992b, Table 3, p. 222). Yet El Salvador depends on agriculture for 45 percent of its exports (FAO 1992b, Appendix Table 11, p. 206). Two-thirds of the land in export crops (and somewhat more than one-third of all cropland) is used as pasture for cattle. Weeks explained, "The extreme land hunger of the Salvadoran peasantry is eloquently explained by the fact that the use of land for cattle raising is proportionally the same in El Salvador and Costa Rica, though population density is almost six times greater in the former country" (1985, p. 102). Lately, civil unrest and war have been the major domestic factors that negatively affected the economic well-being of the country (Bulmer-Thomas 1987).

Before the 1980s, land concentration in El Salvador was one of the most skewed in Latin America, on a par with Guatemala. Although the 1980s witnessed agrarian reform, no census has been undertaken since that of 1971, which showed that 2 percent of the agricultural population held 60 percent of the agricultural land.

Although land was inequitably distributed as a result of Spanish colonization, some of the influence from Iberia was overcome by the mid-nineteenth century since El Salvador was only a remote outpost of the kingdom. Remarkably, visitors to the area spoke of the absence of extreme poverty. One of them, writing in 1869, noted that the major cities of England and southern Europe suffered from worse indigence and misery (Burns 1989, pp. 203–204). In El Salvador, all residents seemed to enjoy access to land; the hacienda existed but did not seem to monopolize the rural economy. As Burns observed, "An absence of the extremes of poverty and wealth bespoke a vague degree of equality" (1989, p. 204).

By the end of the 1850s, Salvadorans came to realize that they could grow coffee not only for the markets of Europe but also for the United States. After a trip to Europe, then-President Gerardo Barrios (1858–1863) claimed that he would "regenerate" the nation by encouraging immigration, building infrastructure, promoting industrialization, and facilitating communications and education. In his vision, the key to progress would be the foreign exchange earned by coffee. Accordingly, an expansion of coffee plantations from 1860 to 1890 affected the tiny nation profoundly. A few Salvadorans with capital invested in coffee, and land appropriate to the crop rose in value.

Land suitable for coffee growing was not always individually owned, however. Sometimes an indigenous community possessed it, but the Indians continued to cultivate their traditional staples, corn and beans, on *tierras comunales*. Towns also held some property in common (*ejidos*), which they apportioned in individual plots to residents. Barrios and his successors, as part of their development goals, promoted the transfer to private hands of lands farmed by Indians and other *campesinos*. President Rafael Zaldivar (1876–1885) was especially adept in this regard. Reminiscent of Ley Lerdo in Mexico, Zaldivar declared *tierras comunales* to be impediments to agricultural development and ordered laws to outlaw them. As these lands were individualized and subsequently taken over by coffee planters, resident *campesinos* were dispossessed. Land consolidation created a landless class, which was now available to pick coffee; on average, *campesinos* became poorer than before the coffee behemoth roared through El Salvador.

Increasingly, public policy was reconfigured to assure that *campesinos* would be available for plantation labor: Antivagrancy laws were enacted in 1881 that required the landless to work a certain number of days on coffee estates under the threat of fines, arrests, and various other punishments (Burns 1989, p. 205); the Agrarian Law of 1907, reflecting the *repartimientos* (forced labor schemes) of the colony, authorized special judges to order *campesinos* to work whenever the planters summoned them. A rural constabulary was established to protect landlords in case of jacquerie; *campesino* rebellions continually erupted in response to land seizures and forced labor, but peasants seldom won these lopsided tests of strength.

This system, held together as it was by escalating use of force, saw the dominant planter elite expand its reach between 1903 and 1931, a period of remarkable political stability. As repression kept the workers and peasants in check, infrastructural investment nourished the economy. Burns commented, "The prosperity and order of the period promoted the rebuilding of the ports, the expansion of the railroad line, the rise of banking, the increase of foreign investment, and the modernization of San Salvador" (1989, p. 206).

The observers from Europe, who Burns (1989) quoted as sensing remarkable egalitarianism in El Salvador, would have seen a radically changed society had they revisited during the 1920s. Planters had become wealthy, well-educated, and cosmopolitan whereas many peasants, who had been separated from their land, existed without steady wage work and were unable to provide a decent subsistence for their families. Far from the vision of Barrios, schooling was not available to all, for planters had found that peasants without education were more compliant workers, less apt to complain or rebel. The social distance between rich and poor had become a gulf. Alberto Masferrer, a Salvadoran intellectual, described the situation as he saw it in 1928:

> Where there is now a voracious estate that consumes hundreds of acres, before there were two hundred small farmers whose plots produced corn, rice, beans, fruits, and vegetables. Now the highlands support only coffee estates and the lowlands cattle ranches. The corn fields are disappearing... Any nation that cannot assure the production and regulate the price of the most vital crop, the daily food of the people, has no right to regard itself as sovereign.... Such has become the case of our nation (quoted in Burns 1989, p. 207).

The worldwide depression in the 1930s exacerbated both rural and urban poverty and led to street demonstrations in San Salvador. Male rural unemployment had reached 40 percent by 1929 and kept on growing through the depression. Much of the peasant rebellion was inspired by college students who sponsored "popular universities" that met in the countryside. The major peasant organizer was Augustín Farabundo Martí, whose resistance movement enjoyed considerable success in the western part of the country. Farabundo Martí's nemesis was General Maximiliano Hernandez Martinez, who, as president, controlled uprisings through repression. Prior to the biggest planned rebellion against Hernandez, Farabundo Martí was captured and shot. The subsequent peasant revolt of January 1932 was dramatic, but casualties were light since towns were stormed one by one. The government counterattack, in contrast, was brutal; Hernandez sent in his troops to join with the private militias of the landlords and slaughter the peasants, often in acts of revenge (Brockett 1990, p. 145). The *matanza* (the massacre), as the event is called in Central America, involved the slaying of some 1 percent of the Salvadoran population, mostly Indians and anyone else to whom the epithet "communist" could be applied.

The *matanza* inaugurated nearly five decades of civil strife (1932 to 1979) during which the peasantry, representing the largest single group of citizens, played little role in El Salvadoran politics and the military, in concert with landowners, governed by force. Landlords, frightened by the *campesino* uprising that preceded the *matanza*, were forewarned and prepared, many forming militias that survive to modern times. The constitution barred strikes and rural unionization, so landlords could call upon the national guard to quell organized "disturbances" if militias were not up to the task.

As early as the Great Depression of the 1930s, some entrepreneurs realized that fiber could be grown locally for manufacture into cloth to replace imported fabrics; a plantation economy in cotton was begun. Appropriate land was converted to plowed fields, and *colonos* (resident hacienda labor), renters, and migrating wage workers provided the labor for planting and harvesting the crop. State land that was still forested began to disappear rapidly during the 1930s; some Salvadorans who had previously staked out pastureland plowed it up and became cotton farmers. Cotton land became increasingly concentrated in the hands of a new elite. Beginning in earnest during the 1940s, cotton represented another wave of modernization that was superimposed on coffee. Central American cotton enjoyed a booming export market during World War II and the Korean conflict. One key to cotton expansion was the formulation of DDT, a dangerous pesticide that made it possible for commercial farmers to eradicate malarial mosquitoes and thus open Pacific coastal plains for cultivation.[2] By the 1960s, the institutional pattern bore a distinct resemblance to the antebellum South of the United States, following a system that fostered the same disdain for *campesinos* that U.S. planters held for black slaves.

In the course of industrialization between 1935 and 1950, the number of cloth-producing factories increased from 4 to 11; the number of looms, from 230 to 1,440; and the number of spindles, from 3,000 to 50,000. By 1959, there were also 11 knitting plants with 125 knitting machines. Meanwhile, village-level weaving died out. Cotton acreage doubled in the 10 years between 1942 and 1951. There was another doubling by 1960; with the completion of a highway running parallel to the coast, the 1960's acreage trebled by 1965 as the remaining coastal forest vanished. By 1964, 90 percent of the cotton crop was exported. Browning concluded:

> In commercial terms, the colonization of the coastal plain was a success... But, as with coffee farming, in social terms the price paid for the commercial achievement has been high. The large, mechanized monocultural plantation has replaced the hacienda, with its associated cattle ranching and tenant farming, and has disrupted the traditional pattern of small-scale cultivation of food crops. A minority of the coastal population is able to work as resident laborers on the new plantations; the majority is obliged to settle where it can, to seek whatever form of precarious living it can find, and has become a poor and dispossessed section of the community. Moreover, the seasonal nature of the labor requirements of the cotton plantations has caused the problems of these people to be neglected; it is considered that any attempt to provide them with a permanent occupation or income must necessarily reduce the numbers of workers available during the short and critical picking season (1971, p. 239).

The spread of mechanization to the cotton fields had enormous social implications. As in the U.S. South, at first planting was mechanized whereas harvesting continued to be accomplished by hand; weed and pest extermination, formerly accomplished by backpack sprayer, soon was performed with airplanes, often with little regard for the humans toiling in the fields below. Mechanization eliminated the need for year-round labor. In cotton picking, however, a large pool of seasonal workers was still required; during the December–March harvest, all available hands were fully occupied. *Campesinos* who had access to land could plant corn and beans to carry themselves through the rainy season, but the many landless laborers remained without means of support for the major portion of the year.

Labor was also impacted by the minimum cash wage in agriculture, legislated in 1965 for adult males (with proportional rates set for women, young people, and children). This legislation had immediate repercussions: some women and children ceased to be offered work; in-kind payment was stopped, which eliminated access to small hacienda parcels for peasants; and other perquisites (such as a noon lunch) formerly offered in lieu of wages were withdrawn. Eventually the landlords found ways (such as instituting piecework) to flagrantly evade the minimum-wage legislation; even so, such laws hastened the process of mechanization, which was already well established in the mid-1960s. Accordingly, underemployment in farming became more acute. White (1973, p. 119) estimates that half of the *colonos* lost their regular jobs as a result of the minimum-wage law; some of them migrated temporarily to harvest crops in Nicaragua until war broke out there.

By the 1960s, rural labor problems erupted more frequently, but this did not deter Alliance for Progress officials from labeling the tiny Salvadoran agrarian reform "a showcase" of the time. But in reality it merely subdivided a few large and relatively unproductive estates that the government owned or bought from willing sellers for eventual purchase by local peasants. This program was rooted in even more insignificant "colonization" program of the 1930s. It was refurbished in the 1960s and accelerated into a highly publicized effort that helped El Salvador compete for U.S. foreign assistance funds and assuage reformist pressure within the country. The number of peasants who were benefited with land (production credit and inputs to support farming activities were unavailable) was minuscule; this "reform" did little to contain the rising aspirations of the peasantry.

Landlords responded to the Alliance for Progress, which conditioned economic assistance on progress toward social reforms, with alarm and indignation. In 1961, the oligarchy sponsored a domestic media blitz that portrayed the Alliance as communist-inspired. Since counterinsurgency was also supported by U.S. policy toward Latin America, the Salvadoran government answered *campesino* pressure for land by founding the Democratic Nationalist Organization (the Spanish acronym was ORDEN, which means "order"). This group was a plainclothes paramilitary force that required members to inform on neighbors who might have insurrectionist tendencies; it ultimately enlisted some 100,000 peasants in its pacification efforts. ORDEN was an auxiliary of the National Guard, assuring that security forces were omnipresent.[3] This divide-and-conquer strategy kept dissatisfied peasants off guard and "loyal" to their landlords. Its major objective was to turn peasants who proclaimed fealty to the government against those who openly expressed a need for change.

Coffee, cotton, sugar, and livestock raising all expanded and modernized during the 1960s and 1970s, giving rise to increased peasant displacement and landlessness. *Campesinos* streamed into the shantytowns around cities. In San Salvador, many came to live in dry riverbeds or *barrancas*.[4]

As the disappearing forest on the eastern lowlands lost its value as a safety valve, Salvadorans migrated in droves to lightly populated Honduras. This strategy was viable until 1969, when a brief war between the two countries gave Honduras the pretext for doing the inevitable: making the border between the two nations impervious. Thousands of Salvadoran families—some estimate as many as 100,000 people—were uprooted by Honduras during the early 1970s and returned to refugee status in their own country, to endure a poverty level far more abject than they had known before.[5]

A distinguishing feature of contemporary El Salvador is the continued absence of a sanctuary for excess population, with the exception of North America, which today serves as home to about 1 million of the country's current or former citizens. El Salvador itself has no more uninhabited forest or unclaimed state property. Neither is there a viable manufacturing sector to employ migrants from rural areas, though there are some export-import duty-free industrial zones. Meanwhile, environmental problems persist. In a very important sense, El Salvador has become the bellwether of Latin America as to what happens when scant attention given to the environment as a large population—among which resources are concentrated in the hands of a few—presses against a limited physical base (Chapin 1990).[6]

By 1969, the government had resurrected the agrarian-reform issue, though in rather abstract terms. One cause for renewed discussion was the opposition Christian Democratic party (Partido Democrático Cristiano, PDC), which began to propose modest land reforms as a means to create a rural equivalent to the urban middle class. Although the proposed reforms were far from radical—as the history of the Christian Democratic party elsewhere in Latin America would demonstrate—party spokespersons gingerly discussed "eliminating" *latifundios* and *minifundios*. When the PDC gained control of the legislature, it convened a National Agrarian Reform Congress that called for a "massive expropriation in favor of the common good" of lands not fulfilling their social function. These words struck terror in the hearts of the country's landowners (Brockett 1990, p. 146). After the PDC lost to the government party in the 1970 elections, young officers within the military government began hinting that agrarian reform might be one way to cope with the mounting refugee problem.[7]

In the 1972 elections, the PDC united with several smaller parties to back José Napoleón Duarte, the longtime mayor of San Salvador, in the presidential race. Duarte's running mate, Guillermo Ungo of the National Revolutionary movement, was the son of one of the founders of the PDC in El Salvador. A major plank of the Duarte-Ungo platform was agrarian reform—expropriation of farms over a predefined limit and redistribution. This was occurring, it should be noted, during the time of the booming agrarian reform of Salvador Allende in Chile and after the PDC term of Eduardo Frei (who began the Chilean reform), a fact not lost on the apprehensive Salvadoran landowning class. When Duarte took the lead on election night, the radio station announcing the returns suddenly fell silent; when it resumed, Colonel Arturo Molina, the government's candidate, was proclaimed the winner. As the only person who might mount a coup against Molina, Duarte was arrested and jailed. The coalition that fielded Duarte, the National Union of the Opposition (Unión Nacional de la Oposición, UNO), then took the public position that more radical agrarian reform than Duarte proposed in his campaign was needed.

The Molina government continued a militaristic strategy of repression, which was little publicized; small reforms in places where confrontations threatened were reported extensively—and in extravagant terms—in the press. In addition to containing peasant pressure, the repression-reform strategy of social control had a tightrope quality: It was contrived to convince the urban middle class of the viability of agrarian reform while making certain that the landlords—whose foreign exchange earnings were the country's lifeblood—remained unscathed.

A more liberal U.S. policy of importing beef (to fortify its dynamic new fast-food industry) brought on the completion of the first USDA-approved Salvadoran packing house in 1972, which was followed by a second in 1973 (Williams 1986). Since cattle raising is a land-extensive form of agriculture, this development (and the fact that cotton land was frequently returned to pasture when the need for fertilizer inputs rose too high and/or cotton prices dropped in cyclical downturns) caused peasant underemployment to rise.

Threatened by an economic crisis from rising petroleum prices, the military evicted more *campesinos* in order to expand cotton production and earn foreign exchange needed for oil imports. By the mid-1970s, peasants had come to feel that their only hope was in organization; they often could count on the active assistance of the Roman Catholic Church, whose liberal wing, after Pope John XXIII, advocated forming "base communities." For its part the government engaged in massive repression of *campesino* movements. Even the universities were not safe. Fearful that leadership of disruptive peasant movements might come from students and professors, the government interrupted the academic calendar to purge the national university of those who championed the peasants' cause.

The government knew that the urban middle class was cognizant of and sympathetic to the peasants' plight, so it persisted in alternating weak agrarian reforms with strong repression. Of course, instituted reforms were subverted as soon as they might have challenged established authority. In 1975, the government created the Salvadoran Institute of Agrarian Transformation (Instituto

Salvadoreña de Transformación Agraria, ISTA), which in 1976 proposed a small-scale agrarian reform for the eastern coastal cotton-belt provinces of San Miguel and Usulután, where *campesino* landlessness was chronic. Inefficiently farmed properties were selected and landlords ordered to sell or be expropriated to make room for 1,200 *campesino* families. The landlords, government promised, would be compensated by foreign funds. Even this demonstration reform, which seemed to enjoy broad support, was adamantly resisted by the landed class. Branding it as communism, landowners caused it to be neutralized and ultimately scrapped.

The late 1970s brought the matter of land reform into clearer focus; even some of the rural members of ORDEN began to speak up for a moderate reform. Organized peasant groups pressed for higher wages and land reforms. The Salvadoran Communal Union (Unión Comunal Salvadoreña, UCS) had been organized by the AFL-CIO-backed American Institute for Free Labor Development (AIFLD). More decidedly left-wing student groups and federations of labor unions became militant in reaction to the government's consistently conservative and repressive policies. The Christian Federation of Salvadoran Peasants (Federación Cristiano de Campesinos Salvadoreñas, FECCAS) grew up around the modern Roman Catholic Church and the outspoken reformist archbishop of San Salvador, Oscar Arnulfo Romero. There were also five groups of armed insurgents advocating very radical change; they united as the Farabundo Martí National Liberation Front (Frente Martí de Liberación Nacional, FMLN).

Government response to increasing peasant activity was far from passive. ORDEN was reined in and directed to maintain support for the government party and opposition to the PDC. According to Diskin and Sharpe, "it freely used coercion against the opposition" (1986, p. 54). Other government security forces began to react more swiftly and severely. Carlos Humberto Romero (no relation to the archbishop) assumed the presidency in 1977 and instituted full press censorship and made sure that outlawed strikes were suppressed, public meetings banned, and judicial proceedings suspended. During his government, the number of people active in peasant protest who simply "disappeared" increased, as did assassinations and death-squad activity. Meanwhile, the left wing also stepped up its response by taking hostages from the rich barrios of San Salvador.

As the 1970s wore on, the lot of the peasantry worsened even though the economy grew at a fairly rapid rate. Real wages of hired rural labor fell by 25 percent between 1973 and 1976 and another 5 percent by 1978, losing ground faster than urban labor. Meanwhile, absolute landlessness for rural families rose from 12 percent in 1961 to 41 percent in 1975 (Brockett 1990, p. 149). In the early 1970s, it was estimated that less than 5 percent of the rural population owned 10 hectares or more of land on average, an amount that White (1973) felt was the minimum needed to give full-time employment to a family in El Salvador. Another study noted that 64 percent of the rural families furnished seasonal and migratory laborers (Jung 1982, pp. 5–13). The peasantry became increasingly aware that its labors were contributing to the wealth of those who were already rich. This feeling of deprivation may have done more than anything else to draw war from insurrection. La Feber summarized:

> The political economy systematically starved the poor. Almost half the land on larger farms (those over 100 acres) was used for pasture or kept fallow. The campesino meanwhile tilled his small plot until it eroded. Thus as cattle prospered, production of the two staples for the peasant diet ... declined. Sorghum, which grew in poorest soil, replaced beans. It became human as well as cattle feed. As one expert phrased it, "Land is a scarce resource in [Salvador] only for the small [land]holders" (1983, p. 243).

As population grew especially rapidly among the poor, the low-quality educational and health facilities in the countryside were overstretched.

The illegitimacy of the country's political process accentuated misery in the countryside. The elections of 1977 were as fraudulent as those of 1972, and the assumption of the presidency by Romero, a man of the far Right, destroyed any hope of even moderate reforms. The coup de grâce came for Romero with the murder of two priests—who advocated peasant participation in the formulation of their own destinies—and the exile, arrest, and torture of others in the wake of the selection of Oscar Romero (who himself fell to an assassin's bullet in March 1980) as the archbishop of San Salvador. In brutally striking at the Catholic Church, the Right slashed at the underpinnings of the country's cultural heritage.

Walter and Williams described the contemporary period of military presidents:

> What the armed forces, as well as the military presidents—from Fidel Sanchez Hernandez (1967–1972) through Arturo Armando Molina (1972–1977) to Carlos Humberto Romero (1977–1979)—were facing was a new enemy: growing numbers of people who (1) were being displaced from their land by the expansion of export agriculture, (2) were being expelled from Honduras (both before and after the disastrous war of 1969), and (3) were being organized by a host of new social actors ranging from priests to students to peasant leaders. The voices of dissent that came out of these masses, however, had no effective, institutionalized channels of expression (1993, pp. 51–52).

In the aftermath of the Sandinistas' ascension to power, Washington began to imagine that "another Nicaragua" might happen in El Salvador. As the United States showed increasing signs of displeasure with the Romero government, a group of military officers saw its chance and engineered a coup in October 1979.

THE CIVIL WAR AND AGRARIAN REFORM

The intransigence of rural elites in the face of these problems had brought the country to the brink of civil war—and then pushed it over the edge. The new government, which took command as a junta in October 1979, was an alliance of civilian reformers and various elements of the right wing, a coalition that did not include *campesinos* or other popular forces. This made government action to institute participatory reforms, or even to halt the continuing violence, a virtual impossibility. Agrarian reform was a matter of concern to the October junta, but when civilian reformers found themselves consistently opposed by an intransigent military, they resigned.

This junta was replaced by another dominated by the PDC, which joined in January 1980 after it had received a commitment from the military that agrarian reform would be permitted (Strasma 1989, p. 408). In March 1980, as leader of the PDC, Duarte was installed on the junta. All this was possible because the Salvadoran armed forces had begun to distance themselves from the landholding oligarchy, an event that "began with the decision of the former to support the land reform program initiated in early 1980. However, additional considerations, emerging over time, were also at work.... [M]ilitary officers increasingly came to view the oligarchy as disloyal and concerned with its own profit. The military looked on angrily as wealthy oligarchs withdrew their capital from the country and sent their sons and daughters abroad when collapse seemed imminent" (Walter and Williams 1993, p. 58). Reform was also emphasized, Brockett (1990) claims, because of the involvement of the United States and its liberal ambassador, Robert White, who was sent to secure the country's political center and avoid another Nicaragua. "This reform was central to U.S. attempts to preempt a popular-leftist victory in El Salvador and to create and perpetuate instead a moderate reformist government" (Walter and Williams 1993, p. 154).

Considering that the key elements of the Salvadoran agrarian-reform coalition were the military and Christian Democrats, it is not surprising that the resultant program was executed from the top down, with little peasant organizational input in either design or implementation. Scofield concluded, "Perhaps the most distinctive feature of the El Salvador land-reform program is the speed with which it was conceived and executed" (1990, p. 142). Indeed, a large military contingent, together with land-reform administrators, traveled in teams to 472 farms that contained, according to government records, more than 500 hectares and declared the properties to belong to the *campesinos* who worked them. The team was responsible for taking a farm inventory, calling farm workers together to elect a management committee, and advising the landlord to go to ISTA in San Salvador to negotiate compensation and reserve rights (landlords were allowed to retain from 100 to 150 hectares, depending on soil type). Great secrecy surrounded movements of these expropriation teams; it was felt that, if they struck swiftly and with stealth, resistance would be minimal. Even so, they often found themselves battling landlords' militias.

As a consequence of this clandestine operation, peasants were as much pawns as they were beneficiaries of the process. And since the plan called for the expropriated properties to be converted immediately to production cooperatives, the daily lives of resident *campesinos* often went unchanged, though they became members of a farming cooperative. Shortly thereafter, it was not unusual to visit an agrarian-reform farm on which peasants had no comprehension that procedures had been reshaped to their benefit via the new co-op.

A wave of 10,000 *campesino* killings, usually attributed to right-wing death squads, occurred in 1980 before overt combat between the army and the guerrillas began in January 1981 (Christian 1992b). Accounts of some observers were graphic. The American Civil Liberties Union (ACLU) noted, "*Campesinos* suffer unspeakable brutality at the hands of military and paramilitary forces.... While there was a sharp controversy in the early 1980s among observers over the extent to which the reform and the repression were analytically distinct, clearly they often were inseparable in practice" (quoted in Brockett 1990, p. 155). Diskin (1989) and others (Simon and Stephens 1982; Chapin 1980) believe that many lives were unnecessarily lost because of the military nature of the expropriation process and its aftermath. "The state of siege ensured a free hand for the military and made monitoring the situation difficult" (Diskin 1989, p. 438). ISTA employees were frequently in physical danger. By September 1981, forty members of the agency's staff had been killed. The head of ISTA was slain with two U.S. AIFLD advisors while dining in a San Salvador hotel. Some estimate that 500 peasant leaders were murdered in the first years of the reform.

Not surprisingly, the ensuing reform was criticized by the Left and the Right. Diskin (1989, p. 438) notes that 96 properties were expropriated on two days in early March 1981; 300 were taken by the end of May. Landowners were to be reimbursed with bonds based mainly at a 6 percent rate of interest on the values declared for purposes of 1976 and 1977 property taxes.[8] Strasma (1989) reports that in the haste with which the reform was accomplished, 238 of these farms were found to belong to owners who did not possess more than 500 hectares, a matter that ultimately forced the government to pay market price for the land in order to avoid a successful appeal to the courts by the landowners. As these cases languished, the land was farmed by beneficiary *campesinos*.

In the postreform period these farms were operated as production cooperatives. In a manner similar to the Chilean *asentamiento*), they were farmed as single firms, much as before the reform. The cooperative organization required that work be done in common under the direction of *campesino*-elected officers and a state-provided manager (*co-gestor*), who would have veto power over the cooperative's board of directors (*junta directiva*) on major farm decisions. In 1990, the *co-gestor* was replaced by a *facilitador*, who had less power.

Takeover of the country's largest farms and their conversion into production cooperatives occurred under what came to be known as Phase I of the agrarian reform. Phase II extended the same process as in Phase I to persons holding 100 to 500 hectares, but it was immediately postponed. Diskin noted that "Salvadorans refer to this [size category] as the 'spinal column' of the country's production structure" (1989, p. 436), since it contains 24 percent of all land in farms and 31 percent of all coffee production (though only 17 percent of the country's cropland). Many observers felt that the delay in implementing Phase II was caused by pressure from the coffee oligarchy. Others felt that the decisive death knell came from the United States, which thought El Salvador's ability to earn foreign exchange would be impaired if Phase II went into effect. Still another group concluded that the delay was unavoidable because the administrative ability of the government and the finances available were already overtaxed by the rest of the reform.

The Constitution of 1983 addressed Phase II specifically by raising the lower limit of any future expropriations to 245 hectares, allowing a two-year minimum before any reforms could be carried out, and permitting those in the 245–500-hectare range to sell or otherwise transfer excess farmland. As a result, the farm-size category Phase II was designed to reform virtually disappeared.

Phase III was a land-to-the-tiller law that allowed *campesino* tenants who farmed up to 7 hectares to file for legal title to the plot they rented. The major criticism of Phase III was that it did not touch the estate sector; in El Salvador, there was no tradition of absentee owners renting out their large properties in small parcels to peasants (as in the agrarian reforms of Taiwan and South Korea, a situation that was easily rectified by cutting the ownership bonds to landlords and proclaiming the independence of peasant producers). Moreover, most of the resident farm laborers on large estates had long since been evicted.

Indeed, most small properties in the country were already in the possession of poor people. Sometimes, however, *campesinos* would pay less mobile peasants to watch the property during the dry season, when they would work for wages elsewhere in the country. A small piece of land rented to a *campesino* could also be the security for which an aged teacher or government employee had saved for a lifetime. It was also common for poor, formerly salaried, government workers to buy a plot of land, rent it to a *campesino* for farming, and live on the rent during retirement. Phase III permitted *campesinos* who were actually farming the land to wrest it from the control of whomever was not farming, regardless of the fact that both were poor (Chapin 1980).

In order to apply, claimants—often illiterate *campesinos*—had to prove they actually rented and worked the land and provide a precise description of the property. Phase III was touted as being "self-administering." In fact, it took an act of some courage for *campesinos* to file a claim, for they immediately put themselves at odds with a peer. Sometimes the result was intimidation and eviction of the new owner by the old one, often with assistance of local authorities. One report notes that one-third of the owners of Phase III properties were not farming their land because "they had been threatened, evicted or had disappeared" (Brockett 1990, p. 159).

As in the mid-1980s, when Sandinistas recognized that concentrating land reform on the small farmers in Nicaragua might motivate *campesinos* to repel counterrevolutionary troops, small-farmer satisfaction with Phase III of the Salvadoran agrarian reform was important to the country's civil war, which raged between the government and the FMLN for twelve years until 1992. It was believed that if *campesinos* felt as though they had gained a measure of security through land ownership, they would be inclined to favor the counterrevolution's side; if not, they might support the FMLN. Because Phase III was "private," "individual" (in contrast to Phase I), and basically counterrevolutionary, the Reagan administration became an ardent supporter. The Christian Democrats, on the other hand, thought it was too expensive and agreed to its implementation only if the U.S. government promised generous subvention.

Phase I, in contrast, benefited only those who had worked full-time on the farm prior to reform; it omitted the poorest within the sector—the landless, the land-poor, and the squatter. Phase III was a partial corrective in that it admitted tenants, sharecroppers, and squatters. Nonetheless, the landless, who made up the poorest and fastest-growing segment of rural society, were largely overlooked; they had little possibility of receiving land. As in the case of the Chilean *asentamiento*, this group often found itself with "new landlords," the agrarian-reform beneficiaries, who were less willing than the former landowners to contract workers and even less prone than former large-estate owners to pay a decent wage. These beneficiaries, like those in Chile, were concerned with protecting land rights for their children and opposed admitting the landless as new cooperative members.[9]

A major criticism of Phase I came from landlords who felt that the cooperatives did not use the land as rationally as they had and produced lower yields. Other detractors criticized the cumbersome bureaucracy required to service land recipients with credit and technical assistance, whereas supporters felt that channeling inputs to some 36,000 new land-enfranchised, independent farm families rather than production cooperatives would be too daunting a task.

Another problem of Phase I cooperatives was the presence of free riders. For each day that members worked on the collective enterprise, they would be paid a wage by the institution that loaned the cooperative its production credit. This "wage advance" against future earnings was then subtracted from the cooperative's gross income as an operating cost. Once the farm's profit was calculated after harvest, the members' shares were determined by dividing it by the days they worked (after subtracting for investment needs of the cooperative). Thus the system separated monetary reward from work accomplished and diluted the incentive to work at capacity. Members were tempted to "free ride." Why work hard when the same monetary reward could be obtained by slacking off?[10]

Since no penalty was imposed on cooperatives that failed to repay all of their production credit or honor their land payments, members routinely voted to increase their current welfare. Vacations, wages during off-season, cooperative-paid clinics, on-farm schools, and other benefits were sometimes charged as operating expenses. Thus many, if not most, of the cooperatives operated at a bookkeeping loss in spite of having reasonably good land and yields.

Whereas the Christian Democrat government of José Napoleón Duarte let problems of accountability slide, the ARENA (Alianza Republicana Nacionalista) government of Alfredo Cristiani, which took over in 1989, insisted on stricter standards of cost accounting. In addition, Cristiani's frequently enunciated goal was to make El Salvador a country of individual landholders: *Hacer un país de propietarios.* As a result, policy on Phase I cooperatives shifted to encourage individual farming.

A write-off of all accumulated production credit occurred in mid-1990 to make banks more attractive for privatization and to assist the cooperatives. In 1991, under the terms of Decree No. 747, a concerted effort was made to establish a collection system to process the payments for the cooperative land. After thirteen years of nonpayment, a mortgage payment was expected from most cooperatives in 1993/1994; a few had made payments in 1992/1993. Land prices, set when the land was acquired by the government in the early 1980s, are currently equivalent to a fraction of its going rate due to inflation (even considering that the market was depressed during the war).[11]

Decree No. 747 also provided that, in exchange for lower mortgage payments, cooperatives would be expected to choose their form of land tenure among available "new options": collective, individual, mixed, or redeemable shares.[12] Under the new options the cooperative can choose partially collective operations or complete parcelization among members. For example, the cooperative could elect to continue under a mixed form of tenure (an individually titled plot with part of the collective enterprise remaining). Another option is *participación real,* where members get individually titled small-house plots (*solares*) on which to grow crops of their own while obtaining redeemable shares in the collective enterprise (which should, theoretically at least, allow them some equity payment if they decide to leave the cooperative).[13] To date, members who exit are refunded only the small amount they paid into the social fund of the cooperative emergency needs; their "sweat equity" over the years is not compensated.

As Table 7.1 shows, 85,227 families benefited from the reforms, about 43 percent of them in Phase I and 50 percent in Phase III, with the remainder comprised of voluntary land transfers. Seventy-three percent of the reformed land is occupied by Phase I beneficiaries, 24 percent by Phase III beneficiaries.

The ISTA beneficiaries have a per-member equivalent of about 6 hectares on which to farm whereas the beneficiaries of the Financiera Nacional de Tierras Agrícolas (FINATA, the agency administering the land-reform program for Phase III beneficiaries) average about 1.6 hectares.

Data comparing land use between the reformed and nonreformed sectors are rough because there is no recent agricultural census. However, the Ministry of

TABLE 7.1   Beneficiaries of Land Reform in El Salvador

Beneficiaries/ Hectares Awarded	Phase I[a]	Phase III[b]	Voluntary Transfers[c]	Totals
Families benefited	36,697	42,489	6,041	85,227
All beneficiaries	194,494	259,183	36,850	490,527
Hectares	215,167	69,605	10,922	295,694
Hectares/family	5.86	1.63	1.81	3.47

[a] Includes all beneficiaries of colonization programs prior to 1980 also. These are sometimes referred to as "Decree 842" properties, and Phase I is sometimes referred to as "Decree 154."

[b] These are sometimes referred to as "Decree 207" properties.

[c] These are properties that were offered in voluntary sale beginning in late 1987. The purpose of the decree facilitating voluntary sale to *campesinos*, that is, Decree 839, was to bring about transfers using the land market. Financiera Nacional de Tierras Agrícolas (FINATA), the government agency in charge of Phase III of the agrarian reform, was then in charge of Decree 839 properties. This authority passed to the Land Bank (Banco de Tierras) upon its founding in 1991. The Land Bank has been fully occupied lately by the Peace Treaty land negotiations, so additions to this category have been negligible recently.

Sources: OSPA-MAG, *XI Evaluación del Proceso de la Reforma Agraria* (San Salvador: División de Seguimiento y Evaluación, Ministerio de Agricultura y Ganadería, December 1992), Cuadro 7, p. 12, and Cuadro 107, p. 135; and FINATA, *FINATA: Diagnóstico y su Proyección* (San Salvador: Financiera Nacional de Tierras Agrícolas, March 1993), Cuadro 3-1, p. 8.

Agriculture and Livestock assembled some data showing land use in the nonreformed sector in 1987/1988, which can be compared with land use on the cooperatives in 1987/1988 and land use on the cooperatives in 1991/1992 (Table 7.2). The cooperative sector shows a higher percentage of land planted to crops than the nonreformed sector. When compared with the nonreformed sector, the reformed sector also shows proportionally less land in pasture for livestock raising, several percent more land in forest, and less unused farmland. Taken together, these data seem to indicate more intensive cropping patterns on the cooperatives than in the nonreformed sector.

On the other hand, the tables show that, over the last five years, the percentage of cooperative land that is cropped has decreased while that used for grazing livestock has increased, with no improvement in utilizing unused farmland. Some increase in forestland on cooperatives is evident.[14]

Yields of major crops on cooperatives (Table 7.3) are higher than the national average, with the exception of coffee, which nearly equals the national norm. This is not surprising, given the fact that Phase I cooperatives are believed to include a somewhat disproportionate share of the best land in the country. Earlier

TABLE 7.2 Land Use, Reformed and Unreformed Sector, El Salvador, 1987/1988 and 1991/1992 (in hectares and percentages)

Land Use	Unreformed Sector, 1987/1988		Reformed Sector, 1987/1988		Reformed Sector, 1991/1992		Total Unreformed, 1987/1988, and Reformed, 1991/1992	
Agriculture	424,515	33.1	156,513	57.6	128,602	47.5	553,117	35.6
Livestock	482,363	37.6	46,130	17.0	53,910	19.9	536,273	34.6
Forest	49,413	3.9	25,949	9.6	33,167	12.2	82,580	5.3
Not usable	70,784	5.5	9,219	3.4	14,552	5.4	85,336	5.5
Infrastructure	54,523	4.3	10,160	3.7	16,813	6.2	71,336	4.6
Unused farmland	199,857	15.6	23,548	8.7	23,608	8.8	223,466	14.4
Total	1,281,455	100.0	271,519	100.0	270,653	100.0	1,552,108	100.0

Sources: Aquiles Montoya, *El Agro Salvadoreño antes y después de la Reforma Agraria*, Cuadernos de investigación, año 2 (San Salvador: Dirección de Investigaciones Económicas y Sociales, Centro de Investigaciones Tecnológicas y Científicas, June 1991), Cuadros no. 7 and 8; OSPA-MAG, "Eighth Census of Agrarian Reform Cooperatives" (San Salvador, 1993).

TABLE 7.3 Yields of Several Major Crops, El Salvador, 1989–1993 (in hectares)

Major Crops	1990/1991 Cooperative Census	1991/1992 Cooperative Census	1991/1992 National Average	1993 Survey
Coffee (quintals/hectare)	18.0	17.4	17.9	25.5
Cane (tons/hectare)	101.2	124.0	72.0	90.0
Hybrid corn (quintals/hectare)	60.7	58.5	39.5	73.0
Rice (quintals/hectare)	76.9	69.3	56.7	94.0

Sources: OSPA-MAG, *XI Evaluación del Proceso de la Reforma Agraria* (San Salvador: División de Seguimiento y Evaluación, Ministerio de Agricultura y Ganadería, December 1992), pp. 39 and 46; OSPA-MAG, "Eighth Census of Agrarian Reform Cooperatives" (San Salvador, 1993); Mitchell A. Seligson, William Thiesenhusen, and Malcolm Childress, "Land Tenure in El Salvador: An Overview and Summary Policy Recommendations," Paper prepared for USAID/San Salvador (Madison, Wisc., 1 September 1993).

reports (Strasma 1989) note that the coffee yield is also higher on cooperative land.

This is not to say, however, that cooperatives use the resources at their disposal in a satisfactory manner. Given the pressing food and the foreign exchange needs of a country as tiny and as densely populated as El Salvador, land appropriate for farming must be worked in a consistent and sustainable fashion. Lack of irrigation on cooperatives in the dry season is just one concern. Though most cooperatives grow some annual crops during the rainy season (*invierno*), most land lies idle during the dry months (*verano*). Of all land on cooperatives, perhaps 18 percent is irrigated (Table 7.4). Few take advantage of irrigation potential and land actually irrigated dropped from 31 percent of the potential in 1990/1991 to 27 percent in 1991/1992. Irrigation systems may be expensive to install (albeit Table 7.4 shows that some land with installed capacity is not being irrigated), but a modern irrigation capability would enable some farms to diversify and intensify their enterprise patterns and, among other possibilities, grow vegetables.

Another suboptimal use of land is natural pasture that grazes only a few head of livestock per 100 hectares. In the judgment of many local technicians, farmland could be used more intensively than it is to remove production pressures from marginal lands that should be allowed to return to natural vegetation. Even without including the war-abandoned ISTA cooperatives, the far western and especially the eastern departments of the country contain a great deal of natural

TABLE 7.4   Farmland Area That Is Irrigable and Irrigated on ISTA Cooperatives, 1990/1991 and 1991/1992 (in hectares)

Distribution	*1990/1991*	*1991/1992*
Potential farmland	144,816	144,284
Irrigable farmland	25,617	25,890
Farmland with installed irriga- tion infrastructure	11,110	11,127
Farmland presently irrigated	7,877	6,929
% of farmland that is irrigable	18%	18%
% of irrigable farmland that is irrigated	31%	27%

Sources: OSPA-MAG, *XI Evaluación del Proceso de la Reforma Agraria* (San Salvador: División de Seguimiento y Evaluación, Ministerio de Agricultura y Ganadería, December 1992); and OSPA-MAG, "Eighth Census of Agrarian Reform Cooperatives" (San Salvador, 1993).

pasture. A recent FAO estimate sets the nationwide figure of unused farmland at 32 percent.[15] Reasons given for this large estimate range from the general unprofitability of farming (cotton prices have dropped precipitously on the world market) to the fact that much land became highly indebted as producers defaulted on production during the war (meaning they cannot obtain production credit today).

PEACE AND LAND REFORM

After many false starts and a number of failed coalitions, a U.N.-mediated peace decree was finally signed on 16 January 1992 and a cease-fire instituted on 1 February 1992. The date on which the FMLN had promised to lay down its arms (later reset to 15 December 1992) proved to be the end of the civil war. Soon thereafter, at least some military officers guilty of atrocities were cashiered. More than 75,000 people died in the dozen years of fighting between the FMLN and the government. According to the peace treaty, half of the 56,000-strong Salvadoran army—the institution that the U.S. government believed it could build and professionalize from an original force of 16,000—was to disband by November 1993, when a new police force controlled by a civilian minister would be appointed. The peace treaty promised elections, to be supervised by the United Nations and other international bodies, in 1994. Judicial reform, too, was part of the peace pact.

The peace in El Salvador, however, is fragile. The president of ISTA is quoted as saying, "Regrettably, the entire [peace] treaty rests on the land issue." At the same time, FMLN leader and peace-commission member Joaquín Villalobos told reporters that the "stability of the nation lies fundamentally in the countryside. If landowners adopt a policy of trying to recuperate their landholdings, it will bring conflict.... If they don't understand that then we have accomplished nothing" (Scott 1992b).

The peace accords stipulate that *tenedores* and former combatants receive land grants, to come from voluntary sales by private owners and cooperatives that have an unfilled membership capacity. Owners of land in former conflict zones can sell their farms to the Land Bank or be relocated to available properties nearby. The Land Bank, which began operations in November 1991 with $3.75 million in U.S. aid, acts as broker and financier for these transactions. When landowners list their properties for sale at the bank, *campesinos* and former soldiers from either side of the conflict are given first preference. The bank offers low down payments and twenty-year terms at market rates of interest.

In conflict zones, many of the original cooperative members left during the heat of battle, some returning after the war. But some *tenedores* took their place (in some cases, of course, the *tenedores* are the remnants of the original cooperative group). The FMLN troops, especially, relied on *tenedores* to feed and shelter them during combat and insisted that they be given land after the war.

The membership capacity of the abandoned cooperatives is negotiated by FMLN, ISTA, and the United Nations. When the capacity is filled, soldiers and *tenedores* will share these farms, but one recent study notes the slowness with which former FMLN members were showing up to be "verified" for land assignment (Joya de Mena et al. 1993). In fact, the European Union (EU) is having somewhat better luck in filling their quotas, apparently because it is granting a small house allowance that will make it possible for former combatants to buy construction materials (the *tenedores* have some crude dwellings, but there are often none for the former combatants). Furthermore, the EU (which is settling 1,500 FMLN and 1,500 Salvadoran armed forces in Usulután) offers somewhat more technical assistance and credit. In addition to lack of housing and technical services, there are other reasons for failure to fill the quotas: (1) many former combatants and *tenedores* do not wish to move from their home communities; (2) former soldiers are not good candidates for farmers (the war was so protracted that many young people learned no other life than the military);[16] (3) many *tenedores* do not welcome groups of strangers to share "their" resources and wish to retain them for their own children (in some cases present *tenedores* have made life difficult for newcomers); (4) logistical difficulties, caused by the fact that each of the five FMLN factions—as well, of course, as the former government combatants—demand to be settled on different properties; and (5) former combatants can opt for government-financed schooling or funding for a small business instead of receiving land. Another possible reason is that the *tenedor* group has defaulted on contracted debts for production credit; these past-due accounts, most feel, will have to be paid by the cooperative as a whole when it is reconstituted.

Meanwhile, peace is bringing a boom in land prices despite low coffee prices. Farmland value overall is estimated to have increased 20 percent in 1993. These higher values in turn limit the number of loans that the relatively undercapitalized Land Bank can finance.

Conflicts between landlords and *campesinos* have kept some owners away from their land for a number of years. Talks are now under way to return landlords safely to their communities, though little progress has been made to date. Some workers will even welcome the return of the old landlords (or, at least the capital they bring with them), provided they are allowed to keep the patch of land they are currently operating and provided that the old landlord invests his capital in agriculture—and creates jobs.

8

Lost Promise: Agrarian Reform and the Latin American *Campesino*

Much of the rural poverty in Latin America originates from inequitable distribution of farmland, which leaves peasants either landless or land-poor. Meanwhile, large landholders throughout Latin America allow substantial portions of their farms to lie idle for much of the year or grow pasture for livestock, one of the most land-extensive agricultural endeavors. Agrarian reforms were expected to help to remedy this inequity with salubrious production results realized by matching, for purposes of employment, landless or land-poor rural people and underutilized land.

Even though the agrarian reforms in Latin America have reached no more than a quarter of those engaged in agriculture in any one country, one imagines that even this level of activity would make income and resource distribution more egalitarian. However, an equitable agrarian structure has not resulted.[1] Although agrarian reform agitated the system and gave clear signals to landlords that their properties—or parts of them—would be expropriated if they did not use land wisely, land ownership in much of the region today remains polarized and unequal. This enduring dualism bespeaks the enormity of the task. It also suggests that reform gave with one hand what it took with the other: reform policies often turned the terms of trade against the new peasant, thereby reclaiming new income, or precipitated inflation. Furthermore, some governments lowered domestic prices of peasant-produced products by increasing imports. Reforms also did not provide beneficiaries with the inputs—credit, technical assistance, fertilizer, improved seeds, and education—they needed to increase their agricultural earnings. Moreover, most agrarian reforms distributed poorer-than-average land to richer-than-average *campesinos*.

However, documenting these suboptimal results should not detract from the fact that reforms did generate secure employment opportunities for some or minimize the difficult political struggle and commitment of idealists willing to make sacrifices to bring it about. Grindle's discussion, however, demonstrated how the constellation of factors set in place in Mexico during the Cárdenas period dissipated:

> The agrarian reform of the 1930s was possible because of committed political leadership, an organized and mobilized peasantry, and a weakened sector of large landowners. By the 1970s and 1980s, political leaders had become uninterested in agrarian reform, the peasantry had become largely co-opted and controlled by the dominant political party, and large landowners had become powerful politically and economically through the successful development of commercial agriculture (1988, pp. 62–63).

Improvements in income equity that resulted from the bulk of the Mexican reforms were eventually reversed: The more equitable distribution of the 1930s eroded in the 1940s as public investment flowed to import-substituting industrialization and capital formation within agriculture increasingly favored the nonreformed sector, going to irrigation facilities, land reclamation, and roads mainly serving commercial farms. By the 1950s, domestic terms of trade in Mexico started to veer away from agriculture and inequalities in the size distribution of farm income returned with a vengeance. Although public rhetoric in Mexico continued its focus on the potential ability of agrarian reform to improve income distribution, maldistribution today is almost as severe as when the reforms were implemented.

Land reforms that took place during the 1960s, 1970s, and 1980s in Latin America demonstrate built-in inequities. Many reforms that occurred after the Bolivian Revolution in 1952 were only as large as they had to be to contain peasant unrest and, as de Janvry (1981) correctly argues, to create stability for purposes of investment. Some of the reforms did propel some rural upper-poor to the middle-class level (an explicit aim at least of Christian Democrats, President Frei in Chile and President Duarte in El Salvador). But as some beneficiaries progressed, others fell once again into poverty as farms were divided with the new generation and needed inputs remained unavailable.

Unforeseen in the planning stages, the lower subclass of rural poor, the nonbeneficiaries, were no better off then before; some of the hard-core rural poor, in fact, even lost ground. In Chile, for example, the government was startlingly unsuccessful in convincing beneficiaries on *asentamientos* (largely former resident farmworkers) to augment their memberships with landless laborers who lived nearby. Strasma (1990) comments that under El Salvador's Phase I production cooperatives could take on about 10,000 more families but that there was resistance to doing so from within the reformed farms. In addition, members of production cooperatives were frequently less-willing employers than the landlords who preceded them and sometimes paid even lower wages. In Chile, the nonreformed sector began to pay higher wages than before to rural labor, apparently reflecting both worker scarcity and a desire to comply with social legislation (and thus avoid expropriation). Moreover, beneficiaries on the cooperatives were just as willing as the old landlord class to substitute capital for labor whenever means would allow. In agrarian reforms that accommodated beneficiaries on individual plots, more *campesinos* were employed per land unit than under the traditional hacienda systems. Such an affirmation cannot be confidently made with reference to the production cooperatives of Chile, El Salvador, Nicaragua, and Peru, however. An inability to incorporate the poorest of the poor, a large and desperate class in Latin America, is one legacy of agrarian reform in the region.

RECENT POLICIES

Notwithstanding these problems, in countries that have implemented substantial reforms distribution is marginally better (or for a time it was) than it would have been with no reform. The poorest resource-and-income distributions exist in Brazil and Paraguay, two countries with the smallest agrarian reforms (Thiesenhusen and Melmed 1990).

It seems to many that the time has now passed for most Latin American countries to address the bulk of the rural poverty problem with agrarian reform; there is a decline of farming as countries industrialize. Since farming now accounts for a much smaller percentage of GDP than it did earlier in the century, targeted policies to diminish poverty must also be sought through employment generation in other sectors of the economy, combined with income transfers, intensification of farming, and education.

In the present climate of neoliberalism, some believe that the primary issue is not whether new agrarian reforms will occur in the region but how fast the current ones will unravel. Countries like Mexico have relaxed poorly administered proscriptions on renting, alienating, and mortgaging reform-sector land; thus displacement of a large number of beneficiaries in the near future is more probable than ever before. *Campesinos* could lose property in a variety of ways: beneficiaries may be physically displaced; they may become wage workers or sharecroppers on what was previously their own land; and they may be forced into idleness and live on rental payments from the more affluent who farm their property. In most of the developed countries (in Europe and North America, especially), small farmers are still romanticized and their stature as custodians of democratic and individualistic values is recognized. They are regarded as essential contributors to the vitality of their communities, as innovators, as producers of inexpensive food, and as the grassroots of the present urban middle class—and thus have been protected by subsidies and other government programs. Latin American countries do not lionize their small farmers or reform beneficiaries in this exaggerated manner.

The current neoliberal policies—for example, freer commodity markets—usually treat agriculture favorably, making exchange rates advantageous for exports and reducing or eliminating food subsidies for urban consumers. But the few countries that support farm prices will also see them retract. One can only speculate what the combination of unfettered trade and free land markets will mean to land-reform beneficiaries and the rural poor over the next decade or so.

MINIMALIST REFORMS

Some of the Latin American agrarian reforms were limited efforts aimed at a combination of (1) obtaining foreign funding; (2) using repression to hold revolting, protesting, or complaining *campesinos* at bay; and (3) satisfying students, clergy, and other socially conscious dissidents that government was indeed enacting policies to assuage rural economic distress. In countries like Chile, El Salvador, and Nicaragua, insignificant reforms were preludes to more ambitious programs. But in Venezuela, Colombia, Brazil, and Paraguay, minimalist reforms were ends in themselves and did not lead to more fundamental alterations of agrarian structure. Governments usually attempted to overstate their tiny reforms by giving them inordinate publicity and downplaying repression when it occurred (as in El Salvador during the 1960s and 1970s and in the Somozas' Nicaragua). Agrarian reform as social control, co-optation of vocal *campesinos* and their leaders, and counterinsurgency has played an uncelebrated but very real part in the recent history of many Latin American countries.

MAJOR REFORMS

Although not devoid of the more pernicious elements of social control, some substantial land reforms in Latin America engendered important social and economic consequences. Those analyzed here fall into several categories: (1) reforms that opened new development paths for agriculture and are today considered potential candidates for radical change; (2) failed reforms that were enacted by one government to mitigate the social ills of the peasantry only to be rolled back by a subsequent administration; and (3) incomplete reforms (of the 1980s) that were born of sharp rural social inequities but were stifled late in civil wars.

Mexico and Bolivia are grouped fairly unambiguously in the first category; Guatemala falls into the second, with Chile bearing some characteristics of both the first and the second classification; El Salvador and Nicaragua make up the third class, though the former's agrarian reform was established by fiat from above whereas the latter's was made operational at the grassroots as a direct result of revolution.

Mexico and Bolivia

In both Mexico and Bolivia, agrarian reforms pacified large numbers of formerly rebellious peasants who lived in an institutional environment rife with carryover elements of servile feudal agriculture. In each instance, reforms made it possible for government to embark upon developing commercial agriculture without concerning itself with issues of rural poverty. In Mexico, modernized farming emerged to a certain degree over the entire country and was often interspersed with *campesino* cultivation and indigenous communities. It was especially prominent in the north on land that became irrigated after the Lázaro Cárdenas administration and on large farms that were exempt from reform or unclaimed by *campesinos*. In Bolivia, once peasants on the altiplano were "stabilized" with agrarian reform, the country's policies focused on clearing farmland in the *Oriente* with the promise of providing export earnings from livestock and tropical and subtropical crops—and securing these lowlands from foreign incursion.

In both countries, agricultural modernization commanded in the commercializing private sector. In Bolivia, lowland agrarian change was in the charge of a new commercial elite that came to challenge the oligarchy in the highlands. Although agricultural production in the Bolivian postreform era grew at a sluggish rate, whatever dynamism existed emanated from these new *Oriente* farms. In Mexico, although the commercial sector took swift advantage of the inputs of the green revolution, its real growth spurt came after agrarian reform and before new high-yielding varieties became available. During the 1950s and 1960s, mechanization, fertilizers, and irrigation were being used on modernized Mexican farms, which flourished despite an increasing macroeconomic policy emphasis on import-substituting industrialization. In a bid to maintain income after some of its land was expropriated, the Mexican landed class responded by increasing productivity on property it still controlled (and also on land the reform could not legally touch), causing rapid agricultural growth from 1934 to 1965. (Progress since 1965 has been much more erratic.) In Bolivia, the old landed class in the highlands also attempted income-maintenance strategies but relatively fewer landowners kept reserves. Rather, Bolivian landlords were more apt to become merchants, purchasing commodities produced by reform beneficiaries in the monopsonistic market open to them because of close personal relations. The de facto result was similar in both countries: former landlords or their children played an important postreform role by becoming more entrepreneurial as the modernizing farm sector became more commercial.

In both Mexico and Bolivia, agrarian reforms were delayed after revolutions. In time, however, *campesinos* and their representatives made it clear they would not permit land reform to be slighted in the new government policy agenda. In both cases *campesinos* were eventually seen as valuable political allies to the government; granting excess land in exchange for votes was an inexpensive proposition for the party in power. Once enfranchised, peasants in both countries could not be bypassed as political actors; the landlord class, substantially weakened through some combination of war, depression, and countervailing power of organized peasants, no longer held complete sway over the *campesino* vote.

Once land was apportioned, however, *campesino* beneficiaries in both Mexico and Bolivia were largely forgotten by public policy. *Campesino* unity was weakened by the success in fighting for and obtaining the land it demanded; organization was co-opted by the now prevailing political parties. So, in the postreform period, beneficiaries were not offered much help with credit, technical assistance, and titling. Once governments had used land to stabilize rural dissidents, they redirected their attention to commercial agriculture and to nonfarm economic growth. The focused political power of the *campesinos* had been spent on the land acquisition itself; none was left to pressure for needed inputs.

Moreover, nonfarm domestic jobs for farm youth failed to materialize after the reforms, so a large number of sons and daughters of beneficiaries (and their families) had to be satisfied with the original reform parcels (though many left farming in both Mexico and Bolivia). What were once family farms were divided among the younger generations, again dissipating the political and economic power of beneficiary peasants. In Mexico, beneficiary-family *campesinos* often became part-time wage laborers for nearby commercial farms or seasonal migrants to the United States; in Bolivia, peasants who settled on the colonization schemes in the *Oriente* provided commercial farmers with a handy source of seasonal labor.

Chile and Guatemala

Chile's reform failed as miserably as that of Guatemala from the *campesino* point of view. Both were overwhelmed by conservative pressure and, in the Chilean case, by inflation during Salvador Allende's populist economic policies (which fueled the backlash). Similarities stop there. Guatemala has remained a low-growth backwater for much of recent history, hobbled by (1) large landowners who proclaimed agrarian reform to be part of a communist plot that would visit dire repercussions on production; (2) unrest generated by dissatisfied peasants combined with a military and paramilitary establishment that severely repressed *campesinos*; and (3) civil war that has bubbled just below the surface for the better part of three decades.

Unlike Guatemala, where agrarian reforms were quickly established and swiftly turned back in counterrevolution to the status quo ante, postreform Chile did not repeat its past. The reform was reversed in a series of steps from the mid- to late 1970s, after Chile had coped with reforms through the 1960s to 1973. Then, after a decade-long recovery from the early rule of military government, a new kind of agriculture made an appearance and made astounding progress in the 1980s. This economic vigor occurred mainly on reserves and on hacienda subdivisions created by landlords to evade expropriation; it typically did not occur on agrarian-reform land except where that property had come into the hands of the new, capitalized, entrepreneurial middle class and elite as reform unraveled.

Although privatization of group farms in Chile was virtually synonymous with the military coup against President Salvador Allende, the reform's reversal in fact had three stages. First, the military government decided that land undergoing expropriation at the time of the 1973 coup would be returned to the original owner. Second, the already established *asentamientos* were physically divided and given to perhaps half of the original assignees on the basis of a point system.[2] Third, a wave of beneficiary failures affected some *campesinos* who entered into possession of individual parcels with financial obligations from the past; they were required to pay the pro-rated debts of the old group farm as well as a mortgage.

Most attention today is focused on the metamorphosis in Chilean agriculture, the emergence of fruit-exporting farms and forestry enterprises (which are capital-intensive and directed by a more vital entrepreneurial class than the large, traditional, temperate-climate, cereal and livestock *fundos* that had dominated the country before the Frei and Allende reforms). As in Mexico and Bolivia, Chile's agrarian reform cleared away institutional debris (for example, noblesse oblige, resident farm labor, in-kind payments, and excessive paternalism) and opened the country to more profitable farming opportunities. Even after agrarian reform abruptly ended in 1973, average farm size, it appears, continued to fall as owners sold land to obtain the capital needed for producing horticultural exports. In an important sense, the Chilean reforms, together with the new and visionary enterprise package of nontraditional exports as well as pragmatic neoliberalism, opened the country to profitable, export-led growth.

Meanwhile, the *campesino* class, some of which included dispossessed former beneficiaries, became employed in wage work. When there was fruit to be picked, employment was at a high level; but harvesting proceeded from the north, where crops ripened early, and crossed many latitudes to the colder south, resulting in a migratory existence and a seasonal work pattern. Whether farm labor in Chile has benefited from Chile's novel (for Latin America) agricultural growth path is still a matter for speculation. Recent commentators remark upon the problematic nature of *campesino* participation in Chile's agricultural growth and the high rate of rural poverty (a product of "exclusionary growth") that still characterizes the farm sector (Carter and Mesbah 1992; Carter et al. 1993).

Nicaragua and El Salvador

The third category encompasses land reforms in the agro-exporting Central American countries—El Salvador and Nicaragua. In El Salvador, agrarian reform was organized in a top-down fashion, resulting (initially) from a pact between the Christian Democratic party and the military. In Nicaragua, the reforms resulted from the relatively brief but very bloody Sandinista revolution and a grassroots, *campesino* empowerment that was heavily government-directed in the 1980s. Both countries found it imperative to strike a balance between instituting distributive reforms and nurturing the agricultural private sector, which earned the majority of foreign exchange and was the lifeblood of the economy (Reinhardt 1989). Of course, foreign exchange was not as scarce in El Salvador, favored as it was (unlike Nicaragua) with American foreign aid. In both countries—Phase III in El Salvador, post-1983 in Nicaragua—individual farms were favored over state farms and production cooperatives during wartime (agrarian reform performed the feat of winning peasant advocates for the government). Today, both countries are left with the great challenge of finding employment, in agriculture or elsewhere, for former combatants and others committed to the struggle who produced food for one side or the other. Again, that task is currently easier in El Salvador because the United States is providing more economic assistance; there are also many more Salvadoran than Nicaraguan expatriates working in North America and returning foreign exchange to their Central American families. Both countries now struggle with sorting out who owns what land after more than a decade of dislocation. Both have problems covering defaults on mortgage and production credit, indemnifying landlords, and paying for inputs and services to beneficiaries, to say nothing of reconstructing social overhead capital (schools and clinics) for rural people.

GRASSROOTS DEMANDS

The various elements of agrarian reform are sometimes best discussed as points along a scale rather than by typology, as above. In that instance, El Salvador and Guatemala would rank equally as countries following the most centralized forms of execution (or the least amount of grassroots control); Nicaragua would probably stand by itself among reforms with the "most grassroots initiative," followed in no special order by Mexico, Bolivia, and Chile. Which reform was most influenced by a charismatic leader? In this case, Zapata and Mexico fall at one end of the spectrum and Guatemala at the other, with the martyred Martí in El Salvador and Sandino in Nicaragua somewhere between. Since so many reform characteristics lie along a range—and are not part of a single typology— other reform issues are covered below in thematic fashion.

Although important to the peasants' middle-class mentors, ideology did not seem to inspire the *campesinos* to revolt and demand the reforms discussed here. Although foreign powers that struggled for a toehold in the region often argued their case in terms of Marxism or anti-Marxism (as did some national and local leaders), *campesinos* fought for the fulfillment of basic needs and a place in modern life.

Until the mid-twentieth century, it was relatively easy for landowners to isolate peasants, thereby prohibiting them from organizing and keeping them illiterate and ignorant of the world to ensure their compliance. In the Mexican and Bolivian agrarian reforms, leaders and organizations had to spread the word about reforms and obtain cooperation from *campesinos*. That situation changed as mass media blossomed, making it possible—even easy—to disseminate ideas to those who could not read. The information transformation occurred rapidly as transistor radios quickly spread to remote parts of the region. Television, because of its expensive receivers, took a somewhat longer period of time to become generally available (though by the 1960s *campesinos* went to nearby towns to view it). Films showed in small towns as well as large cities.

Soon there arrived sophisticated political organizations that courted peasants, who made up large voting blocs in most countries after illiterate *campesinos* received franchise (due to the insistence of the United Nations and human rights groups). Promises of land reform were bandied about in most every campaign. Politicians perceived as successful in bringing agrarian reform to the countryside were revered and even idolized by *campesinos*. In the 1960s, the portrait of John F. Kennedy, often torn from a local newspaper, hung in the homes of many Latin American *campesinos*, perhaps together with that of Fidel Castro, Eduardo Frei, Salvador Allende, Farabundo Martí, or Augusto Sandino. These and other charismatic leaders, such as Mexico's Zapata and Bolivia's Rojas, modeled local leadership; accordingly, many rural communities boasted a spellbinding *campesino* orator who easily held forth on potential improvements to peasant existence that could be wrought by *reforma agraria*.[3] Sometimes, of course, *campesinos* and local leaders who gained power could be as tyrannical as the patrons they replaced, as witnessed by the *caciques* in Mexico and the *sindicato* heads in Bolivia—"landlords with bad table manners," as anthropologist Dwight Heath (1970) called them. Local *campesino* leadership was essential, but it was hardly an automatic guarantee of sudden, egalitarian, and beneficent grassroots democracy.

As the last half of the twentieth century wore on, it became more difficult for landowners and governments to stifle *campesino* association (though as late as the early 1960s union organization was confined in Chile to single farms; some anti-union provisions in Central America were even more strict). Prohibiting rights of assembly proved very difficult; increasingly, organized peasants used meetings to articulate specific grievances regarding land. Lately, wide varieties of nongovernmental organizations have become active, articulate, and often effective on behalf of *campesino* causes (see Bebbington et al. 1993). Middle-class advocates were useful and possibly even necessary to the reforms. They helped *campesinos* organize; indeed, the history of *campesino* progress in Latin America is peppered with assistance from young priests, university students, landlords' sons, local schoolteachers, and youthful *militares*. Some of these, like Archbishop Oscar Romero, Sandino, and Martí, are as eloquent and vital today in legend as they were in life. They lent their names to agrarian-reform institutions and cooperatives, union movements, guerrilla organizations, and even political parties.

Better roads and more reliable bus and truck transportation helped forge the communications network for protesting *campesinos*; large numbers of young people migrated to cities in search of a new life for themselves, experiencing more cosmopolitanism than they ever imagined possible—while often remaining poor. Although few returned permanently to their origins, they continued to visit their farm roots, bringing exaggerated stories of city life unthinkable to those whose urban experience consisted of a trip to the local crossroads town once a year. Widespread literacy and better health care, both of which grew faster than incomes during the 1970s, gave peasants the interest and strength to receive the new ideas. With similar results, some *campesinos* also migrated regularly to and from the United States.[4]

Their isolation broken, the only question was how the awakening generations would assimilate modern ideas. Many *campesinos* chose migration and physical escape from the backwardness and anachronisms of the countryside. Others remained in rural areas to make a better life for themselves. Although the former group performed manual work in cities because lack of education precluded other opportunities, the latter group, as documented here, did not have an easy task either, blocked as it was by ever-more organized landowners, repression, military, plainclothesmen, quasi-intelligence movements, and discriminatory government policies.

Thus the most powerful contemporary force for positive rural change and agrarian reform was the demonstration effect afforded by the vision—emanating from the mass media, interpersonal communication, education, and streamlined organization—that the future could be better than the past. Peasants were driven to rebellion, it appears, when marginal progress was followed by sharp declines in fortunes and renewed bouts with poverty or when they perceived that other classes were enjoying more rapid economic growth. The decade of the 1970s was a time of modest social advancement in education and health. In the 1990s, however, their neglect (during the debt crisis of the 1980s) is acutely felt. How long it will take to rebuild this social infrastructure doubtless depends on how vocal and insistent the peasants become in articulating their needs, how the advantages and disadvantages of neoliberalism affect the rural poor in any one country, and the extent to which politicians take up the *campesinos'* cause in exchange for votes.

Today, this increasing peasant awareness, developed over the last several decades, provides the background for reform's modest accomplishments and bleak failures.

CONFLICT RESOLUTION

The forming of land-reform coalitions is a consistent theme throughout the reform debates. Thus it is logical to ask: What is the nature of conflict resolution in communities in which landowners and *campesinos* confront each other? Inter alia, Paige (1975) addresses two major classes, "small proprietors" and "wage workers." However, this simplistic categorization does not adequately capture the Latin American situation, where there are resident farmworkers, migratory rural wage workers, *minifundistas*, urban-based rural wage workers, sharecroppers, squatters, and so on. More serious, some agrarian subclasses perform several quite different seasonal roles, operating as wage workers during part of the year and as small farm operators (*minifundistas*) at another time. Together they make up the "semiproletarians" of Kautsky (1976) and de Janvry (1981), ready to perform the labor of capitalism on a part-time basis, supported when there is no wage work by plots too small to produce year-round family sustenance. There is also the issue of locationally specific land tenure, typified by the Guatemalan peasant, who is a *minifundista* at home in the highlands and a wage worker when picking cotton on the southern coast, and the migratory worker in Chile, who may have a *minifundio* but follows the southward-advancing harvest. In some countries, "following the harvest" has an international dimension—Salvadoran peasants pick coffee in Nicaragua and Mexicans harvest produce in the United States. In some places (like Chile), open worker migration is discouraged by nontransient laborers who live in rural slums while awaiting the harvest and are not anxious to see competition.

Distance from home base may influence how the semiproletarian behaves in conflict situations, but here we have only questions. Are wage-earning rural workers more radical or more passive in fighting for their rights when far from home? Can and do landowners take advantage of the transient nature of wage labor, which requires the frequent absence of the breadwinner, to dissipate demands for land the semiproletarian might make? The problem for typologies based largely on land-tenure categories such as Paige's (1975) is how to determine which set of allegiances defines the underlying loyalties and divines the actions of the split-location or split-job *campesino*. Are semiproletarians conservative, aiming to preserve only small pieces of land? Or do they demand more land *and* better working conditions and wages (or both at different times), and does a divided appeal dilute the overall pressure they exert on the existing institutional structure? Evidence seems at least to imply that the two situations effectively cancel each other out as semiproletarians try to preserve the plot in current possession. In the region to date, the class of semiproletarians—to which increasing numbers of land-reform beneficiaries have been added over decades as parcels are divided—has not played much of a political role in enunciating clear demands for change. Perhaps the increase in semiproletarians is the reason why many of the rural poor in Latin America did not articulate grievances in a way that engendered much change during part of the 1980s and early 1990s (with, of course, a few obvious exceptions). De Janvry and Sadoulet also noted this situation: "Surprisingly, the poor have retreated to the household instead of voicing political demands" (1992, p. 5); at best, they speculate, the "new poor" may judge their economic shortcoming as individual rather than systemic or institutional failure.

The primary impact of agrarian conflict and its resolution in Latin America in the 1960s and 1970s fell on neither the wage worker nor the landed peasant but on a meld of the two: the resident farmworker on estates, a *campesino* who was offered year-round employment and given a plot to farm on the hacienda, a small cash wage, and sometimes payments in-kind. This corvée laborer has, for all intents and purposes, disappeared from the Latin American landscape of the 1990s: Some *campesinos* were defined out of the category as they benefited from agrarian reform. Most, however, were driven off farms by increased commercialization of agriculture and rising prices for land (land became too valuable for landowners not to cultivate themselves, and day labor could be hired cheaply). In the 1960s, land reform occurred more often on properties on which there were substantial numbers of resident farm laborers, an easily organized pressure group. Landlords were correct in anticipating that occurrence; consequently, they evicted *colonos* and *inquilinos*—many of whom had lived there for generations—in their determination to protect their farms from reform, using any pretext that might carry legal validity. Mechanization of farming and the few efforts at instituting a minimum wage sealed the fate of the resident farmworker characteristic of haciendas in mid-century. Labor needs were thus converted into highly seasonal patterns (for example, with cotton planting mechanized, manual labor was required only for weeding and harvesting).

Paige (1975) also sets up the case of landlords in conflict with *minifundistas*. He notes that, since both are intransigent actors, no progress toward conflict resolution that favors peasants is possible unless peasants are well organized and landowners are weakened (as during the depression of the 1930s when the Cárdenas reforms took place in Mexico, for example). The usual case pitted strong landowners against unorganized peasants (as in Mexico prior to the revolution, when owners sometimes moved fences to include land of indigenous peoples), forcing them into wage labor. Such quiet landlord victories were an enduring feature of Latin American history in the 1800s after "liberal" laws made church ownership of land illegal (as was, by implication, any communal ownership of property). Today's critics of privatization of land reforms in Latin America sometimes worriedly point to this era, fearing a repeat of its disastrous effects on the rural poor.

But past conflicts sometimes predetermine circumstances that will inevitably lead to future conflicts. The Latin American "liberal" reform case set the stage for the later conflicts that occurred after Zapata had organized groups of small, individual proprietors-cum-wage-laborers to countervail landlords. These transformations occur over a long period. In El Salvador, the *matanza* of the 1930s took place, as an increasingly organized landed class reacted to peasant uprising, in a particularly brutal fashion. In time the legacy of that conflict evolved into a test of wills between capital-intensive landlords and increasingly organized peasants dominated by wage laborers; the long guerrilla war of the

1980s was the ultimate result. The rural movements in Nicaragua proceeded along a similar trajectory, beginning with a strong, brutal reaction by the oligarchy in the 1930s, followed by a lengthy dictatorship that led to the revolution and counterrevolution of the late 1970s and 1980s. The typical Latin American case was no reform or little reform, the reason being that, as the peasants organized, planters changed also, evolving from landed aristocrats to capital-intensive, large-scale farmers.

Because steps to modernize and commercialize agriculture usually preceded reforms, de Janvry and Sadoulet concluded that these Latin American countries lost their opportunity

> to create net social gains via redistributive land reform because they chose to first modernize medium and large farms, using expropriation as a threat instead of proceeding with outright expropriation and redistribution. This threat ... led to defensive strategies on the part of landlords. These included excess modernization, manipulating the state into making the promise of nonexpropriation-if-modernization credible, and effective rent seeking [such as favorable exchange rates, better access to credit, and so forth], that made subsequent redistributive land reforms socially uneconomical (1989b, p. 1398).

Transformed medium- and large-scale commercial farmers took on additional political strength as they became economically stronger (de Janvry and Sadoulet 1989b, p. 1398). If redistribution was really to have been a serious goal of Latin American reforms, de Janvry and Sadoulet (1989b, p. 1398) believe that it should have taken place before commercial agriculture acquired such political strength and obtained so many governmental concessions. Instead, the good that reform contributed was to commercialize farming, breaking the fetters that held archaic institutions in place.

LAND REFORM MULTIFOCUSES

Because land-tenure patterns in Latin America reflect and are reflected by regional social systems, agrarian reforms that imply social change have been difficult and costly undertakings in which organized and politicized *campesinos* confront organized and modernizing landlords.

Those who expected to find easy solutions to rural poverty in Latin America and see measurable progress toward poverty alleviation must surely be disappointed by agrarian-reform programs throughout the twentieth century. Although agrarian reforms carry the potential to ameliorate poverty, that relief has not been forthcoming. Farm production ultimately increased in countries where gains can be measured, but any gain is largely attributable to modernization in the nonreform sector. Governments that have focused on the *campesino*'s need for land and enacted reformist policies have often strayed from their course, buffeted by more politically compelling imperatives.

Indeed, a great difficulty is that reform is expected to address so many problems at once: add to production, give jobs to *campesinos*, bring about equitable distribution of resources and income, and add to effective demand for nonfarm goods. Helping conserve the environment has recently been added to this list. But these are only the explicit goals of agrarian reforms, the ones found only in the rhetoric of politicians. At one time or another in Latin America, land reforms were meant to serve more opaque and less frequently articulated ends: strengthen capitalism, neutralize *campesinos* as an opposition political force, win votes, fend off extremist ideologies, provide an effective counterinsurgency tool, and foster social stability needed for a secure investment environment.

Any policy expected to accomplish so much will naturally be seen as falling short or failing when progress toward any single goal is examined. In fact, measuring progress toward any one target in an objective fashion is difficult. It is not especially hard to survey agricultural production on a piece of land before and after it has been "reformed." But attributing general successes in agriculture to agrarian reforms is more difficult. In Mexico, for example, was the progress in agriculture during the 1950s and early 1960s made possible by the agrarian reforms of the 1930s? Some say that shaking off feudal relationships opened the way for entrepreneurial action, technological innovation, and capital formation. But agrarian reform also restricted much of the *campesino* laboring class to *ejidos* while making mechanization and other labor-saving technology possible in the nonreformed sector, which then commercialized quickly. Mexico is an excellent example of a country that changed the nonreformed subsector to foster mechanization while ignoring the overall problem of excess labor, which was then relegated to agrarian reform communities. So constituted, land reform mollified rural workers for several decades. After population growth, however, rural labor again rebelled in the 1970s, only to be repressed and then mollified once again through new government spending programs and reform.[5] In 1994 there was renewed jacquerie in Chiapas. As Grindle wrote of contemporary Mexico,

> [G]overnment investment in agriculture has been heavily skewed toward the zones of large-scale and irrigated agriculture.... Since 1940 government policy has sought to promote "capitalist" farming as the sector with the greatest potential rather than the "socialist" *ejido* sector. Credit, technical assistance, improved and appropriate technology, market facilities, and other services have been directed away from the heirs of the agrarian reform toward zones and groups thought to have greater production potential (1988, p. 60).

Bolivian agriculture in the *Oriente* might not have flourished if the peasants had not been stabilized on land of their own in the altiplano and high valleys so that state resources could be concentrated in the eastern lowlands. In Chile, the remarkable progress in exporting fruit during the 1980s might not have happened had reduced-size properties not "flowed" from the agrarian-reform sector to the "new entrepreneurs" and had there not been similarly scaled-down "reserves" and *huertas* created as part of (or in fear of) the agrarian-reform process itself.

WHOSE REFORM IS IT?

Land reform in Latin America is thus closely associated with increasing agricultural commercialization. Indeed, creating a modern commercial agriculture—not increasing *campesino* welfare—is probably the most important and enduring economic effect of land reform. In a very important sense, most land reform has been manipulated by the privileged members of a new entrepreneurial class to enhance their own status and to assure that the social structure is not altered in any fundamental way. For their part, *campesinos* have been relegated into the half of a dualistic structure that government chose not to aid and were expected to supply the bulk of the country's staples and more and more labor to the nonreformed sector as beneficiary plots were divided over generations (de Janvry 1981).

Although a few *campesino* entrepreneurs (one might call them middle-class farmers) have emerged from the masses to assemble larger, more capitalized farms (Forster 1989), most *campesino* beneficiaries rely increasingly on wage work as farms shrink with generational division. At the same time, commercial agriculture's appetite for wage labor grows as modernizing farming depends more and more on nontraditional exports. For example, workers are needed in the Central Valley of Chile and in highland Central America to plant, tend, and harvest fruit, vegetables, and flowers—nontraditional agricultural export crops. Commercial agriculture benefits when laborers have at least some land nearby to which they can return during off-seasons (de Janvry 1981). Whether wage workers enjoy higher standards of living as a result of nontraditional crops is a matter for speculation. Some believe that, even though more labor is used, wage rates have not risen much, there is still a long "dead period," and that transience harms stable family life; others hold that labor has greatly benefited from the expansion of nontraditional exports in terms of more wages and jobs, not only at the farm level but also in the needed agro-packing and agro-processing.

But reforms always guaranteed that a controlling niche of the local economy remained with the landlord. In Bolivia, for instance, landlords marketed the products of beneficiary families. In countries where land reserves were provided, landlords coveted the best land and received the bulk of credit and inputs that accompanied the reforms (plus any subsidies) as well as access to a labor force unable to completely earn its living on the assigned land.

Reforms to existing reform schemes in the region are now being made to pull *campesino* land into more commercial agriculture and fuel economic growth. During the 1970s and 1980s, in countries like Peru (see Lastarria-Cornhiel 1989; Carter and Alvarez 1989), Chile, Honduras (see Stringer 1989), and the Dominican Republic (see Meyer 1989; Stanfield 1989), many agrarian-reform communities individualized their holdings (or had them individualized by decree) from the original production cooperatives. Even after individualization (including countries like Bolivia where beneficiary farming was always individual), most reform beneficiaries could not legally rent, buy, sell, or mortgage their properties as collateral for loans (though these provisions were often ignored). Today usufructuary properties are converted into private farm units that can legally be bought, sold, divided, rented out, mortgaged, and so forth. Developing a full-fledged land market is an official policy in Mexico, Peru, Honduras, and the Dominican Republic (and is being debated in Bolivia). One concern, based on a fear that beneficiary *campesinos* will sell out their birthright holdings, is how an economically (and politically) weak group of fee-simple *campesinos* will fare under the new system: Will they lose their land to stronger peers, middle- and upper-class landowners, and even foreign individuals and companies, and will the process yet again give birth to a wave of dissatisfied land-hungry peasants? The capitalist-minded feel that the strong will prevail and agriculture will become more efficient as land is transferred to commercial management, engendering productivity gains that will more than compensate the displacement of *campesinos*. Some peasants, of course, will never leave their land because most of their alternatives are less inviting.

These initiatives, which make the sale of *campesino* property within the reform sector a legal option, continue a well-established trend toward smoothing the way to a commercial and modern agriculture. The problem is that, as land develops into a more mobile factor of production, *campesinos* are likely to bear the full brunt of privatization; they will either become landless or be hired back as workers on their former properties (and those with capital will call the shots as "entrepreneurs"). Establishing an open land market would not be so troublesome for *campesinos* if there were provided opportunities in public works programs or off-farm jobs. Whether Mexico's "Solidarity" program will be up to the task is an open question. For its part, Bolivia has no such welfare program and no prospect of initiating one. If countries do not establish safeguards, a completely open land market may allow the entire agricultural sector, which is not segmented now, to develop in a capital-intensive manner that bypasses the *campesinos* who are rendered landless. In this case governments must decide whether widespread destitution is too high a price to pay for an "efficient" and commercial agricultural sector. As worker displacement takes place, unemployed laborers may crowd into the slums surrounding cities, international migration may increase, and settlement of the displaced may occur within ecologically fragile frontier land.

It is also quite possible that these new reforms will lead to an underpublicized economic-refugee problem in the 1990s almost as serious in fact as the dramatic political-refugee problem of wartime Central America in the 1980s, a problem that will only be amplified if the few existing subsidies to *campesinos* are withdrawn too rapidly.

The regional reforms have foundered as formerly vigorous coalitions weaken during the interim when land is allocated but inputs are not yet available. For example, the *campesino* middle-class alliance was supplanted by the new "commercial class" of agriculturists. Middle-class allies of *campesinos*, not versed in or preoccupied by the exigencies of agricultural production, often considered the job of agrarian reform to be complete with land delivery. General Velasco in Peru, for instance, made it clear that, once the peasants were settled on land, no further favors would be forthcoming. Furthermore, peasant coalitions become shaky once land is distributed because of diverging goals among *campesino* groups themselves. During the Mexican and Bolivian revolutions, most of the rural poor could loosely combine over the issue of land (but remember that even Francisco Villa pushed his movement by founding schools, not by calling for land reform). During their early reforms, peasants were probably more united by their common experience and aspirations than the class-divided individuals who participated in reforms after 1960. By then, sharp differences had emerged between farm wage laborers, *minifundistas*, resident laborers, and sharecroppers. And as resident farm laborers came to be primary beneficiaries they proved themselves unwilling to help their coworkers (day laborers, for example) acquire land. As in the cases of Chile and El Salvador, estate workers wanted excess capacity on reformed farms reserved for their own heirs. After all, they reasoned, it was they who paid the price for reform through years of working for landlords; organizing, petitioning, and striking for reforms; and exposing themselves and their families to repression and retaliation.

Whereas resident farm laborers virtually disappeared in a process beginning in 1970, the wage-worker class grew rapidly and class divisions between *campesinos* widened. Thus a large, peasant-oriented, wage-earning group will probably fight for better wages and improved working conditions rather than land. Increasing differentiation, with ever-sharper class definition, seems to have weakened the cry for land reform in Latin America. The experience of dissatisfied beneficiaries—who found it difficult to make land payments, let alone invest much capital in their farms—provoked another response: Is owning land really beneficial when working capital is not forthcoming?

Organized peasants now confront commercial capitalists and innovative landowners, not the old-style landlords of legend, and have lessened their demands for agrarian reform (de Janvry 1984; Paige 1975). To split up undercapitalized farms where value is represented mostly by the land itself makes some sense; to destroy the coherence and rationality of a newly capitalized business unit by dividing it does not. Accordingly, capitalist farmers have gained political strength and the tools (wage settlements, hour adjustments, and the like) to buy off or co-opt peasant groups. In *The Death of Artemio Cruz*, Carlos Fuentes showed there is room for negotiation and maneuvering when one character says to a landlord: "You cannot stop events. Let's go on and give up those fields to the peasants. After all, it is land that is dry-farmed. You will lose very little. We give it up, so that the Indians will go on raising only patch-crops. And you will see that when they are obliged to us, they'll leave their patches to be hoed by women, and return to working our irrigated fields for wages. Look: you pass for a hero of the agrarian reform, and it costs you nothing" (1964, p. 49).

With the resurgence of the military and selective press controls in some Latin American countries, "divide and conquer" is the rule: It is relatively easy to repress *campesino* groups fighting for land in isolation. Of course, isolation can vanish. One need only look to the dramatic, well-heralded, and publicized marches for land, like those to Quito and La Paz in the early 1990s, led by indigenous peoples who most assuredly could not be publicly repressed on the 500th anniversary of Columbus's voyage. The events in Chiapas that began on 1 January 1994 also demonstrate that few places in the region remain genuinely isolated.

In Latin America, land reform became a policy by which only "rich" and articulate peasants benefited; governments granted land to the most vocal malcontents who were most able and willing to rebel. This target-and-benefit policy did not benefit the most stubbornly rural poor who were less organized. Moreover, any gains realized by small beneficiary groups were overpublicized by government. The standard of living of the unorganized masses may have been hurt each time a smattering of better-off peers was advanced.

AGRARIAN REFORM NEUTRALIZED

The state role in neutralizing agrarian reform may sometimes be blatant, like the complete reversals in Guatemala and Chile, but is usually subtle and surreptitious, occurring through macroeconomic policies that take away by stealth what a well-publicized effort conferred with a flourish. Paige (1975), Huntington (1968), and others have noted that giving peasants land makes them conservative and robs them of the desire to organize and petition the government. Thus beneficiary peasants are unlikely to oppose government policies that erode the potential economic power that land has given them, especially early in the process when they are unsure of their ability to hold on to the land. But soon after settlement governments frequently fail to provide the technical inputs—fertilizer, seed, irrigation water, knowledge, and credit—that the land-reform beneficiaries need to succeed.

The history of reform shows that government, whether by intent or inadvertence, may turn the domestic terms of trade against agriculture. It may allow imports to drive down the prices of crops that reform beneficiaries produce while it subsidizes the urban consumer. If it overvalues exchange rates (thereby hampering exports), it might assure that capital equipment (which replaces labor) is imported. Sometimes this happens as the state attempts to give redress to groups overlooked during the land-reform process. In Mexico, governments after Cárdenas underwrote the demanding industrial sector in cities and the commercial farming sector. Sometimes this compensatory treatment is politically justifiable. When Guatemala's Arbenz left out cities in his zeal for agrarian reform, urban dwellers united in a coalition that helped reverse it. In Chile, much of the reaction against Allende came from the urban middle class, which tired of bearing what it perceived as the inflationary price of agrarian reform. Although the political cost of ignoring an outspoken urban group in the course of land reform is usually high, the economic cost of satisfying urban and rural sectors concurrently is usually astronomical.

Another important technique that governments used to neutralize reforms was economic populism. To pay up-front costs of reform and attendant welfare expenses elsewhere in the economy, without matching expenditures with savings and with a cavalier attitude toward foreign exchange reserves, governments fueled inflation. This harmed the beneficiaries and all but devastated the nonbeneficiary rural poor, for whom inflation was a body blow. There are two recent cases where land reform played an obvious role in economic populism: the end of Allende's rule in Chile and the late 1980s in Sandinista Nicaragua. In both countries agrarian reform was an important part of programs aimed at assisting the poor; in both cases hyperinflation flared as savings fell far short of expenditures.

In this sense, Mexico's reform was a fortuitous exception; the Cárdenas reforms enjoyed extraordinarily good luck. Inflation was minimized because no public funds were really laid out for land. Also, Cárdenas's reforms took place during a depression, when public-sector spending helped revive the economy. Agrarian reform in Mexico in the 1930s was a relatively low-cost component of the economic populism occurring at the time. The philosophy emphasized an enormous expansion of the state as economic actor: A large number of state enterprises were organized, oil was nationalized, and the state continued to finance infrastructure. During the 1930s, public investment was supported largely with internal resources; by 1939, internal savings financed 85 percent of total investment (Navarrete R. 1967, pp. 115–118). Since tax collections were insufficient, the government resorted to bonds and budget-deficit overdrafts on the central bank. The accumulated deficit from 1936 to 1939 was small and by 1939 had been steadily reduced in relative terms. Because economic activity stayed at a relatively low level during the reform period, deficit financing generated increases in production and employment without seriously raising prices. Production rose by 58 percent from 1929, employment by 11 percent. "But more significantly, important infrastructural investments were made that increased the productive capacity of the economy and that, together with an intensified agrarian reform and the nationalization of private sectors stimulated the development of productive forces" (Navarrete R. 1967, p. 117). Of course, the period was also marked by capital flight because of labor disputes in the petroleum industry and its later expropriation.

In contrast, expansion in Chile was marked with extraordinary growth in Allende's first year followed by a quick drawdown of foreign exchange reserves and crippling inflation during his last two years. Similarly, the Sandinistas in Nicaragua embarked on an extensive literacy program, constructed health clinics and schools, brought potable water to the countryside, and enacted agrarian reforms. Initially there were ample foreign resources to finance these programs, and since the Somoza properties could be taken over, no indemnification had to be paid to landowners in this early stage. Tax collection also increased, reaching a peak in 1984. The government deficit was 8.9 percent of GDP in 1978 and remained there through 1981. Wage increases were discouraged to stimulate private-farmer investment in agriculture and to maintain exports. Indeed, inflation did not reach 100 percent until 1985, when a number of problems began to affect the economy adversely. These all caused the country to run an enormous deficit on its current and foreign account: (1) The private sector did not respond to incentives for increased production for exports; it was alarmed to inaction by rhetoric that increasingly threatened expropriation; (2) as the government became more radical, foreign exchange grants and loans tended to evaporate; (3) the embargo on imports to and exports from the United States curtailed foreign exchange; (4) cotton and coffee, which made up three-fifths of Nicaraguan exports, dropped in price; (5) the currency was overvalued; and (6) beginning in 1983, half of the national budget was devoted to the *contra* war, so the government deficit soared. Social spending dropped as the war continued; conflict exacerbated labor shortages, production shortfalls appeared, export earnings were diverted to weapons, imported parts and fertilizers for agriculture became unavailable, and infrastructure was destroyed by rebel attacks. The government continued to build schools and health clinics, albeit at a slower rate. It cut agrarian-reform costs by simply granting individual titles to squatters. Meanwhile, urban wages fell precipitously. By 1986, consumption had fallen to one-third of its prerevolutionary level and the government relied on printing money to cover the deficit. By 1988, inflation advanced to 11,500 percent and output fell back to levels of the 1960s. The Sandinistas lost the 1990 election largely because of these severe economic problems.

It should be emphasized that populism does not need to include land reform; it surely did not under Perón in Argentina and under Vargas in Brazil after 1945. Indeed, under these versions of populism the terms of trade turned sharply against agriculture as state policy favored industry. The point is that it makes no difference where deficits are created—in the rural sector or in cities. The overall macroeconomic problem remains if savings do not increase to finance the spending programs.

Precisely who benefits within the *campesino* class is also important. As recounted here, the Latin American reforms granted land to those who were better off economically—those in the upper echelons of farmworkers—those who were organized, already lived on haciendas, had at least some usufructuary access to land, and could coordinate political action. This type of "rural populism," therefore, had unmistakable similarities to the previous urban populism that helped unionized workers (or at least those with manufacturing jobs—that is, those near the top rungs of the social ladder in towns and cities). Frequently forgotten in this milieu is that the poorest of the poor may suffer twice from economic populist policies—once from being omitted from the original entitlement policy and again in the hyperinflation that follows.

Since populist experiments end in inflation, which ultimately hurts the intended beneficiaries, why have Latin American governments repeated the same misbegotten policies in so many different forms? The answer, of course, lies in politics and the extremely unequal pattern of development that has historically plagued Latin America. Perhaps populist policies are set in place by leaders who, desperate for some redistribution, are confident of being "rescued" by outside funding. (Also these policies can sometimes be timed so that the inflationary effects will not manifest themselves until someone else has taken over the reins of government.)

IS LAND REFORM STILL RELEVANT? TWO VIEWS

One could argue that land reform is irrelevant to Latin America in the 1990s on the following grounds: (1) Capital and technology are now more important than land; (2) the *colono* class of corvée labor has largely been eliminated in favor of day labor—higher wages and better working conditions are primary goals of this new group of wage workers, not land reform, so no credible coalitions favoring agrarian reform can be stitched together; (3) the youth of the region feels that almost any alternative is preferable to working on a small farm given the riskiness of the endeavor, the difficulty of obtaining credit and inputs, the general lack of amenities, and the problem of meeting mortgage payments; (4) large capitalized farmers are stronger and better organized than ever whereas *campesino* groups that might demand land reform are less organized as waves of repression and reform take their toll; (5) repressive forces (the military and the police) have enjoyed something of a resurgence, and though land invasions were sometimes settled in favor of *campesinos* in the past, this is not likely in the future; and (6) as the agricultural sector shrinks, land reform as a policy tool will become less important.

Others claim that land reform is likely to have a meaningful role in the future of Latin America: (1) Civil wars have left some land issues festering and so agrarian reforms are needed to ward off future conflicts; (2) though few opportunities exist for creating jobs, the excess capacity in farming can generate additional employment—that is, manufacturing creates insufficient new jobs, the informal sector is already overburdened and can offer only very low-income employment, international migration is becoming more risky and there is unused agricultural land remaining to be farmed; (3) resettling people on unused agricultural land seems a sustainable alternative that would prevent further deterioration of the fragile land that *minifundistas* currently farm and would keep others from moving to the frontier (which surely would be deforested upon their relocation); (4) in the absence of social security or other safety nets, idle land could be regarded as a component of the welfare system and one way to protect the interests of the rural poor, the weak, and the aged with little added governmental expense; and (5) a "new" group of rural poor—the indigenous peoples who were largely omitted from previous reforms—is presently making organized claims on the current system.

THE FUTURE OF AGRARIAN REFORMS

Although an end to land reforms in Latin America is not predicted here, the coalitions that bring them to pass will look quite different in the future. It has been argued that many large farms still contain fallow land that is appropriate for agriculture even as *campesinos* either farm the poorest plots in an ever-more intensive manner or relocate to the ecologically fragile frontier to carve out farms for themselves. These efforts epitomize nonsustainability; into the 1990s, environmental groups and intellectuals conscious of this problem will become more vocal in demanding that large owners use land wisely. Eventually the state may yield to this pressure and require landowners, perhaps through the taxation system, to use land wisely for agricultural purposes or else forfeit it to those who will. If governments refuse to tackle the problem, nongovernmental organizations and bilateral and multilateral aid donors could add their voices to those who favor rational land-use policies that protect the environment. Meanwhile, on the remaining frontier in the region, forest destruction continues apace as governments encourage despoliation of resources (sometimes displacing indigenous peoples). Displaced *campesinos* today have no choice but to establish farms in fragile areas.

In addition to conservationists and indigenous forest-dwelling peoples, middle-class urban dwellers in Latin America might come to support land reforms either as a matter of conscience or as cities become more and more ungovernable due to rural migration. In-migration from farm to city places an intolerable strain on urban infrastructure and creates social disorganization on an enormous scale. Whereas strikes in the countryside are easily contained and do not disturb city life, urban well-being is quickly disrupted when electric service fails, garbage is not collected, sanitation facilities do not work, and water supplies are rationed. When rural areas have excess capacity in terms of unused agricultural land despite commercialization, why should urban areas be overtaxed by resettlement and frontier zones be environmentally compromised?

Furthermore, as economic refugees move in increasing numbers to developed parts of Latin America (and to the United States and Canada), international pressure and economic aid for new agrarian reforms might develop as they have for family-planning programs. Conservation groups in the more advanced countries will surely join the chorus as the environment of the hemisphere suffers because peasants are forced to farm in fragile areas.

Notes

CHAPTER 2

1. The disappearing common village land was called the *ejido*, and later agrarian reform communities took this name.

2. Blasier (1985, p. 75) estimates that some 2 million hectares of U.S.-owned land in Mexico was ultimately expropriated.

3. In the 1940s and 1950s, investments in the north were encouraged with public funds, often for reclamation of desert land and extensive road and dam construction—investments that tended to redound to the benefit of a new breed of commercial farmers who established themselves there. Many areas in the north, in fact, were as untouched by the reforms as they were influenced by the United States. Not without coincidence, this part of the country, site of the Northern Front in revolutionary days, had the most conservative politics and exhibited increasing right-wing opposition to PRI governance into the 1990s.

4. Through the years numerous regulations, some of them contradictory and ambiguous, have been designed to implement Article 27, but it was not substantially amended until 1992.

5. Emiliano Zapata had originally thought that he could work within the system to obtain the return of farmland. In Cuautla, in Morelos, local *hacendados* had taken over the land, reducing its former owners to workers on encroaching sugar estates. Zapata participated in a local council for the defense of these village lands and later went to Mexico City to persuade Díaz to return land to the village. Zapata got no real satisfaction until the revolution gave him scope for the land reform that he had carried out in Morelos, an activity not recognized by the state until much later.

6. Some remnant farms remained large after the reform because landlord families were sizable and landlords could retain 100 hectares of irrigated land for each family member. Mexican sages tell of land being illegally claimed for dead relatives and even for family pets.

7. This rather antediluvian provision was not modified until 1990; the revised law provided that ranchers whose property exceeded 200 rain-fed hectares would be free to combine ranching and crop-raising if total revenue from the two activities did not exceed the income from 100 hectares of irrigated cropland—still a production deterrent and an ambiguous one at that.

8. The *agraristas* had successfully argued that if land could be mortgaged, rented, or sold it might be returned to the haciendas, and unless individual *ejido* parcels were passed to heirs undivided they would become no more viable than *minifundios*.

9. Other agrarian reforms in Latin America have shown that when governments abandon the idea of group farming they can destroy the collective spirit by withdrawing group services.

10. Functional shares must be used because of the absence of data on the size distribution of income before 1950.

11. An emergent concern is that *ejidos* that reorganize in this manner may experience underemployment as members try to live on rent or wages from land they formerly farmed.

12. The Salinas announcement and the Cárdenas retorts spawned a much wider debate in Mexico, outlines of which have just begun to appear. See, for example, Paz Sánchez et al. 1992; Medellín 1991a; Correa 1991; *Excelsior* 1992; Morett Sánchez 1991a; *Proceso* 1991; Téllez K. 1991; Morett Sánchez 1992; Medellín 1991b; Morett Sánchez 1991b; *Diario de Chihuahua* 1991a; Azcoitía 1991; *Diario de Chihuahua* 1991b; *Diario de Chihuahua* 1991c.

CHAPTER 3

1. On this matter there was a rather celebrated argument among several U.S. anthropologists in the 1960s, including Richard Patch (1965), who believed that agrarian reform occurred primarily as the result of a grassroots uprising, and Dwight Heath (1963), who thought that land reform came mainly from party and government initiatives with little assistance from the rural pressure of *campesino* unions.

Dandler (1967) mediated this matter. He showed how Patch conceded there had been considerable interaction between *campesino* unions and the party in the law's formulation and that as peasant unions of the Cliza-Ucureña areas became more militantly organized under the direction of José Rojas, the national leadership lost control of the movement, forcing the government to respond with land reform more complete and "extreme" than might otherwise have occurred. Dandler also urged writers to better define the geographic areas they were studying. Although interaction between *campesinos*, the party, and the government was important as the law was formulated following the clashes in Cliza-Ucureña, once promulgated, it looked like a central government imposition. The argument was that grassroots actions near Cochabamba importantly shaped the agrarian reform (later generalized to become a law proclaimed by the MNR government when it saw that land reform could not be evaded).

2. This provision for exceptionally large farms in the *Oriente* was later used to support charges of land-grabbing and graft.

3. The law set indemnification levels at the land values declared by owners for tax purposes, but few landlords had either reported a value or paid land taxes.

4. Recent rumors allege that trafficking in land is occurring (*Hoy* 1992), stemming from the story that CNRA—in abrogation of its original mandate—has lately been favoring large farmers in the *Oriente*.

5. This seems to have been due to a stroke of luck. President Eisenhower, himself unable to visit after his election, sent his brother to various Latin American countries. Sympathetic to the revolution, Milton Eisenhower was fascinated with Bolivia's uprising and, as an agriculturist, with its land reform. Not caught up with the anticommunist fervor that was sweeping the United States at the time, he also was able to put the revolution into some academic perspective. As he noted to his brother, "We should not confuse each move in Latin America toward socialization with Marxism, land reform with communism, or even anti-Yankeeism with pro-Sovietism" (Zondag 1982, p. 28). Several other factors

worked in Bolivia's favor in the delicate days after the revolution: The U.S. ambassador in Bolivia had prior experience with technical assistance there and was favorably inclined to the country. Conversely, the ambassador from Bolivia to the United States was well received (Zondag 1982, pp. 27–28; Wilkie 1969, pp. 8–9).

CHAPTER 4

1. The right to vote still excepted illiterate women, who made up three-quarters of the female population in the country (Jonas 1991, p. 23).

2. By 1947, the Arévalo government had scrapped both the labor code that defined workers' rights and the antivagrancy legislation.

3. If a competitive infrastructural system were built, he reasoned, the grip of the foreigners might be broken.

4. Lack of judicial review brought the entire program to the verge of a crisis when, in two split decisions, the Supreme Court claimed the process was unconstitutional and that private lands were being expropriated illegally. This brought the process to a temporary halt, but Arbenz pleaded with Congress to put the reforms on track again. Obedient to a fault, the Congress impeached the errant court members on the basis of "ignorance of the law" and replaced them with judges who were favorably inclined to the agrarian reform and willing to reverse the former ruling (Gleijeses 1989, pp. 464–465).

5. In a recent article, Manning (1990, p. 57) interviews a congressman who claims, "Nobody in Guatemala dares to mention the idea of redistributing wealth.... Everybody knows it should be done ... to provide more services to the poor. But if you say that too loudly you scare the *finqueros* and the army.... The gap between rich and poor remains. And so does the raison d'etre for the guerillas."

6. After Haiti, Guatemala has the lowest rate of taxation in Latin America.

7. Evidence indicates that this is because of the increasing unprofitability of growing staples and the fact that the terms of trade had turned sharply against domestic agriculture. An anthropologist (Krueger 1989, p. 2) provided anecdotal evidence:

One peasant after another told us that it is now cheaper to buy corn than to grow it.... Why? Because the people can no longer afford fertilizer, given its increased costs and their own impoverishment. Growing corn without fertilizer reduced yields to perhaps half their previous levels. The consequences? More cash is needed to purchase corn in the market. Paid work is less available; when it is available, the purchasing power of wages is a fraction of what it was 10 years ago.... Beans which cost [four to five times the price of corn], have already been eliminated as a regular part of the diet. Subsidies have been removed from medicines and from gasoline, so that as sickness increases, medicine is less accessible. Higher transportation costs inflate the prices of goods that are not self-produced and of migrating to look for work.

8. A memorandum from the Agency for International Development's agricultural development office in Guatemala several years ago illustrates this support: "As nontraditional crops, export vegetables appear to be a promising option for development due to their high labor intensity and expanding demand in industrial countries.... Farms which

diversified ... earned three times the net income than farms which did not" (Wing 1988, pp. 17–18).

Painter (1987, pp. 56–57) sketched the bleaker picture for nontraditional agricultural exports:

> Guatemala became the centre of operations for the USAID-financed LAAD [Latin American Agribusiness Development] Corporation. This was founded in 1970 by a consortium of 15 mainly agribusiness transnationals.... By the mid-1980s there were over 60 LAAD businesses in Guatemala, the most important of which was ALCOSA, a subsidiary of Hanover Brands, which processes and freezes vegetables like broccoli and cauliflower for the U.S. market. USAID funds a number of projects to persuade small Indian producers to grow new export crops for ALCOSA and other U.S. companies, when such crops are known to displace Indian staple crops and to involve more risks and expenses than traditional farming.

9. There are, of course, groups within Guatemala that argue against the necessity of land reform. See, for example, Aguirre B. et al. (1989) and Schneider et al. (1989). These recent publications, tailored mainly by landlord groups, seem to be responses to a rather forthright 1988 statement by the Guatemalan Roman Catholic Church on the need for land reform in Guatemala. This statement (CEG 1988, p. 32) concluded that Guatemala needed to "[l]egislate an equitable distribution of land beginning with the vast state-owned farms and poorly worked properties favoring those who have the capacity to cultivate them" [translation by author]. The statement also advocated just salaries for rural workers as well as credit, education, inputs, just prices, and organization for beneficiary *campesinos*. The bishops also contrast the situation of the powerful agro-exporting landowners with that of the *campesinos*. They denounce "the inhuman and merciless exploitation" of workers by landowners who do not even pay the minimum daily wage. See especially the articles by Rosada Granados (1988) and Sandoval Villeda (1988) in the *Revista de la Universidad de San Carlos*.

CHAPTER 5

1. These Alliance-motivated agrarian reforms showed that, when it comes to changes closely related to a country's social structure, outside prodding is not of much help if faced with strong internal opposition. On the other hand, if there is domestic political will favoring the reforms, U.S. support at critical times can be useful.

2. For discussion of the Peruvian reform, see Alvarez 1980a, 1980b; Brandenius 1976; Caballero 1976; Carter and Alvarez 1989; Handelman 1975; Horton 1974; Lastarria-Cornhiel 1989; Lastarria C. and Havens 1976; Mallon 1972; McClintock 1983; Rudolph 1992; Schydlowsky and Wicht 1983; and Webb and Figueroa 1975. Since very few reliable, recent data are available, the agrarian reform in Peru is omitted from this volume.

3. In fact, entails were abolished in the Constitution of 1828, restored in the Charter of 1833, and finally lifted in 1852.

4. We use the terms hacienda and *fundo* interchangeably in this chapter.

5. Women had been granted the franchise in 1949.

6. The settlement—named "John F. Kennedy"—was a good day trip for representatives of agencies offering economic assistance to Chile. In fact, it was a Potemkin village in

which only a few formerly landless *campesinos* got parcels of land and intensive farming assistance. More importantly, it was not a useful and affordable pilot project from which to draw lessons for the reforms to come.

7. Indeed, experimental reforms were carried out on church lands (Thiesenhusen 1966).

CHAPTER 6

1. There ensued the odd episode of William Walker, a U.S. citizen who, with a tiny number of American troops, helped the Liberals defeat the Conservatives (perhaps more to the point, Walker, in the name of manifest destiny, made a fortune in land development). Walker, in his effort to "expand democracy" (Booth 1985, p. 18), soon found himself at the vortex of power in Nicaragua: He was elected president of the country in 1856. Soon, however, he ran afoul of the Conservatives, who thought that the conclusion of the escapade might be U.S. annexation of the entire isthmus. In 1856, Walker's Liberals ruthlessly fought side-by-side with imported proslavery Southerners who favored annexation. In 1857, at war with a Guatemalan army that represented Conservatives, he accepted a truce—but later attempted three more times to return to Nicaragua. Eventually he was executed in Honduras. All of this discredited the Liberals, and the Conservatives then ruled in Nicaragua, a fact that helped account for the three decades of stability that followed.

2. Both Sandino and Anastasio Somoza were considered "generals" by virtue of the fact that each had raised a small "army" to fight the Conservatives, and in 1927 both were asked for their affirmation. As Booth (1985, p. 41) wrote, "From this moment forward the destinies of these two men and Nicaragua became inextricably entwined."

3. From 1910 to 1920, the government continued to sell national lands to large planters, displacing squatting *campesinos* in the process.

4. Booth (1985) reports that one device that Anastasio Somoza used early in his dictatorship was to receive rebates for the granting of concessions. When he granted a gold, rubber, or timber concession in the 1940s, for example, he would receive "additional contributions," executive levies, or presidential commissions. Also, he extracted bribes from otherwise illegal operations. He earned enormous profits from illegally exporting his own cattle to Costa Rica and Panama, for example, and secured "commissions" from other cattle producers for letting them break the same laws (Booth 1985, p. 67).

5. Anti-German legislation passed in Nicaragua to mollify the United States during World War II allowed Somoza to purchase the German coffee estates.

6. For example, after Somoza obtained the country's only pasteurizing plant, he manipulated the congress into passing legislation that required all milk to be pasteurized before sale (Booth 1985, p. 68).

7. Their personalities complemented each other, making a perfect good cop–bad cop act.

8. The U.S. administration felt that governments could be prodded to remain noncommunist with the help of military and economic aid. With the Alliance for Progress, economic assistance doubled and military help increased sevenfold. It was not until Richard Nixon resigned as president that U.S. support for Somoza began seriously to unravel.

9. The indigenous, ethnic groups living on the Atlantic coast had never been completely integrated into the country's mainstream; the Rama road was a step in this direction.

10. There were few causes that drove U.S. foreign policy toward Latin America in the 1980s more than Nicaragua's bloody revolution and the subsequent decade-long counterrevolution. Nicaragua conditioned relations between North America and Latin America during the entire Reagan presidency. The agrarian origin of this conflict was often forgotten in a single-minded effort by the U.S. government and its detractors to focus on whether the revolutionaries were helping the rebels in El Salvador and the extent to which the Eastern bloc was fostering a new beachhead in the Western world. While U.S. conservatives fervently denounced the Sandinistas, liberals were often uncritical in their praise, transfixed by the promises the new government in Managua seemed to offer for the prospects of development in the third world.

11. The ambivalence of the Carter administration in reaction to Somoza's fall from power is documented in Blasier (1985, pp. 291–292).

12. After the revolution the state sector found itself with 15 percent of the cotton production in the country, 12 percent of the coffee, and 8 percent of the livestock. The state was the majority producer for tobacco.

13. Many managers of agricultural properties, identified as they were with Somoza, fled in the revolution. Untrained substitutes, often with no farm background, had good intentions but little knowledge of agriculture.

14. This history is chronicled in Luciak (1987, pp. 271–341).

15. Brockett (1990) finds individual grants of land increasing almost tenfold between 1984 and 1985. He also notes that some state farms were privatized in this period, especially in the war zones of the north.

16. Kaimowitz (1989) documents that regionalization was a partial antidote to the overcentralization of the early years of reform, when costly decisions had been made without adequate attention to local conditions.

17. Although the Enríquez (1991) figure on total beneficiary families is probably nearer the mark, Martinez (1993), who divides the 1980s into six distinct and somewhat overlapping periods, sets the number at 120,000.

18. Data from Utting (1987); and FAO (1992a), tables 12, 20, 67, 78, and 87, pp. 55, 79, 156, 173, and 184.

19. Collins et al. (1982, p. 145) blame "decapitalization," in which the majority of private farmers preferred to let their "farm and equipment run down to sending [their] money to a Miami bank.... Under Somoza over 80 percent of investment came from the private sector; by 1981, only 10 percent."

20. As a result, when the somewhat larger producers who worked on the more productive soil of the Pacific coast were given more help with growing corn, they diverted inputs to more profitable cash crops such as vegetables.

21. This includes an enhanced role for women. See Deere (1983).

22. At time of writing, this is an unresolved dilemma.

23. Whether former landowners will be able to find validation satisfactory to the review commission is still not known.

CHAPTER 7

1. Before the agrarian reform, none of these crops was typically produced by *campesinos*, who usually grow the country's staples—corn, rice, beans—on their small farms.

2. In 1870, the Frenchman Lafarrière observed that the coastal area "is visited constantly by innumerable fevers and to see the faces of the natives there, yellow, emaciated, flaccid and withered, one understands immediately that a long stay would be fatal for people who have not been acclimatized over a long period of time" (Browning 1971, p. 227).

3. Although rumors and conspiracy theories were common, most people could only speculate on how all-pervasive the organization was—no one knew for sure whether or not their neighbors were ORDEN members.

4. Although these riverbed communities were habitable during most of the year, they flooded during the rainy season, when their residents retreated to higher ground. But since they were mostly out of the line of sight, their poor inhabitants were "invisible"—though by day they often worked in wealthy San Salvadoran neighborhoods, where they served as maids and cooks. Nonresidents sometimes descended into these warrens (to purchase tortillas—it was known that the best ones were made by the poor), remarking all the while on the ugliness of the lifestyle there.

5. In the 1970s, many of these refugees could be found camping along main roads, not knowing where they would work the next day.

6. In taking some fields out of production for a time and allowing natural vegetation to grow back, the war provided a respite to this problem, which will now grow more serious by the year.

7. But also in 1970, an irrigation-district law was passed that set size limits for properties within its boundaries. The landed oligarchy and the military right wing found such legislation anathema, for they believed that if the government could make farm-size limits hold in an irrigation district, it could do the same in an agrarian reform. Consequently, implementation of this law was glacial.

8. The bonds had maturities of 7, 20, 25, and 30 years. Most paid 6 percent interest, but some paid more and some less. Maturity and interest rate depended on the type of land use and the reason for expropriation. Annual coupons could be used in payment of any taxes if the government had failed to provide funds to the Central Bank with which to pay the interest; the same was true of bonds not paid upon maturity. As a result, although the government did not provide funds for compensation of most of these bonds and interest, it did wind up paying them indirectly when they were presented as payment for taxes. The bonds were fully negotiable, and traded mostly at about 40–60 percent of nominal value (John Strasma, personal memorandum to author, August 1993).

9. Although sometimes regarded as a homogeneous class in El Salvador, as elsewhere in Latin America *campesinos* are actually differentiated into distinct subclasses. As Strasma (1989, p. 425) noted, "many resident workers consider themselves relatively high on the rural social scale. For generations they have looked down on the migrants ... rather than seeing them as fellow campesinos." Experience shows that no land-reform program can incorporate the different types of *campesino*—squatters, migratory wage workers, resident laborers, and so forth—unless it devises a plan of how that will be accomplished.

10. An argument is sometimes made that peer pressure keeps members working on production cooperatives that are exceptionally well organized. In cases where dividends are actually paid, members may see some correspondence between effort and reward.

11. Effects of a new and further reduced asking price, now being instituted by ISTA, will entail another substantial subsidy to cooperative members (Thiesenhusen 1993).

12. Although not specified in the law (see ISTA 1991), in practice some amount of private property usually accrues to individual members in the process of choosing under this program, if only a very small house plot, even if the cooperative picks the "collective" option. Selecting to farm under a new option enables the cooperative to take advantage of the lower mortgage payment; the old mortgage terms for land and other accumulated debts prevail if cooperatives decide not to participate in new options. Thus the incentives augur well for fairly widespread adoption of the program.

13. As soon as is practicable after the cooperative has selected a tenure form, ISTA measures the private plots, either the *solares* or the parcels, and draws up titles. Individual tracts may be transferred to others by rental or purchase, but any new holders must work in agriculture and must not own a farm larger than 7 hectares already; they must, in other words, be bona fide *campesinos* as defined by Salvadoran law (a stipulation that is almost impossible to monitor). New members must also be acceptable to the established membership. When the cooperative selects its new option, it obtains its refigured mortgage based on the cost of renting an equivalent amount of land in the area. The ISTA encourages cooperatives to select rather quickly under the *nuevas opciones* program. After having begun this process in 1990 (before Decree No. 747 was enacted), by January 1993, only 72 cooperatives had made the choice (though 22 of these had already parceled extralegally well before that time); by 1 July 1993, 158 out of 319 had chosen.

14. An explanation for the latter development is that some land designated as *matorral* or "brush"—usually categorized as "unused farmland"—was reclassified as "forestland." Left alone long enough, fallow land in the tropics returns naturally to trees.

15. Interview with Luis Lopez Córdovez, FAO/CEPAL, San Salvador, 5 July 1993.

16. It may be speculated that the long hours of waiting for action followed by bursts of intense activity do not train a young person very well for the steady work pace required for farming.

CHAPTER 8

1. This chapter will not summarize how land reforms might be better administered since that has been done in other publications. See, for example, Dorner (1971); Thiesenhusen (1989); Prosterman et al. (1990).

2. The point system gave high scores to *campesinos* with the most seniority on the original *fundo*, the largest families, and no record of social protest against the previous owner.

3. In order to operate successfully in the national arena, politicians learned to switch comfortably from thoughtful advocates of reform for the middle-class audience to plain-spoken sermonizers for the grassroots audience.

4. Mexican migrants forced back home during the Great Depression (because they were taking jobs from U.S. citizens) were at the forefront of the *campesino* organizations required by the successful Cárdenas reforms.

5. An advantage of the "rolling horizon" of the Mexican land reform was that reform could be accelerated to tranquilize peasant pressure for change.

Bibliography

Adelman, Irma. 1989. "Industrialization and Poverty." Address to the Sri Lanka Economics Association, Colombo. Mimeographed.

Aguirre Batres, Francisco, Ernesto Rodrigues B., and Rene Arturo Orellana M. 1989. *La Situación Agraria en Guatemala: Enfoque Estadístico*. Guatemala: Asociación de Amigos del País.

Alexander, Robert J. 1962. *Labor Relations in Argentina, Brazil, and Chile*. New York: McGraw-Hill.

Alvarez, Elena. 1980a. *Política Agraria y Estancamiento de la Agricultura, 1969–1977*. Lima: Instituto de Estudios Peruanos.

_____. 1980b. "Política agraria del gobierno militar y su posible impacto sobre la población, 1969–1979." Paper prepared for seminar, "Políticos públicos y su incidencia en la dinámica poblacional," El Bosque, Peru, 16–19 June 1980.

Angel Garza, Luis. 1991. "Vaquerías: Primer intento de transnacionalizar el campo, a medias por falta de agua e interés." *Proceso*, no. 788, 25 November.

Antezana, Luis, and Hugo Romero. 1973. *Historia de los Sindicatos Campesinos*. La Paz: Servicio Nacional de Reforma Agraria.

Arulpragasam, L.C. 1966. "A Consideration of the Problems Arising from the Size and Subdivision of Paddy Holdings in Ceylon." *Ceylon Journal of Historical and Social Studies* 4: 59–70.

Asman, David. 1991. "The Salinas Reforms Take Root." *Wall Street Journal*, 2 December.

Azcoitía, Víctor Manuel. 1991. "'Error histórico el cambio al 27': CAP." *Heraldo de Chihuahua*, 9 November.

Barham, Bradford, Michael Carter, and Wayne Sigelko. 1992. "Adoption and Accumulation Patterns in Guatemala's Latest Agro-Export Boom." SSRI Working Paper, no. 9216. Madison: Social Science Research Institute, University of Wisconsin.

Barkin, David, and Blanca Suárez. 1982. *El Fin de la Autosuficiencia Alimentaria*. Mexico, D.F.: Nueva Imagen.

Barnes, Grenville. 1992. "Technical and Institutional Issues Related to Land Tenure, Titling, and the Cadastre in Bolivia." Draft report. Columbus, Ohio, 20 August.

Barraclough, Solon. 1973. *Agrarian Structure in Latin America*. Lexington, Mass.: Lexington Books.

_____. 1991. *An End to Hunger? The Social Origins of Food Strategies*. London: Zed Books [on behalf of UNRISD and the South Center].

Barraclough, Solon L., and Arthur L. Domike. 1966. "Agrarian Structure in Seven Latin American Countries." *Land Economics* 42: 391–424.

Bauer, Arnold J. 1992. "Chilean Rural Society and Politics in Comparative Perspective." In *Development and Social Change in the Chilean Countryside: From the Pre-Land*

Reform Period to the Democratic Transition, edited by Cristóbal Kay and Patricio Silva, pp. 19–31. Amsterdam: Centre for Latin American Research and Documentation.

Bebbington, Anthony, Graham Thiele, Penelope Davies, Martin Prager, and Hernando Riveros. 1993. *Non-Governmental Organizations and the State in Latin America: Rethinking Roles in Sustainable Agricultural Development*. London: Routledge [for the Overseas Development Institute].

Berry, R. Albert, and William S. Cline. 1979. *Agrarian Structure and Productivity in Developing Countries*. Baltimore: Johns Hopkins University Press.

Black, George. 1981. *Triumph of the People: The Sandinista Revolution in Nicaragua*. London: Zed Press.

Blasier, Cole. 1985. *The Hovering Giant: U.S. Responses to Revolutionary Change in Latin America, 1919–1985*. Rev. ed. Pittsburgh: University of Pittsburgh Press.

Bloom, Reynold Joseph. 1973. "The Influence of Agrarian Reform on Small Holder Communities in Chile's Central Valley, 1965–1970." Ph.D. dissertation, University of California at Los Angeles.

Booth, John A. 1985. *The End and the Beginning: The Nicaraguan Revolution*. Boulder, Colo.: Westview Press.

Brandenius, Claes. 1976. "Structural Changes in the Peruvian Economy 1968–1975." Discussion Paper, no. 104. Lund, Sweden: Research Policy Program, University of Lund, September.

Bray, James O. 1961. *The Agrarian Problem in Chile*. Santiago, Chile: Economic Research Center, Catholic University.

_____. 1962. "Demand and the Supply of Food in Chile." *Journal of Farm Economics* 44: 1005–1020.

Brockett, Charles D. 1990. *Land, Power, and Poverty: Agrarian Transformation and Political Conflict in Central America*. Boston: Unwin Hyman.

Bromley, Daniel W. 1984. "The Role of Land Reform in Economic Development: Comment." In *Agricultural Development in the Third World*, edited by Carl K. Eicher and John M. Staaz, pp. 275–277. Baltimore: Johns Hopkins University Press.

_____. 1989. "Property Relations and Economic Development: The Other Land Reform." *World Development* 17: 867–877.

Brooks, James. 1992. "Ecuador Gives Indian Group Title to Big Amazon Rain-Forest Area." *New York Times*, 5 September.

Brown, Marion R. 1989. "Radical Reformism in Chile: 1964–1973." In *Searching for Agrarian Reform in Latin America*, edited by William C. Thiesenhusen, pp. 216–239. Boston: Unwin Hyman.

Browning, David. 1971. *El Salvador: Landscape and Society*. Oxford: Clarendon Press.

Brundtland Commission (World Commission on Environment and Development). 1987. *Our Common Future*. Oxford: Oxford University Press.

Bulmer-Thomas, Victor. 1987. *The Political Economy of Central America Since 1920*. Cambridge: Cambridge University Press.

Burke, Melvin. 1971. "Land Reform in the Lake Titicaca Region." In *Beyond the Revolution: Bolivia Since 1952*, edited by James M. Malloy and Richard S. Thorn, pp. 301–339. Pittsburgh: University of Pittsburgh Press.

Burns, E. Bradford. 1989. "Establishing the Patterns of Progress and Poverty in Central America." In *Studies of Development and Change in the Modern World*, edited by

Michael T. Martin and Terry R. Kandal, pp. 202–215. New York: Oxford University Press.

Caballero, José Maria. 1976. "Reformas y reestructuración agraria en el Perú." CISEPA Documento de Trabajo, no. 34. Lima: Pontificia Universidad Católica del Perú, December.

Campos-Dudley, Liliana. 1992. "Beni: Surviving the Crosswinds of Conservation." *Americas*, 44(3), pp. 6–15.

Cariaga, Juan L. 1982. "The Economic Structure of Bolivia After 1964." In *Modern-Day Bolivia: Legacy of the Revolution and Prospects for the Future*, edited by Jerry R. Ladman, pp. 147–163. Tempe: Center for Latin American Studies, Arizona State University.

Carter, Michael R., and W.C. Walker. 1988. "The Evolution of Agrarian Structure in Latin America: An Econometric Investigation of Brazil." Agricultural Economics Staff Paper Series, no. 298. Madison: Department of Agricultural Economics, University of Wisconsin, December.

Carter, Michael R., and Elena Alvarez. 1989. "Changing Paths: The Decollectivization of Agrarian Reform Agriculture in Coastal Peru." In *Searching for Agrarian Reform in Latin America*, edited by William C. Thiesenhusen, pp. 156–187. Boston: Unwin Hyman.

Carter, Michael R., and Dina Mesbah. 1992. "Can Land Market Reform Mitigate the Exclusionary Aspects of Rapid Agro-Export Growth?" Draft. Madison: Department of Agricultural Economics, University of Wisconsin, January.

Carter, Michael R., Bradford B. Barham, Dina Mesbah, and Denise Stanley. 1993. "Agro-Exports and the Rural Resource Poor in Latin America: Policy Options for Achieving Broadly-Based Growth." Draft. Madison: Department of Agricultural Economics, University of Wisconsin, 18 March.

CEG (Comisión Episcopal para Guatemala). 1988. *Carta Pastoral Colectiva, USAC: Revista de la Universidad de San Carlos*, no. 4, December.

Chapin, Mac. 1990. "El Salvador's Environment: Problems and Institutional Responses." Background paper. Mimeographed. Boston: Cultural Survival, August.

Chapin, Norman. 1980. "A Few Comments on Land Tenure and the Course of Agrarian Reform in El Salvador." In "El Salvador Project Paper: Agricultural Reform Organization, AID/LAC/P-060, Annex II.A." Mimeographed. Washington, D.C.: U.S. Agency for International Development.

Chonchol, Jacques. 1970. "Eight Fundamental Conditions of Agrarian Reform in Latin America." In *Agrarian Problems and Peasant Movements in Latin America*, edited by Rodolfo Stavenhagen, pp. 159–172. Garden City, N.Y.: Doubleday and Company.

_____. 1971. "La Política agraria en una economía de transición: El Caso chileno." In *El Pensamiento Económico del Gobierno de Allende*, pp. 217–244. Santiago: Editorial Universitaria.

Christian, Shirley. 1992a. "Dispute over Land Becomes Obstacle to Salvador Peace." *New York Times*, 7 September.

_____. 1992b. "Salvadoran Landowners and Peasants Also Learn to Live with One Another." *New York Times*, 27 January.

CIDA (Comité Interamericano de Desarrollo Agrícola). 1966. *Chile: Tenencia de la Tierra y Desarrollo Socio-Económico del Sector Agrícola*. Santiago: Talleres Gráficos Hispano Suiza.

Ciriacy-Wantrup, S.V., and Richard Bishop. 1975. "'Common Property' as a Concept in Natural Resource Policy." *Natural Resources Journal* 15: 713–727.

Clark, Ronald J. 1968. "Land Reform and Peasant Market Participation on the Northern Highlands of Bolivia." *Land Economics* 44: 153–172.

Cline, Howard F. 1963. *Mexico: Revolution to Evolution: 1940–1960.* Oxford: Oxford University Press.

COHA (Council on Hemispheric Affairs). 1992. "Mexican Land Policies Shift Political Terrain." *COHA's Washington Report on the Hemisphere,* 29 July.

Colburn, Forrest. 1986. *Post-Revolutionary Nicaragua: State, Class and the Dilemmas of Agrarian Policy.* Berkeley: University of California Press.

Cole, William E., and Richard D. Sanders. 1970. "Income Distribution, Profits and Savings in the Recent Economic Experience of Mexico." *Inter-American Economic Affairs* 24: 49–63.

Collins, Joseph, Frances Moore Lappé, and Nick Allen. 1982. *What Difference Could a Revolution Make? Food and Farming in the New Nicaragua.* San Francisco: Institute for Food and Development Policy.

Coone, Tim. 1990. "The Sandinistas Lose Office But Not Power." *World Press Review,* 37:4, pp. 22–25.

Cornelius, Wayne A. 1992. "The Politics and Economics of Reforming the *Ejido* Sector in Mexico: An Overview and Research Agenda." *LASA Forum,* 23(3), pp. 3–10.

Cornia, G.A. 1985. "Farm Size, Yields and the Agricultural Production Function: An Analysis for Fifteen Developing Countries." *World Development* 13: 513–534.

Correa, Guillermo. 1991. "El Ejido sobrevive de nombre, pero se acerca la privatización." *Proceso,* 4 November.

Couriel, Alberto. 1984. "Poverty and Underemployment in Latin America." *CEPAL Review,* no. 24, December, pp. 39–62.

Cox, Isaac Joslin. 1963. "Chile." In *Argentina, Brazil and Chile Since Independence,* vol. 3, edited by A. Curtis Wilgus, pp. 277–414. New York: Russel and Russel.

Craig, Ann L. 1983. *The First Agraristas: An Oral History of a Mexican Agrarian Reform Movement.* Berkeley: University of California Press.

Crosson, Pierre. 1970. *Agricultural Development and Productivity: Lessons from the Chilean Experience.* Baltimore: Johns Hopkins University Press.

Cruz, María Elena. 1992. "From Inquilino to Temporary Worker; From Hacienda to Rural Settlement." In *Development and Social Change in the Chilean Countryside: From the Pre-Land Reform Period to the Democratic Transition,* edited by Cristóbal Kay and Patricio Silva, pp. 247–262. Amsterdam: Centre for Latin American Research and Documentation.

Dandler, Jorge. 1967. "Local Group, Community, and Nation: A Study of Changing Structure in Ureureña, Bolivia (1935–1952)." Master's thesis, University of Wisconsin-Madison.

De Cordoba, José. 1993. "Battle for Properties Keeps Nicaraguans on Verge of Anarchy." *Wall Street Journal,* 12 November.

Deere, Carmen Diana. 1983. "Cooperative Development and Women's Participation in the Nicaraguan Agrarian Reform." *American Journal of Agricultural Economics* 65: 1043–1048.

De Janvry, Alain. 1981. *The Agrarian Question and Reformism in Latin America.* Baltimore: Johns Hopkins University Press.

_____. 1984. "The Role of Land Reform in Economic Development: Policies and Politics." In *Agricultural Development in the Third World*, edited by Carl K. Eicher and John M. Staatz, pp. 263–274. Baltimore: Johns Hopkins University Press.

De Janvry, Alain, and Elisabeth Sadoulet. 1989a. "Investment Strategies to Combat Rural Poverty: A Proposal for Latin America." *World Development* 17: 1203–1221.

_____. 1989b. "A Study in Resistance to Institutional Change: The Lost Game of Latin American Land Reform." *World Development* 17: 1397–1407.

_____. 1992. "Market, State and Civil Organization in Latin America Beyond the Debt Crisis: The Context for Rural Development." Paper presented at LAC-TECH Planning Workshop, Agency for International Development, Washington, D.C., 9–11 December 1992.

De Soto, Hernando. 1987. *El Otro Sendero: La Revolución Informal.* 6th ed. Bogotá: Editorial La Oveja Negra.

Diario de Chihuahua. 1991a. "Privatización del ejido, 'arma de doble file,' afirma delegado de CNC," 4 November.

_____. 1991b. "Polémica en Chihuahua por la reforma al 27 constitucional," 9 November.

_____. 1991c. "Reforma ejidal afectará control político: FDC," 10 November.

Diskin, Martin. 1989. "El Salvador: Reform Prevents Change." In *Searching for Agrarian Reform in Latin America*, edited by William C. Thiesenhusen, pp. 429–450. Boston: Unwin Hyman.

Diskin, Martin, and Kenneth E. Sharpe. 1986. "El Salvador." In *Confronting Revolution: Security Through Diplomacy in Central America*, edited by Morris J. Blachman, William M. Leogrande, and Kenneth Sharpe, pp. 50–87. New York: Pantheon Books.

Dornbusch, Rudiger, and Sebastian Edwards. 1989. "The Macroeconomics of Populism in Latin America." World Bank, Working Papers on Macroeconomic Adjustment and Growth, no. WPS 316. Washington, D.C.: World Bank, Country Economics Department, December.

Dorner, Peter. 1992. *Latin American Land Reforms in Theory and Practice: A Retrospective Analysis.* Madison: University of Wisconsin Press.

Dorner, Peter, ed. 1971. *Land Reform in Latin America: Issues and Cases. Land Economics* Monograph Series, no. 3. Madison: Published by *Land Economics* for the Land Tenure Center at the University of Wisconsin.

Dorner, Peter, and Don Kanel. 1971. "The Economic Case for Land Reform." In *Land Reform in Latin America: Issues and Cases*, edited by Peter Dorner, pp. 41–56. *Land Economics* Monograph Series, no. 3. Madison: Published by *Land Economics* for the Land Tenure Center at the University of Wisconsin.

Dorner, Peter, and William C. Thiesenhusen. 1990. "Selected Land Reforms in East and Southeast Asia: Their Origins and Impacts." *Asian-Pacific Economic Literature* 4: 65–95.

_____. 1992. "Land Tenure and Deforestation: Interactions and Environmental Implications." UNRISD Discussion Paper, no. 34. Geneva: United Nations Research Institute for Social Development, April.

Dorsey, Joseph F. 1975. "Bolivia Country Report." Draft. Madison: Land Tenure Center, University of Wisconsin, for the International Bank for Reconstruction and Development.

_____. 1984. "Changes in the Use of Labor on Large Haciendas in Chile's Central Valley: 1965, 1970 and 1976." Ph.D. dissertation, University of Wisconsin–Madison.

Echenique, J., and N. Rolando. No date. *Tierras de Parceleros. ¿Dónde Están?* Santiago: Agraria.

Economist. 1992. "Latin America Cheers Up," 18 April.

Ellsworth, P.T. 1945. *Chile: An Economy in Transition.* New York: Macmillan Company.

Enríquez, Laura J. 1991. *Harvesting Change: Labor and Agrarian Reform in Nicaragua, 1979–1990.* Chapel Hill: University of North Carolina Press.

Excelsior. 1992. "Ideas," 28 February.

Falcoff, Mark. 1989. *Modern Chile, 1970–1989: A Critical History.* London: Transaction Books.

FAO (Food and Agriculture Organization of the United Nations). 1992a. *Production Yearbook, 1991.* Rome: FAO.

_____. 1992b. *The State of Food and Agriculture, 1991.* Rome: FAO.

Felix, David. 1961. "Chile." In *Economic Development: Analysis and Case Studies,* edited by Adamantios Pepelasis, Leon Mears, and Irma Adelman, pp. 288–325. New York: Harper and Brothers.

FINATA (Financiera Nacional de Tierras Agrícolas). 1993. *FINATA: Diagnóstico y su Proyección.* San Salvador: FINATA, March.

Forster, Nancy R. 1989. "*Minifundistas* in Tungurahua, Ecuador: Survival on the Agricultural Ladder." In *Searching for Agrarian Reform in Latin America,* edited by William C. Thiesenhusen, pp. 92–126. Boston: Unwin Hyman.

Fuentes, Carlos. 1964. *The Death of Artemio Cruz.* Translated from the Spanish by Sam Hileman. New York: Farrar, Straus and Giroux.

Gannon, J.D. 1988. "New Look to Contra Negotiators," *Christian Science Monitor,* 25 May.

Galbraith, John Kenneth. 1990. "The Rush to Capitalism." *New York Review of Books,* 25 October, pp. 51–52.

Gasperini, William. 1990. "Nicaragua's Economic Slide." *Christian Science Monitor,* 19 September.

Gilbert, Dennis. 1986. "Nicaragua." In *Confronting Revolution: Security Through Diplomacy in Central America,* edited by Morris J. Blachman, William M. Leogrande, and Kenneth Sharpe, pp. 88–124. New York: Pantheon Books.

Gleijeses, Piero. 1989. "The Agrarian Reform of Jacobo Arbenz." *Journal of Latin American Studies* 21: 413–480.

_____. 1991. *Shattered Hope: The Guatemalan Revolution and the United States, 1944–1954.* Princeton, N.J.: Princeton University Press.

Golden, Tim. 1991. "The Dream of Land Dies Hard in Mexico." *New York Times,* 27 November.

_____. 1992. "Mexican President Outlines Program for Change." *New York Times,* 2 November.

Gomez, Sergio. 1981. "Participation Experience in the Countryside: A Case Study in Chile." World Employment Programme, Research Working Paper, WEP 10/WP 20. Geneva: International Labour Office.

Góngora, Mario. 1960. *Origen de los Inquilinos de Chile Central.* Santiago: Editorial Universitaria.

Grindle, Merilee S. 1988. *Searching for Rural Development: Labor Migration and Employment in Mexico*. Ithaca, N.Y.: Cornell University Press.

Handelman, Howard. 1975. *Struggle in the Andes: Peasant Mobilization in Peru*. Austin: University of Texas Press.

Haney Jr., Emil B., and Wava G. Haney. 1989. "The Agrarian Transition in Highland Ecuador: From Precapitalism to Agrarian Capitalism in Chimborazo." In *Searching for Agrarian Reform in Latin America*, edited by William C. Thiesenhusen, pp. 70–91. Boston: Unwin Hyman.

Hardin, Garrett. 1968. "The Tragedy of the Commons." *Science*, 13 December.

Heath, Dwight B. 1963. "Land Reform and Social Revolution in Bolivia." Paper read at 62nd annual meeting of American Anthropological Association, San Francisco, California, 21–24 November 1963.

_____. 1970. "Hacendados with Bad Table Manners: Campesino Syndicates as Surrogate Landlords in Bolivia." *Inter-American Economic Affairs* 24: 3–13.

_____. 1990. "Land Reform, Revolution and Development: A Longitudinal Study of the Case of Bolivia." *Economic Quarterly* 25: 3–15.

Heath, John Richard. 1990. "Enhancing the Contribution of Land Reform to Mexican Agricultural Development." Working Paper of the World Bank, Country Department II, WPS 185. Washington, D.C.: World Bank, Latin American and Caribbean Regional Office, Agriculture and Rural Development Department, February.

_____. 1992. "Evaluating the Impact of Mexico's Land Reform and Agricultural Productivity." *World Development* 20: 695–711.

Hellman, Judith Adler. 1983. *Mexico in Crisis*. 2nd ed. New York: Holmes and Meier.

Hendrix, Steven E. 1992a. "Thoughts on Tenure, Poverty and the Environment." Memorandum to Environmental Officer, USAID/La Paz. Washington, D.C., 17 September.

_____. 1992b. "The Crisis of Land Law and Policy in Nicaragua." Draft. Washington, D.C., 20 April.

Herring, Ronald J. 1983. *Land to the Tiller: The Political Economy of Agrarian Reform in South Asia*. New Haven, Conn.: Yale University Press.

Horton, Douglas. 1974. "Land Reform and Reform Enterprises in Peru." Report submitted to the Land Tenure Center, University of Wisconsin–Madison, and the World Bank. Mimeographed. Madison, Wisconsin.

Hough, R. et al. 1982. "Land and Labor in Guatemala: An Assessment." Typescript. Washington, D.C.: AID/Washington and Development Associates.

Hoy (La Paz), 22 October 1992.

Hull, Jennifer Bingham. 1991a. "Chamorro Struggles to Settle Nicaragua's Complex Land Claims." *Christian Science Monitor*, 24 June.

_____. 1991b. "Chamorro's Nicaragua at Year One." *Christian Science Monitor*, 25 April.

Huntington, Samuel P. 1968. *Political Order in Changing Societies*. New Haven, Conn.: Yale University Press.

IDB (Inter-American Development Bank). 1990. *Economic and Social Progress in Latin America: 1990 Report*. Washington, D.C.: Distributed by Johns Hopkins University Press for Inter-American Development Bank, October.

_____. 1991. *Economic and Social Progress in Latin America, 1991 Report*. Washington, D.C.: Distributed by Johns Hopkins University Press for Inter-American Development Bank, October.

_____. 1992. *Economic and Social Progress in Latin America, 1992 Report*. Washington, D.C.: Distributed by Johns Hopkins University Press for Inter-American Development Bank, October.

_____. 1993. *Economic and Social Progress in Latin America: 1993 Report*. Washington, D.C.: Distributed by Johns Hopkins University Press for Inter-American Development Bank, October.

IICA (Instituto Interamericano de Cooperación para la Agricultura). 1992. "Pobreza rural persistente: Desafío para el año 2000, linjeamentos de una estrategía para combatirla." Paper prepared for workshop on rural poverty and civil society, sponsored by IICA and Grupo ESQUEL, São Paulo, Brazil, 13–15 April 1992. Preliminary version. San José: IICA, April.

INEGI (Instituto Nacional de Estadística, Geografía e Informática). 1986. *Estadísticos Históricos de México*. Vol. 1. Mexico City: SPP.

ISTA (Instituto Salvadoreño de Transformación Agraria). 1991. *Ley del Régimen Especial del Dominio en la Reforma Agraria y su Reglamento*. San Salvador: ISTA, 12 April.

Jarvis, Lovell S. 1985. *Chilean Agriculture Under Military Rule: From Reform to Reaction, 1973–1980*. Berkeley: Institute of International Studies, University of California.

_____. 1989. "The Unraveling of Chile's Agrarian Reform, 1973–1986." In *Searching for Agrarian Reform in Latin America*, edited by William C. Thiesenhusen, pp. 240–275. Boston: Unwin Hyman.

Johnston, Bruce F. 1966. "Agriculture and Economic Development: The Relevance of the Japanese Experience." *Food Research Institute Studies* 6: 251–312.

Johnston, Bruce F., and William C. Clarke. 1982. *Redesigning Rural Development: A Strategic Perspective*. Baltimore: Johns Hopkins University Press.

Jonas, Susanne. 1991. *The Battle for Guatemala: Rebels, Death Squads and U.S. Power*. Boulder, Colo.: Westview Press.

Jones, James. 1990. "A Native Movement and March in Eastern Bolivia: Rationale and Response." *Bulletin of the Institute for Development Anthropology*, 8(2), pp. 1–8.

Joya de Mena, Ana Luz, Maria Latino de Rodrigues, Rodolfo Cristales, and Michael L. Wise. 1993. "A Survey of Thirty-Six Properties Transferred Under the Peace Accord Program of Land Tenure." Typescript. San Salvador: U.S. Agency for International Development, 10 June.

Jung, Harold. 1982. "The Civil War in El Salvador." *Boletín de Estudios Latinoamericanos y del Caribe*, June, pp. 5–13.

Kaimowitz, David. 1989. "The Role of Decentralization in the Recent Nicaraguan Agrarian Reform." In *Searching for Agrarian Reform in Latin America*, edited by William C. Thiesenhusen, pp. 384–408. Boston: Unwin Hyman.

Kaldor, Nicolas. 1959. "Problemas económicas de Chile." *Trimestre Económico*, no. 102, April–June, pp. 170–221.

Kanel, Don. 1971. "Land Tenure Reform as a Policy Issue in the Modernization of Traditional Societies." In *Land Reform in Latin America: Issues and Cases*, edited by Peter Dorner, pp. 23–35. *Land Economics* Monograph Series, no. 3. Madison: Published by *Land Economics* for the Land Tenure Center at the University of Wisconsin.

Kautsky, Karl. 1976. *La Cuestión Agraria*. Bogotá: Editorial Latina.

Kay, Cristóbal. 1992a. "Political Economy, Class Alliances, and Agrarian Change." In
   *Development and Social Change in the Chilean Countryside: From the Pre-Land Reform
   Period to the Democratic Transition*, edited by Cristóbal Kay and Patricio Silva,
   pp. 93–108. Amsterdam: Centre for Latin American Research and Documentation.
_____. 1992b. "The Development of the Hacienda System." In *Development and Social
   Change in the Chilean Countryside: From the Pre-Land Reform Period to the
   Democratic Transition*, edited by Cristóbal Kay and Patricio Silva, pp. 33–53.
   Amsterdam: Centre for Latin American Research and Documentation.
_____. 1992c. "Agrarian Reform and the Class Struggle." In *Development and Social
   Change in the Chilean Countryside: From the Pre-Land Reform Period to the
   Democratic Transition*, edited by Cristóbal Kay and Patricio Silva, pp. 129–151.
   Amsterdam: Centre for Latin American Research and Documentation.
Kay, Cristóbal, and Patricio Silva. 1992. "Rural Development, Social Change, and the
   Democratic Transition." In *Development and Social Change in the Chilean Countryside:
   From the Pre-Land Reform Period to the Democratic Transition*, edited by Cristóbal
   Kay and Patricio Silva, pp. 291–299. Amsterdam: Centre for Latin American Research
   and Documentation.
Keller R., Carlos. 1963. "Minifundios y latifundios." In *Chile: Su Futuro Alimentación*.
   Santiago: Editorial Nascimiento.
Klein, Herbert S. 1982. "Bolivia Prior to the 1952 Revolution." In *Modern-Day Bolivia:
   Legacy of the Revolution and Prospects for the Future*, edited by Jerry R. Ladman,
   pp. 15–25. Tempe: Center for Latin American Studies, Arizona State University.
Krueger, Kris. 1989. "Development and Politics in Rural Guatemala." *Development
   Anthropology Network* 7: 1–6.
LAC TECH Bulletin. 1994. No. 3. Washington, D.C.: Agriculture and Rural Development
   Technical Services Project, March.
Ladman, Jerry R., and Ronald L. Tinnermeier. 1979. "The Political Economy of Bolivian
   Agricultural Credit." Columbus: Department of Agricultural Economics and Rural
   Sociology, Ohio State University, 1979. Paper presented at Latin American Studies
   Meetings, Pittsburgh, 5–7 April 1979.
La Feber, Walter. 1983. *Inevitable Revolutions: The United States and Central America*.
   New York: W.W. Norton and Company.
Lago, María Soledad. 1992. "Rural Women and the Neo-Liberal Model." In *Development
   and Social Change in the Chilean Countryside: From the Pre-Land Reform Period
   to the Democratic Transition*, edited by Cristóbal Kay and Patricio Silva, pp. 263–274.
   Amsterdam: Centre for Latin American Research and Documentation.
Lagos, Maria Laura. 1988. *Pathways to Autonomy, Roads to Power: Peasant-Elite
   Relations in Cochabamba (Bolivia), 1900–1985*. New York: Columbia University Press.
Lastarria-Cornhiel, Susana. 1989. "Agrarian Reforms of the 1960s and 1970s in Peru."
   In *Searching for Agrarian Reform in Latin America*, edited by William C. Thiesen-
   husen, pp. 127–155. Boston: Unwin Hyman.
Lastarria C., Susana, and A. Eugene Havens. 1976. "Agrarian Structure, Agrarian
   Reform, and Peru's 'Revolution.'" Draft. Lima, April.
LARR (Latin America Regional Reports). 1987a. "No High Marks for Cerezo." *Latin
   American Regional Reports: Mexico and Central America*, 20 August, p. 6.
_____. 1987b. "Business Attacks New Tax Package." *Latin American Regional Reports:
   Mexico and Central America*, 24 September, p. 6.

López Cordovez, Luis. 1982. "Trends and Recent Changes in the Latin American Food and Agriculture Situation." *CEPAL Review*, no. 16, April, pp. 7–41.

Loveman, Brian. 1976. "The Transformation of the Chilean Countryside." In *Chile: Politics and Society*, edited by Arturo Valenzuela and J. Samuel Valenzuela, pp. 238–296. New Brunswick, N.J.: Transaction Books.

Luciak, Ilja A. 1987. "The Sandinista Revolution and the Poor: Basic Needs and Political Participation in Nicaragua." Ph.D. dissertation, University of Iowa, Iowa City.

Lynch, John V., and Paul J. Ferree. 1961. *The Agricultural Economy of Bolivia*. ERS-Foreign 1. Washington, D.C.: U.S. Department of Agriculture, Economic Research Service, May.

Mallon, Richard D. 1972. "Reforming Property Ownership and Income Distribution in Peru." Mimeographed. N.p., December.

Mamalakis, Markos. 1969. *Sectoral Coalitions and Clashes in Chile, 1880–1930*. Milwaukee: Latin American Center, University of Wisconsin.

Manning, Michael. 1990. "The New Game in Guatemala." *New York Review of Books*, 25 October, pp. 53–57.

Martinez, Philip R. 1993. "Peasant Policy Within the Nicaraguan Agrarian Reform, 1979–1989." *World Development* 21: 475–487

Martins, José Pedro. 1992. "Land Reform Problems Continue in Brazil." *Latinamerica Press*, 10 September.

McBride, George McCutchen. 1936. *Chile: Land and Society*. New York: American Geographical Society.

McClintock, Cynthia. 1983. "Velasco, Officers, and Citizens: The Politics of Stealth." In *The Peruvian Experiment Reconsidered*, edited by Cynthia McClintock and Abraham F. Lowenthal, pp. 275–308. Princeton, N.J.: Princeton University Press.

McEwen, W. 1974. *Changing Rural Society: A Study of Communities in Bolivia*. New York: Oxford University Press.

McGranahan, Gordon. 1991. "Fuelwood, Subsistence Foraging, and the Decline of Common Property." *World Development* 19: 1275–1287.

Medellín, Rodrigo A. 1991a. "Debate sobre el ejido." *Perfil de la Jornada*, 26 November.
_____. 1991b. "La Iniciativa presidencial." *Perfil de la Jornada*, 26 November.

Meyer, Carrie A. 1989. *Land Reform in Latin America: The Dominican Case*. New York: Praeger.

Montoya, Aquiles. 1991. *El Agro Salvadoreño antes y Después de la Reforma Agraria*. Cuadernos de investigación, año 2. San Salvador: Dirección de Investigaciones Económicas y Sociales, Centro de Investigaciones Tecnológicas y Científicas, June.

Morett Sánchez, Jesús Carlos. 1991a. "Modernización política del campo y transformación productiva de la unidad ejidal." *Excelsior* (Mexico City), 4 January.
_____. 1991b. "No Tuvo la culpa el ejido sino quien lo hizo compadre." *Perfil de la Jornada*, 26 November.
_____. 1992. *Alternativas de Modernización del Ejido*. Mexico, D.F.: Editorial Diana.

Nairn, Allan. 1983. "Choices on Guatemala." *New York Times*, 4 April.

Nash, Nathaniel C. 1992. "Latin Informal Economy Saves Day." *New York Times*, 21 March.

Navarrete R., Alfredo. 1967. "The Financing of Economic Development." In *Mexico's Recent Economic Growth: The Mexican View*, edited by Enrique Perez Lopez et al., pp. 105–130. Latin American Monograph, no. 10. Austin: Institute of Latin American Studies, University of Texas.

Ortega, Emiliano. 1982. "Peasant Agriculture in Latin America: Situations and Trends." *CEPAL Review*, no. 16, April, pp. 75–111.

_____. 1985. "Campesinado y producción agrícola: La Agricultura campesino en América Latina." Typescript. Santiago.

OSPA-MAG (Oficina Sectoral de Planificación Agrícola-Ministerio de Agricultura y Ganadería). 1992. *XI Evaluación del Proceso de la Reforma Agraria*. San Salvador: División de Seguimiento y Evaluación, Ministerio de Agricultura y Ganadería, December.

_____. 1993. "Eighth Census of Agrarian Reform Cooperatives." San Salvador.

Otero, Gerardo. 1989. "Agrarian Reform in Mexico: Capitalism and the State." In *Searching for Agrarian Reform in Latin America*, edited by William C. Thiesenhusen, pp. 276–304. Boston: Unwin Hyman.

Paige, Jeffery M. 1975. *Agrarian Revolution: Social Movements and Export Agriculture in the Underdeveloped World*. New York: Free Press.

Painter, James. 1987. *Guatemala: False Hope, False Freedom*. London: Catholic Institute for International Relations.

Parthasarathy, Gorgula. 1979. "Understanding Agriculture: Growth and Current Concerns." Mimeograph. Rome.

Patch, Richard W. 1965. *A Note on Bolivia and Peru: Social Change in a Political Context*. AUFS Reports, West Coast South America Series, vol. 12, no. 2. New York: American Universities Field Staff.

PDC (Partido Democrata Cristiano). 1964. *El Libro de la Tierra: Movimiento Nacional de Liberación Campesina*. Santiago: PDC.

Pino, Hugo Noe, and Andrew Thorpe, comp. 1992. *Honduras: El Ajuste Estructural y la Reforma Agraria*. Tegucigalpa: Centro de Documentación de Honduras y Postgraduado Centroamericano en Economía y Planificación del Desarrollo.

Pinto Santa Cruz, Aníbal. 1962. *Chile: Un Caso de Desarrollo Frustrado*. Santiago: Editorial Universitaria.

Paz Sánchez, Fernando, Felipe Torres Torres, Julio Moguel, José Luis Calva, Cuahtémoc González Pacheo, and Bernardo Olemedo Carranza. 1992. "Opiniones y comentarios: México: Modificaciones al Art. 27 constitucional. La Nueva etapa capitalista en el campo." *Problemas del Desarrollo: Revista Latinoamericana de Economía*, vol. 23, April–June.

Proceso. 1991. "La Revolución mexicana va para atrasa: Tronó el campo," no. 784, 11 November.

Prosterman, Roy L., Mary N. Temple, and Timothy M. Hanstad. 1990. *Agrarian Reform and Grassroots Development: Ten Case Studies*. Boulder, Colo.: Lynne Rienner Publishers.

PRSP (Proyecto Regional para la Superación de la Pobreza, PNUD). 1992. "Magnitud y evolución de la pobreza en América Latina." *Comercio Exterior* 42: 380-392.

Queister Morales, Waltraud, and Harry E. Vanden. 1985. "Relations with the Non-Aligned Movement." In *Nicaragua: The First Five Years*, edited by Thomas W. Walker, pp. 467–484. New York: Praeger.

Reinhardt, Nola. 1989. "Contrast and Congruence in the Agrarian Reforms of El Salvador and Nicaragua." In *Searching for Agrarian Reform in Latin America*, edited by William C. Thiesenhusen, pp. 451–482. Boston: Unwin Hyman.

Reynolds, Clark W. 1970. *The Mexican Economy: Twentieth-Century Structure and Growth*. New Haven, Conn.: Yale University Press.

Ringlein, Wayne. 1971. "Economic Effects of Chilean National Expropriation Policy on the Private Commercial Farm Sector, 1964–1969." Ph.D. dissertation, University of Maryland.

Robinson, Linda, and Andrea Dabrowski. 1992. "The Unfinished Revolution." *U.S. News and World Report*, 27 June, pp. 45–46.

Romero Loza, José. 1974. *Bolivia: Nación en Desarrollo*. La Paz-Cochabamba: Editorial Los Amigos del Libro.

Rosada Granados, H.C. 1988. "Reforma agraria en Guatemala." *Carta Pastoral Colectiva, USAC: Revista de la Universidad de San Carlos*, no. 4, December.

Ross, John. 1991. "Mexican Land Reform Threatened by Privatization." *Latinamerica Press*, 23(45), 5 December.

Ruben, Raúl. 1989. "Notas sobre la cuestión agraria en Honduras." San José, Costa Rica: Consultorías para el Desarrollo Rural en Centroamerica y el Caribe, with Free University of Amsterdam, 20 July.

Rudolph, James D. 1992. *Peru: The Evolution of a Crisis*. Westport, Conn: Praeger.

Salinas de Gortari, Carlos. 1991. "III Informe de gobierno." Address presented at Los Pinos, Mexico City, 1 November.

Sanderson, Steven E. 1986. *The Transformation of Mexican Agriculture: International Structure and the Politics of Rural Change*. Princeton, N.J.: Princeton University Press.

Sandoval Villeda, Leopoldo. 1988. "Reforma agraria en Guatemala: Condiciones y posibilidades." *Carta Pastoral Colectiva, USAC: Revista de la Universidad de San Carlos*, no. 4, December, pp. 50–77.

Schlesinger, Stephen, and Stephen Kinzer. 1982. *Bitter Fruit: The Untold Story of the American Coup in Guatemala*. Garden City, N.Y.: Doubleday and Company.

Schneider, Pablo R. et al. 1989. *El Mito de la Reforma Agraria*. Guatemala City: Centro de Investigaciones Económicas Nacionales, March.

Schuh, G. Edward, and Antonio Salazar P. Branadão. 1985. "The Theory, Empirical Evidence, and Debates on Agricultural Development Issues in Latin America: A Selective Survey." Typescript for *A Survey of Agricultural Economics Literature*, vol. 4.

_____. 1991. "Latin American Agriculture: The Crises of the 1980s and the Challenges of the 1990s." In *Latin America: The Crisis of the Eighties and the Opportunities of the Nineties*, edited by Werner Baer et al., pp. 173–192. Urbana: Bureau of Economic and Business Research, University of Illinois at Urbana-Champaign.

Schultz, Theodore W. 1964. *Transforming Traditional Agriculture*. New Haven, Conn.: Yale University Press.

Schweigert, Thomas E. 1990. "Land Distribution and Land Use in Guatemala." Ph.D. dissertation, University of Wisconsin-Madison.

Schydlowsky, Daniel M., and Juan J. Wicht. 1983. "The Anatomy of an Economic Failure." In *The Peruvian Experiment Reconsidered*, edited by Cynthia McClintock and Abraham F. Lowenthal, pp. 94–143. Princeton, N.J.: Princeton University Press.

Scofield, Rupert W. 1990. "Land Reform in Central America." In *Agrarian Reform and Grassroots Development: Ten Case Studies*, edited by Roy L. Prosterman, Mary N. Temple, and Timothy M. Hanstad, pp. 139–177. Boulder, Colo.: Lynne Rienner Publishers.

Scott, David Clark. 1992a. "Mexico's Reforms Transform Agrarian Sector." *Christian Science Monitor*, 12 November.

_____. 1992b. "Salvadorans Face Off Over Land Reform Issue." *Christian Science Monitor*, 13 February.

Seligson, Mitchell A., William Thiesenhusen, and Malcolm Childress. 1993. "Land Tenure in El Salvador: An Overview and Summary Policy Recommendations." Paper prepared for USAID/San Salvador. Madison, Wisc., 1 September.

Simmons, Roger. 1974. *Palca and Pulcara: A Study of the Effects of Revolution in Two Bolivian Haciendas*. University of California Publications in Anthropology, vol. 6. Berkeley: University of California Press.

Simon, Jean-Marie. 1988. *Guatemala: Eternal Spring, Eternal Tyranny*. New York: W.W. Norton.

Simon, Lawrence R., and James C. Stephens. 1982. *El Salvador Land Reform, 1980–1981: Impact Audit*. Boston: Oxfam-America.

Singer, Morris. 1969. *Growth, Equality, and the Mexican Experience*. Austin: University of Texas Press.

Smith, Carol A. 1990. "The Militarization of Civil Society in Guatemala: Economic Reorganization as a Continuation of War." *Latin American Perspectives*, 17 (Fall), pp. 8–41.

Solis, Dianne. 1991a. "Agricultural Reform in Mexico Leaves Farmers Wanting, and Fearing, Change." *Wall Street Journal*, 29 November.

_____. 1991b. "Corn May Be Snag in Trade Talks by Mexico, U.S." *Wall Street Journal*, 12 December.

_____. 1993. "Agricultural Crisis in Mexico Deepens as More Farmers Face Loan Delinquency." *Wall Street Journal*, 13 September.

Stanfield, J. David. 1989. "Agrarian Reform in the Dominican Republic." In *Searching for Agrarian Reform in Latin America*, edited by William C. Thiesenhusen, pp. 305–337. Boston: Unwin Hyman.

_____. 1992. "The Insecurity of Land Tenure in Nicaragua." Draft for discussion. Madison: Land Tenure Center, University of Wisconsin, 18 October.

Steenland, Kyle. 1977. *Agrarian Reform Under Allende: Peasant Revolt in the South*. Albuquerque: University of New Mexico Press.

Sternberg, Marvin J. 1962. "Chilean Land Tenure and Land Reform." Ph.D. dissertation, University of California at Berkeley.

Strasma, John. 1989. "Unfinished Business: Consolidating Land Reform in El Salvador." In *Searching for Agrarian Reform in Latin America*, edited by William C. Thiesenhusen, pp. 408–428. Boston: Unwin Hyman.

_____. 1990. "Reforming the 1980 Land Reform: An Analysis of Proposals to Consolidate Debts and Allow Beneficiaries to Decide on Land Ownership and Production in Land Reform Projects in El Salvador." Typescript. Madison: Department of Agricultural Economics, University of Wisconsin, June.

Stringer, Randy. 1989. "Honduras: Toward Conflict and Agrarian Reform." In *Searching for Agrarian Reform in Latin America*, edited by William C. Thiesenhusen, pp. 358–383. Boston: Unwin Hyman.

Subercaseaux, Benjamín. 1943. *Chile: A Geographic Extravaganza*. New York: Macmillan Company.

Tannenbaum, Frank. 1962. *Ten Keys to Latin America*. New York: Alfred A. Knopf.

Taylor, James Robert. 1968. "Agricultural Settlement and Development in Eastern Nicaragua." Ph.D. dissertation, University of Wisconsin●Madison.

Téllez K., Luis. 1991. "El Cambio estructural en el campo mexicano." *Examen*, 27 June.

Thiesenhusen, William C. 1966. *Chile's Experiments in Agrarian Reform*. Madison: University of Wisconsin Press for *Land Economics*.

_____. 1984. "The Illusory Goal of Equity in Latin American Agrarian Reform." In *International Dimensions of Land Reform*, edited by John D. Montgomery, pp. 31–62. Boulder, Colo.: Westview Press.

_____. 1990. "Human Rights, Affirmative Action, and Land Reform in Latin America." In *The Political Economy of Ethnic Discrimination and Affirmative Action: A Comparative Perspective*, edited by Michael L. Wyzan, pp. 25–48. New York: Praeger.

_____. 1991. "Implications of the Rural Land Tenure System for the Environmental Debate: Three Scenarios." *Journal of Developing Areas* 26: 1–23.

_____. 1993. "Agrarian Reform in El Salvador: A Contemporary Assessment." Typescript. Madison, Wisc., 1 September.

Thiesenhusen, William C., ed. 1989. *Searching for Agrarian Reform in Latin America*. Boston: Unwin Hyman.

Thiesenhusen, William C., and Jolyne Melmed-Sanjak. 1990. "Brazil's Agrarian Structure: Changes from 1970 Through 1980." *World Development* 18: 393–415.

Thome, Joseph. 1970. "Expropriation and Title Distribution Under the Bolivian Agrarian Reform: 1953–1967." Typescript. La Paz, December.

_____. 1989. "Law, Conflict, and Change: Frei's Law and Allende's Agrarian Reform." In *Searching for Agrarian Reform in Latin America*, edited by William C. Thiesenhusen, pp. 188–215. Boston: Unwin Hyman.

Thome, Joseph R., and David Kaimowitz. 1985. "Agrarian Reform." In *Nicaragua: The First Five Years*, edited by Thomas W. Walker, pp. 299–316. New York: Praeger.

Troncoso, Hernán. 1957. *Trade Union Freedom*. (Pamphlet prepared for Congreso de Abogados de Concepción, Chile). Santiago: Acción Sindical Chilena.

UNDP (United Nations Development Programme). 1993. *Human Development Report, 1993*. New York: Oxford University Press.

UNICEF (United Nations Children's Fund). 1990. *The State of the World's Children, 1990*. Geneva: Oxford University Press.

Utting, Peter. 1987. "Domestic Supply and Food Shortages." In *The Political Economy of Revolutionary Nicaragua*, edited by Rose Spaulding, pp. 127–148. London: Allen and Unwin.

Vargas, Alberto. 1992. "Economic, Ecological and Social Aspects of Forest Management in Peasant Organized Communities in Quintana Roo, Mexico." Dissertation proposal, University of Wisconsin–Madison, 3 August.

Walter, Knut, and Phillip J. Williams. 1993. "The Military and Democratization in El Salvador." *Journal of Interamerican Studies and World Affairs* 35: 39–88.

Webb, Richard, and Adolfo Figueroa. 1975. *Distribución del Ingreso en el Perú*. Lima: Instituto de Estudios Peruanos.

Weeks, John. 1985. *The Economies of Central America*. New York: Holmes and Meier.

Whitaker, Morris D., and E. Boyd Wennergren. 1982. "Bolivia's Agriculture Since 1960: Assessment and Prognosis." In *Modern-Day Bolivia: Legacy of the Revolution and Prospects for the Future*, edited by Jerry R. Ladman, pp. 233–254. Tempe: Center for Latin American Studies, Arizona State University.

White, Alastair. 1973. *El Salvador*. London: E. Benn.

Wilkie, James W. 1969. *The Bolivian Revolution and U.S. Aid Since 1952*. Los Angeles: Latin American Center, University of California at Los Angeles.

Williams, Robert G. 1986. *Export Agriculture and the Crisis in Central America*. Chapel Hill: University of North Carolina Press.

Wing, Harry E. 1988. *USAID/Guatemala Agriculture Sector Development Strategy, 1988–1992*. Office of Rural Development Report, no. 25. Guatemala City: USAID/Guatemala.

Womack Jr., John. 1967. *Zapata and the Mexican Revolution*. New York: Random House.

World Bank. 1990. *World Development Report, 1990*. Oxford: Published for World Bank by Oxford University Press.

_____. 1992a. *Bolivia: Agricultural Sector Review*. Report no. 9882-BO. Washington, D.C.: Country Department III, Latin America and the Caribbean Regional Office, 6 April.

_____. 1992b. *World Development Report, 1992*. Oxford: Published for World Bank by Oxford University Press.

_____. 1993. *World Development Report, 1993*. Oxford: Published for World Bank by Oxford University Press.

Zondag, Cornelius H. 1982. "Bolivia's 1952 Revolution: Initial Impact and U.S. Involvement." In *Modern-Day Bolivia: Legacy of the Revolution and Prospects for the Future*, edited by Jerry R. Ladman, pp. 27–40. Tempe: Center for Latin American Studies, Arizona State University.

About the Book
and Author

Two defining features of agriculture in Latin America are unequal resource distribution and poverty among peasant farmers or *campesinos*. Agrarian reform—which grants land rights to *campesinos* together with production credit, inputs, and training—is often seen as a measure that will foster equity and social justice. Although some claim that agrarian reform will lower farm production by fundamentally altering the structure of agriculture, others argue that production will rise as *campesinos* get a stake in the system.

This book presents a historical and analytical interpretation of agrarian reforms in six Latin American countries: Mexico, Bolivia, Guatemala, Chile, El Salvador, and Nicaragua. Dr. Thiesenhusen offers an examination of the accomplishments and failures of these reform efforts, concluding that governments have frequently announced bold policies that have proved to be ineffectual or that have been quietly neutralized by other actions. He shows that although most *campesinos* in these countries received no property at all from the reforms, those who did get land were unable to obtain the inputs needed to farm efficiently. In addition, inflation and unfavorable terms of trade have further eroded reform benefits.

The book illustrates how agrarian reform is related to environmental issues in Latin America, explaining that small farmers often intensively cultivate steep hillsides, while large farmers leave rich bottom land idle. Thiesenhusen concludes with an evaluation of how the current emphasis on privatization is changing the lives of *campesino* land recipients once again.

William C. Thiesenhusen is professor of agricultural economics and agricultural journalism and director of the Land Tenure Center at the University of Wisconsin–Madison.

Index

ACLU. *See* American Civil Liberties Union
Adelman, Irma, 24
Affonso, Almino, 101
Africa, 4, 9(table)
Afuerinos, 8, 93, 94, 102, 106, 113
AGA. *See* Asociación General de Agricultores
Agency for International Development (U.S.), 81
Agrarian Law (1907) (El Salvador), 141
Agrarian reform, 3, 26, 180–181
  beneficiaries, 3, 4, 11, 12, 16, 23, 26, 131, 159, 176
  and equity, 11, 159
  and foreign aid, 162
  and government policy, 14, 15, 16, 162, 172, 174, 176–179, 180
  and grassroots initiatives, 166–168
  impact, 3, 4, 26–27, 171–175
  interest groups, 8, 167, 180, 181
  maintenance, 11
  minimalist, 87, 161, 162
  and production, 10–11, 26
  as social control, 162, 164, 173, 179
  and women, 113
  and youth, 179
  See also Land; *under individual countries*
Agrarian reform centers. *See* Centros de reforma agraria
Agrarian structuralists, 91
Agrarian structure. *See Latifundios; Minifundios*
Agraristas, 35, 43
Agribusiness, 15, 16, 22, 42, 46
Agricultural Bank of Bolivia (BAB), 65
Agricultural capitalism, 16, 22, 91
Agricultural enterprise (Bolivia), 60
Agricultural estates (Guatemala), 70

Agricultural product rate, 20, 127
Agricultural research, 64
Agriculture, 10
  commercialization, 4, 8, 11, 12, 20, 37, 38, 42, 51, 59, 61, 65, 73, 111, 122, 163, 171, 173, 174
  exports, 8, 15–17, 22, 24, 26, 38, 83
  GDP share, 161
  GNP share, 60
  inputs, 8, 12, 14, 22, 23, 25, 26, 64, 92, 159
  labor, 24
  labor absorption, 2, 20, 101
  markets, 12
  mechanized, 8, 17, 47, 61, 83, 91, 93, 101, 107, 143–144, 171
  private investment in, 37
  production, 10, 11, 24, 26
  productivity, 23
  small-scale, 22, 39
  subsidies, 14, 65
  subsistence, 45, 51, 64, 70, 82, 126, 135
  See also Farms; *under individual countries*
AIFLD. *See* American Institute for Free Labor Development
Alcoholism, 126
Alessandri, Arturo, 95
Alessandri, Jorge, 95, 96
Alianza Republicana Nacionalista (ARENA) (El Salvador), 153
Aljería, 54
Allende, Salvador, 95, 98, 100, 102, 103, 104, 106, 107–109, 110, 164, 165, 167
Alliance for Progress (1960s), 67, 125
  and land reform, 87, 95, 96, 123, 144

209